The ART *of*
EMPATHY

KARLA McLAREN, M.Ed.

The ART of EMPATHY

A Complete
Guide to
Life's Most
Essential
Skill

sounds true
BOULDER, COLORADO

Sounds True, Inc.
Boulder, CO 80306

Published 2013

The excerpt on pages 274 and 275 is from *The Social Conquest of Earth* by Edward O. Wilson, © 2012. Used by permission from Liveright Publishing Company.

Cover and book design by Rachael Murray
Cover photo © Shooter from Shutterstock.com

Printed in the United States of America

BK03712

Library of Congress Cataloging-in-Publication Data
McLaren, Karla.
  The art of empathy : a complete guide to life's most essential skill / Karla McLaren.
     pages cm
  Includes bibliographical references and index.
  ISBN 978-1-62203-061-3
  1. Empathy. I. Title.
  BF575.E55M39 2013
  152.4'1—dc23
                            2013010780

Ebook ISBN: 978-1-62203-067-5
10 9 8 7 6 5 4 3 2

For you who long to connect deeply, to understand clearly,
to respond perceptively, and to engage authentically, I welcome you.

Empathy is an art, but *you* are the artist.
Thank you for bringing your unique empathic artistry
to our waiting world.

Contents

A Note to You

WE ALL LONG to be seen and understood, to be valued and honored, and to be loved for exactly who we are. We also want to connect deeply with others, understand them clearly, and respond skillfully to their wants and needs. We want to navigate through difficulties and conflicts with grace, and we want our relationships to be a source of healing, strength, humor, and love. We want *empathy,* and we want to know how to offer our empathy to others.

Luckily, each of us already has an innate talent for empathy, and most of us developed our capacity for fully compassionate and empathic engagement when we were just toddlers (research suggests that our empathic skills can develop before we're two years old; we'll explore that research in this book). We humans are a deeply and intrinsically empathic species—we can tune into the emotions, wishes, thoughts, intentions, and hopes of others, and we can make intelligent decisions about how we'll respond to the information we receive. Through our empathic skills, we can get into sync with others, understand them, and meet their needs in ingenious ways. Empathy helps us witness, engage with, and respond skillfully not only to humans and animals, but also to nature, art, music, ideas, ideologies (such as traditionalism, existentialism, etc.), and even structures (such as buildings, public spaces, and living and working areas).

Empathy is everywhere: it's the air you breathe and the ground you walk on; it makes relationships, communities, and societies work. And yet, empathy can also be something of a mystery. Because empathy is such a central part of everything you do, you can overlook it and almost ignore the processes that make empathy work (or stop working). This is actually an important part of how empathy functions, because you don't want to have to think about every piece of empathic information you pick up, then catalog all of it, then reflect on each piece, and then plod through all of your possible responses. In fact, it's *good* that empathy is generally hidden from your conscious notice! But when you want to consciously work with your empathy—either to increase it or to calm it down—it's very important to be able to enter into that hidden world and understand the processes of empathy very clearly.

In this book, you'll learn how to access the often-hidden world of empathy, emotional awareness, and the interactional space that surrounds you. You'll also learn how to bring skills and organization to your empathy so that it will become a dependable and valuable resource for you and your friends, your family, your loved ones, your colleagues, and our waiting world.

But before we begin, we must attend to three pieces of empathic business. First, your health and happiness are important to me. Empathy and emotional sensitivity are essential capacities, but in a relatively insensitive and emotion-averse culture, both can be difficult to manage. This book offers support, ideas, and strategies to help you work with emotions and empathy and to become a healthy and happy empath. But it is important to note that not all aspects of emotional and empathic sensitivity should be addressed through self-help. Therapy, counseling, and (in conditions such as repetitive anxieties, depressions, or rage disorders) medical support are often necessary. Please reach out for the help of professionals if your situation becomes uncomfortable.

Second, the health and happiness of the people I've worked with are important to me, too. Although this book is based on my lifetime study of emotions and empathy, and by my four decades of empathic work with others, you won't find stories about those individuals here. My empathic work occurs in a private and strongly enclosed sacred space where *all* emotions are welcomed. As such, things can get very deep, very quickly, and I'm not there trying to gather anecdotes for my books. My work is clearly deepened and informed by all of the wonderful people I've consulted with, but their stories belong to them. As you read, you may notice that I write vignettes about myself, which may seem egocentric; however, I've chosen to use myself as an example because mine is the only story I have the ethical right to tell. If I do write about others, I protect their identities or I get their permission, or both.

And third, in this post-Internet world, the rules and conventions about using material from blog posts are becoming more formal. Some of the material on empathy and emotions in this book first appeared (in a less detailed form) on my blog at karlamclaren.com or on my author's page at Facebook.

Blogging and status writing are special forms of writing that allow me to quickly sketch out ideas (or answer readers' questions), and often, those sketches provide an excellent template for the more fully detailed explorations that books allow. In this book, I borrow from and incorporate some of my previous writing; when I do, I'll tell you about it.

In our work together, we'll enter into the hidden world of empathy so that you can learn how to become a healthy, happy, and intentional empath who works *with* emotions instead of working *against* them—and instead of being worked over *by* them! I'm happy to tell you that it doesn't matter where you start, what your empathy training was like in childhood, or where you currently reside on the continuum from low empathy to high empathy. No matter where you are, you're a member of an extensively empathic and intrinsically emotive species, and the tools you need to become a skilled empath are waiting inside you. Welcome!

PART ONE

Welcoming Empathy into Your Life

Chapter 1

What Is Empathy,
and Why Is It Important?

THIS BOOK ABOUT empathy is being written in the second decade of the twenty-first century, when intensive research on empathy is occurring in more than half a dozen academic disciplines. Empathy is *hot;* it's a major topic, and it's currently the focus of extensive review, research, and debate. Researchers all over the world are focusing tremendous attention on defining empathy, and many competing views of the components of empathy are being argued about in academic journals and conferences (we'll explore many of these views in this book). Empathy is a major topic of multidisciplinary and international interest right now.

Empathy is also a major topic of interest in your personal and professional life, where it helps you understand others well enough to successfully communicate and work with them. Empathy is also an essential part of love (though you don't have to love others to empathize with them skillfully—you don't even have to know them). Empathy helps you connect with others, feel alongside them, understand them, work with them, meet their needs, love them, and be loved by them. Empathy is essential for the health of your relationships, and empathy is fundamental to your social and emotional skills.

Empathy—or rather the *lack* of empathy—is also a central feature of modern American politics, where our profoundly polarized political parties are perfect examples of how too much identification with "our side" and a corresponding lack of empathy for the "other side" (and even the willingness to create another side) lead directly to unworkable, conflict-based posturing that has essentially paralyzed our entire political process. As we

3

can clearly see by its absence, empathy is crucial to the functioning of all social structures—large, small, intimate, local, national, and international. So what, exactly, is empathy?

DEFINING EMPATHY

If you and I sat together in a café, comfortable and congenial, we could probably come up with a fairly clear definition of *empathy*. We would likely agree that empathy is a social and emotional skill that helps us feel and comprehend the emotions, wishes, intentions, thoughts, and needs of others. We would also want to include a capacity to help others in our definition, because empathy tends to involve some form of action that allows us to interact with and offer support, assistance, or a listening ear to people we empathize with. In our definition, we'd probably conclude that empathy makes us aware of and available to the emotions, circumstances, and needs of others so that we can interact with them skillfully.

We would also probably agree that we'd prefer to be with an empathic person who could understand, connect to, interact with, and support us skillfully, as opposed to an unempathic person who did not know how to get into sync with us. In our relaxed café discussion, we might take fewer than five minutes to define empathy in a way that made sense to both of us, and yet we'd be jumping the gun. As I mentioned, researchers and theorists are engaged in an extensive rethinking of the definition and the function of empathy, and it is currently the topic of intense review and debate.

We'll visit these debates in Chapter 2, and we'll deepen our definition of empathy throughout this book. However, as we commence with our study of empathy, let's define it this way:

> *Empathy* is a social and emotional skill that helps us feel and understand the emotions, circumstances, intentions, thoughts, and needs of others, such that we can offer sensitive, perceptive, and appropriate communication and support.

In a way, we could call empathy the social and emotional glue that helps us create and maintain our relationships. It's a skill and a trait that we all possess in varying degrees—and it's a trait that's shared by many of our animal friends. It's also a skill and a trait that's very strong in certain people—while some of us struggle to empathize with clarity, others are exceptionally

4

sensitive to the emotions, circumstances, and needs of everyone and every-thing around them. I identify these latter people as *empaths*.

IDENTIFYING EMPATHS

What is an empath? Well, you are (in your own way) an empath. I am as well, and as the proto-empath (I was the first person to have claimed the title professionally in the late 1970s, and I started writing books about being an empath back in 1997), I've spent my life learning to work with, understand, define, redefine, and study emotions, empathy, and empaths. So, my current definition is this:

> An *empath* is someone who is aware that he or she reads emotions,
> nuances, subtexts, undercurrents, intentions, thoughts, social space,
> interactions, relational behaviors, body language, and gestural
> language to a greater degree than is deemed normal.

We're all empathic;[1] we have to be in order to navigate our way through the social world. We all read emotions, intentions, nuances, and so on, because empathy (as I am defining it—we'll explore more in the next chapter) is central to our capacity to connect to, interact with, and understand others and the social world.

The difference between being empathic and being an empath is one of intent and awareness. For me, emotions, nuances, subtexts, and so forth are the things I notice first in any situation. Words are interesting, but in many cases they tend to hide and obscure the more honest parts of communication and social interaction. For me, there's a wonderfully surprising world that exists in the space between words, and it's the space where my attention is nearly always drawn. Let me show you what I mean so you can understand this in a more tangible way. I'm going to invite you to sit inside my head as I people watch in a regular, everyday situation where I can't hear what's being said. (Is this the world's first *empath-cam*? Yes!) I chose this scene carefully, because it invites you into a level of empathy that's intentional, simple, and fun. (I masked the identities of everyone but my husband, Tino, and myself.)

Empathy wasn't always simple or fun for me. When I was young, my intense empathic and emotional receptivity made me feel as if I were on fire with the emotions of others. I picked up so many emotions and so much nonverbal social information from everyone around me that I often didn't know who I was or what I felt. The unprotected empathic receptivity I experienced in childhood was overwhelming for me. Too much information came barreling in at me, and I couldn't organize it, separate from it, manage it, or understand it. Part of my intense interpersonal receptivity, or *hyperempathy,* was a response to abuse that had occurred in my early childhood (I'll gently touch on that story in Chapter 2). But another part of my struggle came directly from our everyday training about emotions.

Most of us learn in very early childhood to distrust emotions, to categorize them as positive or negative, and to be suspicious about—and frankly afraid of—most of them.[2] I learned through cultural training that receiving emotions from others (unless those emotions were based on happiness) was something to guard against, because emotions were constantly portrayed as unwelcome, irrational, and even dangerous. This training didn't help me in any way, and as I grew up and learned how to live as a hyperempath, I had to actually veer away from almost all of our cultural training about emotions so that I could understand them empathically and work with them intelligently. Now, thankfully, after a lifetime of learning how to recognize, comprehend, and work with emotions empathically and how to understand and manage my hyperempathy, both have become useful tools that I can demonstrate without overwhelming you.

In the following scene, I'll walk you through a safe and grounded situation in which my strong empathy and emotional sensitivity are now helpful traits and not horrendous problems. I'll slow everything down so that you can identify, think about, catalog, reflect on, and predict some possible actions, emotions, and responses—but I'll rein myself in so that this people-watching scene won't exhaust you with too many details.

Note that I'll refer to emotions in a way that may seem unusual to you, but don't worry. We'll learn about my empathic approach to emotions in Chapters 3 and 4. For now, just come along with me:

It's almost closing time at the gym. I'm sitting relaxed and alone in the lobby after my swim, waiting for my husband, Tino, to come out of the locker room. The pool behind the large plate-glass window next to me is empty, and the normally noisy building is quiet and settling down after a long day.

Joseph, the maintenance man, enters the lobby and walks to the front desk, pushing a large cart filled with towels and cleaning supplies. He holds himself tall and proud—never subservient or slightly apologetic, but straightforward and dignified, with a good connection to his healthy anger and contentment. He nods and smiles at me, happily, and then turns and stops at the front desk on his way down the hallway. I can't quite make out what he's saying to Iris, the front desk attendant, as she works to close up shop, but I can see his back and his gestures, as well as her face as she interacts with him.

Joseph is talking about their shared work, and he's using analogies from the Bible to engage with Iris. I know this not just because I've heard Joseph bless me and other people, but also because he's using the rhythms and cadences of the Southern Baptist church. I don't know if Iris is a religious woman, and I'm concerned and apprehensive that he might offend her, so I watch her respond to Joseph as he sways slightly and gestures in a gracefully theatrical way.

Iris doesn't break his gaze to look at me with any sort of apology or irritation, so I gather that she's not offended or embarrassed. However, she holds her body a bit rigid, not matching Joseph's swaying rhythm. She displays a hint of anger and smiles at him, but it's not a big smile, if you know what I mean. She's engaging with him, yet she's keeping her distance, cool and somewhat businesslike, as she works to close down her desk for the night. Uh-oh! I feel my faint apprehension return. I'm not sure yet if her subtle anger is a function of their possibly unequal statuses within the workplace, their racial and cultural differences (Joseph is black; Iris is white), or perhaps some interpersonal problem between them.

Joseph displays a momentary bit of wariness—a soft form of fear that he follows quickly with a light display of happiness. Then he shifts his body and his story, turning slightly away from Iris and almost addressing an invisible audience. Oh, nice! I feel calmer, and I feel respect for Joseph's social skills. Joseph has oriented to her anger signal, and he has corrected his approach by applying a split second of appropriate shame to his behavior. Iris now has the space she needs to focus on her work. Joseph still wants to tell his inspirational story, but he has picked up her signaling and responded to it with empathic skill; he's created a win-win situation. I know this because happiness arises in Iris as she smiles a bit wider, and though she breaks his gaze to attend to her closing duties, she begins swaying with

7

Joseph—slightly, almost imperceptibly, but it's there. She's dropped a boundary, and she's engaging with him willingly. This tells me that they're not having an ongoing interpersonal problem (because he was so quickly able to repair the situation, and she was so willing to let the repair happen) and that their workplace status appears to be fairly equal (because he understood her need to get back to work and didn't monopolize her time as a superior might have). However, I'm still interested in the cultural and racial divide between them.

As the conversation between Joseph and Iris continues, Iris sweeps her gaze toward me with some wariness—soft fear and a bit of appropriate shame (because she's not working "properly" in front of a gym member). I look down quickly and pretend not to be watching them. This is the end of a long day for them, and they need a sense of their own private time. Even though I'm just a few yards away, I intentionally ignore Iris to create a kind of privacy wall between us. Iris turns back toward Joseph, and her soft fear and shame subside, because she's satisfied that I'm not a problem she needs to attend to.

Joseph reaches a natural pause in his story, and Iris leans toward him happily and adds her own piece about some biblical character. Okay, so she's religious, and she's not offended by his biblical references. But as she speaks, I see Joseph's back tense up slightly—with small amounts of anger and shock—and he shifts his body sideways, away from her, tilting his head as if he's listening to something that he is not quite sure of. *Ouch!* I wonder if Iris has made a faux pas; perhaps she's mentioned the wrong part of the Bible or the wrong character. Joseph knows his Bible, it's clear, and I wait with some apprehension to see how he'll respond.

Will Joseph correct Iris in a paternal, shaming way (and shut her down)? Will he argue with her (and create conflict between them)? Or will he shun and disengage from her (and hurt her feelings)? *Yow!* This could go sideways very quickly! I scan the room: Will I need to create a pretense to get up and move into their relational space—maybe to get a drink of water—if one or both of them gets stuck and needs some social support or a way to disengage?

At the end of her comment, Iris waits (so do I!). Although she may not be able to consciously identify the signals Joseph's body language is sending, she's aware that something is off and that she's done something wrong. She looks down and flushes with shame almost imperceptibly, and then she covers her embarrassment by leaning toward Joseph wordlessly, smiling in a broad but faintly apologetic way, and slightly lowering her entire body below his in a shame-submissive, sadness- and fear-moderated shrugging gesture.

I realize that I'm holding my breath, concerned and apprehensive. But Iris's adroit gestures of contrition shift everything. Joseph immediately leans in toward her, moving his head downward and joining her in the submissive space she has created, and with his head, he makes a kind of scooping upward gesture as he engages, "Yes!" and weaves her story into his own. Iris rises with him out of the submissive space—almost as if Joseph were pulling her upward with the movement of his head—and they are equals again, happy together, swaying together as the story continues. *Whew!* Nice social repair, Joseph and Iris! My apprehension subsides, and I begin to breathe again as I look away, relaxed and a bit dreamy.

Tino walks into the lobby from the locker room and sees Joseph and Iris talking. Although he feels appropriate shame as he looks down and attempts to walk gently past them to give them their privacy, Joseph stops his story and greets Tino jovially. Iris also stops what she's doing, and Tino slows down to address each of them with a happy smile and open, though faintly apologetic, gestures. As Tino passes them, Joseph and Iris look at each other and nod silently in unison to end their interaction and get back to work. Tino approaches me with a smile of happiness and relief, sees my absorption and curiosity, and asks, "Whatcha doin'?"

"Oh, nothin'."

Nothing indeed. The interaction I watched between Joseph and Iris took fewer than two minutes. However, as I mentioned earlier, I had to rein myself in as I wrote about it for you, because it was filled with enough social, emotional, interactional, cultural, gestural, and subtextual information to fill this book. There's a fascinating, deep, endlessly surprising richness that exists in the interactional space between people—and though we all swim in, live with, trip over, and depend utterly upon this space for our social existence, our knowledge of it exists in a hidden and unspoken area that only specialists seem to be able to access consciously.

Actors, musicians, dancers, choreographers, composers, animal trainers, performance artists, and martial artists are some of the specialists who have knowledge of this interactional space. So do novelists, poets, creative writers, and playwrights. Social scientists and behaviorists study this space intensively, and psychologists and counselors work to help us understand and become skillful in regard to it. This book adds another category to this list of interaction specialists: *empaths*.

You're already an empathic person, because your awareness of emotions, nuance, gestural language, and interaction is a function of being a member of our highly social species. *The Art of Empathy* will not magically turn you into an empath—you were born with these skills, and you use them every day. What this book will do is help you become a healthy, effective, and *intentional* empath so that you can understand emotions, use your empathy comfortably, and pilot successfully through the richness of interactional space.

You already use your nonverbal empathic skills every day—when you socialize, read body language, work with animals and infants, listen to music, laugh at physical comedy, and appreciate art and drama. You also use your verbal empathic skills when you speak and when you decipher spoken and written language, because you actually cannot make sense of verbal or written communication if you can't decipher subtext, context, nonverbal cues, and the multiple meanings behind words. Empathic skills make you verbally and nonverbally sensitive to and aware of yourself, others, and the social world.

If you're highly empathic, you might appear to be magically and supernaturally aware of others. For many years, I mistakenly thought that my intense hyperempathic abilities meant that I was a psychic (I realized my mistake and ended my entire psychic healing career in 2003). If you can read and decipher emotions, intentions, nuances, social space, and nonverbal language, you can see deeply into people's lives. You can see the issues people think they're hiding, you can quickly understand how people approach life and relationships, and you can become very skilled at getting down to the essence of who people are.

A quick example: I was an intensely active and fidgety child, and I had trouble with language (a stutter and other verbal-processing issues). I had wildly sensitive hearing and vision, recurrent nightmares, and great difficulties regulating my emotions. When I was four, my mother took me to a neurologist to see if he could help me. When he first met us, this doctor came into the consulting room in his nice white lab coat and smiled warmly as he sat down. I studied him for a few seconds and said, "Why are you so grouchy?"

"Hmmm," he said, meeting my eyes willingly. "Do I look grouchy to you?"

"No," I replied. "You don't *look* grouchy; you *are* grouchy."

He laughed and sent me to play in the waiting room while he talked to my mom. Mom told me that he sort of patted her on the head in commiseration and explained that I had no filters, that I was unusually sensitive to every possible form of input—visual, auditory, tactile (he knew this from preliminary testing by my pediatrician), and emotional—and that she was going to have to protect me from the world until I learned how to manage all of my intense sensitivities. He made this diagnosis in a few seconds, empathic man that he was, because I had read through his smile and his calm demeanor and picked up on the emotional residues of a fight that he had had with his wife on the phone earlier that morning. I marvel at how lucky I was to be seen by this doctor. Another doctor might have been offended by such an impertinent child; another doctor might have lied or not even remembered the fight. But this doctor validated my strong empathic capacity and set my mom and me onto a path of trying to create a healthy, nurturing environment for an intensely sensitive person. (This book is filled with information on how you can create a similar healthy environment for yourself and your loved ones.)

With strong empathic skills, you can get to know people very deeply in a seemingly magical period of time, and it can seem as if you have access to some sort of paranormal skill. But empathic skills aren't magical; they're normal human abilities—even when they're very highly developed.

After a sea change in my understanding of what it means to be an empath, as well as a return to college to study the social sciences, I now know that empathic abilities are not in any way paranormal. I apologize for having been so confused about that, because framing empathy as a mystical skill made it into something special and unobtainable—and that isn't something I ever felt comfortable about. Empathic awareness that is highly developed can look mystical, but it's not. Although the world that empathy reveals *is* a hidden world of undercurrent, subtext, and nonverbal cues, it is not a mystical world; rather, it is the social interactional world—and it is a world that we can all learn to understand more clearly.

A vital part of that understanding comes from learning how to work with (not against) emotions. Of all the things we pick up from others empathically, emotions can be the most problematic. When we lose our empathy for others, it's not usually because we don't agree with their subtext, their nuance, or their gestural language. No, when we lose our empathy and shut people out, it's usually because we sense an emotion (or an emotional tone) that makes us uncomfortable.

For me, learning how to maintain my empathy in the face of any and all emotions has been a real game changer, and it has made being an empath infinitely easier. Empathy is a fundamentally emotional skill, and understanding emotions empathically—as vital parts of cognition—is a key to understanding the often-obscured processes that make empathy work. Thankfully, empathy isn't a hidden world for me now—the processes aren't mysterious, the emotions don't knock me out of commission, the extensive information I pick up isn't concealed from my conscious awareness, and the decisions I make about what to do in response to my empathic observations are not random. This is the approach to empathy that I'll be sharing with you.

Empathy helps you comprehend, connect to, and care about others; it helps you create healthy relationships, healthy communities, and a healthy society. As our world becomes ever more multicultural, we can all see the chilling effects of people becoming intentionally less empathic about the *other*, whoever that other may be. Racism, sexism, religious intolerance, homophobia, ageism, ableism (insensitivity and discrimination toward the disabled), and political polarization are all results of a breakdown in empathy, and each leads directly to misery and injustice. Empathy for the seeming other is the magical ingredient that can help us learn to live more peacefully with ourselves; with our friends, family, and community; and, most especially, with people who are nothing at all like us.

BUT FIRST, HOW EMPATHIC ARE YOU?

Empathy is a vital skill that we all possess to varying degrees, and the good news is that it can be worked with and developed throughout our lives. Empathic abilities can also be increased or calmed down (in the case of hyperempathy) at any age. I'm providing this informal empathic inventory for you, but rather than treating it as the final word on your empathic skills, please look at it as a snapshot of your current situation. Your empathic capacity is actually fluid and malleable throughout your life span.

If you have a low empathy score, this book will help you increase your empathic abilities; if you have a very high score, this book will help you moderate your hyperempathy so that you can live more comfortably. As you'll learn, there's a sweet spot with empathic skills—a *juuust right* place where your empathy is neither too cold nor too hot. So as you answer yes or no to each statement that follows, understand that in most cases, you can modify each capacity. Empathy is a skill, and it's a pliable skill at that.

YOUR EMPATHIC INVENTORY

_____ I tend to know how others are feeling, even (or especially *if)* they are trying to hide it.

_____ I tend to avoid conflict because I don't want to hurt others or make them feel embarrassed.

_____ People (and animals) and their relationships and interactions are endlessly interesting to me.

_____ I do *not* need to see other's faces to read their emotions.

_____ I am drawn to situations of injustice, and I spend a lot of time thinking about how to alleviate suffering.

_____ I often mimic the mannerisms, accents, and body language of others without meaning to.

_____ I tend to think about interpersonal issues by imagining myself in the place of those involved.

_____ I have a very easy time reading between the lines, under the surface, and behind the obvious.

_____ I feel beauty palpably; beauty creates a sense of delight and expansiveness in my body.

_____ Interpersonal conflict—even when it does not involve me personally—often feels physically painful to me.

_____ I do not like black-and-white polarization; the truth usually resides somewhere in the middle.

_____ When I make a social blunder, I feel extremely disturbed, and I work hard to make things right again.

_____ I feel the emotions of others viscerally, as if the emotions belong to me.

_____ I can sense and identify multiple simultaneous emotions in myself, in others, and in interactions between duos or groups.

_____ I can sense and identify the relative intensity of multiple emotions in myself, in others, and in interactions between duos or groups.

_____ I consider the needs and feelings of others in decisions I make, often to the point of ignoring my own needs and feelings.

_____ I love to watch interactions, especially when the people or animals are unaware of me.

_____ I enjoy drama, movies, good television shows, and well-told stories.

_____ I love good literature, well-written characters, and well-paced stories.

_____ I love to play with and interact lovingly with people and animals.

_____ I have an easy, natural ability in one or more art forms.

_____ I have a good, and often silly, sense of humor.

_____ I am good with shy people.

_____ I am good with children.

_____ I am good with animals.

_____ In an emergency, I can focus on what's important and provide assistance.

_____ I often feel tender, protective feelings toward others—even complete strangers.

_____ Art, music, and literature touch me very deeply.

_____ I am very sensitive to foods and tend to respond markedly to dietary changes.

_____ I have an intense capacity to focus on activities that delight and engage me.

_____ When I'm in conflict with others, I tend to talk deeply about it with third parties so that I can sort out the many issues that have led to the conflict.

_____ I love to talk about and think about interpersonal issues and social structures.

_____ I have a rich interior life, and I enjoy being alone with my thoughts and ideas.

_____ I often need to get away from the needs of others and recharge my emotional batteries.

_____ I am deeply sensitive to things like sounds, colors, textures, scents, shapes, and spatial relationships between objects.

_____ I am able to stay present (for myself and others) in the face of intense emotions like grief, rage, and despair.

_____ I tend to physically feel the emotions of fear and anxiety of others in my own body, especially when others are unwilling or unable to admit to feeling them.

_____ I enjoy thinking about, searching for, and finding the perfect gift for others.

_____ I regularly feel alongside others; I feel their emotions and share their concerns.

_____ I tend to approach problems tangibly, using my hands and body as I think about and walk through the issues involved.

_____ I gesture a great deal when I communicate, and my face is often very animated.

_____ With those closest to me, I tend to rely upon gestures and eye contact (rather than words) during conversations.

_____ I am very aware of the personal space of others.

SCORING YOUR ANSWERS

1–20 yes responses: If you answered yes to twenty or fewer of these questions, you can consider yourself to be somewhat low in empathic ability at this moment. However, the reasons for this are different for each person. This score may mean that you're relatively uninterested in or unaware of the emotions and situations of others. But sometimes, a low score can mean that you're actually hyperempathic but currently unable to organize your sensitivities and your concern for others in a way that works for you. In hyperempathy, you may experience overwhelm in the presence of emotions or interactions, and you may shut down as a protective response. In either case, this book can help you. If you're insensitive to emotions and interactions, this book will help you become more aware of and skillful with them; and if you're overwhelmed by emotions and interactions, this book will help you organize and address your sensitivities so that you can live more comfortably in the social world.

21–32 yes responses: This midrange of yes responses may place you in that *juuust right* empathic sweet spot I mentioned—where your empathic abilities are neither too cold nor too hot. However, there may be areas where you need some support in increasing or decreasing specific sensitivities. We want this sweet spot to be comfortable, so that you can be a healthy and happy empathic presence in a world that needs you!

33–43 yes responses: This number of yes responses places you in the high empathy category, which can lead you into hyperempathy if you haven't yet learned to create effective boundaries, work gracefully with emotions, and use self-regulation skills when you're overwhelmed. As it is with any talent or tendency, high levels of ability can be a double-edged sword. Although it can be very easy for you to empathize, the steps involved in healthy empathizing may be hidden from you because you didn't really ever learn *how* to do it. In this book, we'll explore each of the specific and connected aspects of empathy so that you'll have the tools you need to understand and manage your empathic abilities.

As you read through the discussion of your own score, think about people in your life who you would currently label as being low in empathy or high in empathy and then read through those categories as well. People who seem to be very low in empathy can sometimes be covering up an uncomfortable amount of hypersensitivity or an uncomfortably deep level of concern for others, which means they could use some gentleness and accommodation from others. On the other side of the coin, people who seem to be very high in empathy can be heading for burnout, because their empathic skills are *too* activated, which means they could use some gentleness and accommodation as well.

Wherever you currently stand with your empathic skills, I welcome you, and I appreciate your willingness to explore and deepen these vital social and emotional capacities. In this book, we'll work together to help you find your own version of that *just right* place where your empathic skills and sensitivities are accessible, understandable, workable, and comfortable for you.

Thank you for embarking upon this empathic journey, and thank you for being willing to bring your emotional awareness and your healthy empathy to a waiting world. I appreciate you!

CHAPTER 2

Defining and
Redefining Empathy

An Empathic Approach

IN THE JANUARY 2012 issue of the academic journal *Emotion Review,* scholars from around the globe and across the disciplines came together to share current research on empathy. Surprisingly, there is not yet a clear, agreed-upon definition of *empathy* or of the differing facets that constitute empathy. (As for *empaths*? Forget that! They're not even a topic of scientific notice.) In fact, debates about empathy are in full flower in the fields of philosophy, psychology, anthropology, sociology, social work, primatology, evolutionary biology, and cognitive neuroscience—and the precise functional definition of empathy is currently being argued about all over the world.

This is not actually a problem (in most cases), because this kind of dynamic, multifaceted, and often-contentious interaction is what you want to see in a healthy scientific pursuit, especially in regard to something as crucial as empathy. In many disciplines, research on emotions and empathy is currently undergoing tremendous upheaval and renewal as we continually reassess human evolution and human (and animal) behavior—and as we increase our capacity to understand the inner workings of the brain.

Some researchers are looking at the words we use to describe empathy. They're doing a kind of linguistic reorganization of words such as *sympathy, compassion,* and *altruism,*[3] such that most current definitions of empathy now encompass the compassionate actions and responses that you and I included in the short café discussion we had just a few pages ago. This is an interesting transition, because in some older definitions, empathy was specifically restricted to the capacity to share emotions with others and did not include a compassionate action component (such as responding to the emotions you sense and doing something thoughtful for another). Today, this empathic action component is being redefined as a sign of empathy that is fully realized. This is an especially important distinction in empathy research with infants and toddlers,[4] where children's age-linked attainment of the capacity to *do something helpful* about the emotions they sense is treated as a sign that they have arrived at a specific developmental stage. At this point in our understanding of empathy, it's not enough to merely share an emotion with another; you also have to be able to do something helpful and compassionate in response.

Other researchers are working to create, validate, or modify tests for empathy; identify whether primates and other animals have empathy (yes, they do) and in what amounts; determine when infants develop empathy and in what forms; and understand how empathy develops (and what impedes or supports its development). There is also a great deal of interest in how empathy works in the brain and whether (or if) neurological structures called *mirror neurons* and the hormone oxytocin are central to empathy. Other researchers and philosophers are arguing about whether certain kinds of people can be categorized as either highly empathic or unempathic; while still others are looking at how empathy is related to the very formation of our species as an emotionally expressive and empathically connected band of highly social primates. The quest to understand empathy is an intensive, multinational enterprise.

The fact that you and I created a definition of empathy in our imagined café discussion a few pages back is useful for our purposes, but I do want you to know that we're ahead of the curve here. The study of empathy is ongoing, and the academic definition is in flux. My approach comes not just from the academic literature but also from a lifetime of learning how to survive and thrive as a hyperempath and helping others learn how to thrive as well. As we move forward, we'll rely upon the research, but we'll focus on the lived experience of what it is to be an empath.

However, before we enter more deeply into our empathic study of empathy, there are a few problems we need to clear up. Some of these problems come from everyday prejudices, but some actually come from the research itself, and we need to address these problems directly.

WELCOMING THOSE WHO HAVE BEEN EXILED

An unfortunate offshoot of all of this intense interest in empathy is that there's been a facile and frankly unempathic quest to exclude entire categories of humans from the empathic community. As an empath, I challenge these exclusions wholeheartedly, and I absolutely won't perpetuate them in this book. Certainly, in popular culture, there's a deeply sexist notion that empathy is a female skill and that males are constitutionally less empathic or less emotive than females are. This terrible idea has created untold suffering for boys and men, who are often not taught much about emotions and are not treated as fully emotive and sensitive beings. I can't tell you how many times I've given talks and had men come up to me afterward and whisper, as if they don't even have the right to say it, "I think I'm an empath." What? *Of course men are empaths!*

Certainly, many males have been excluded from an understanding of emotions and empathy, and sexist ideas about men are absolutely commonplace, but they're not true. So let's look at our definition of empathy again, specifically in terms of men and boys:

Empathy is a social and emotional skill that helps us feel and understand the emotions, circumstances, intentions, thoughts, and needs of others, such that we can offer sensitive, perceptive, and appropriate communication and support.

This definition does not exclude men or boys, and it doesn't suggest that feeling or understanding emotions is a female skill. Males can easily understand the feelings, circumstances, thoughts, and needs of others. Males can also offer sensitive, perceptive, and appropriate communication and support. Empathy is not a gendered skill—it's a human skill! The alleged problem of male empathy doesn't come from inside the male body; there is no male-specific defect of empathy or emotional awareness; and there are no male-specific differences in early emotional development. Little boys love cuddling and love and emotions and empathy. So do men.

But tragically, we don't tend to raise boys (or men) as if they're fully empathic and fully emotive beings. As a direct result, males in our heavily gendered society may experience emotions more intensely than females do. However, because they've been socialized to view themselves as unemotional, many males may believe that their normal human emotions are strange or out of place. In general, males are not socially permitted to express a full range of emotions or to chat with friends about those emotions (as females are socially allowed to do), which leaves males with very few healthy or fully conscious outlets for their emotions. In our social training and our social myth making, we've created an appallingly unempathic environment for most males.

I wrote a piece on my website[5] about this in connection to the wonderful book *Pink Brain, Blue Brain,* by neurologist Lise Eliot. She busts sexist myths about boys and girls, and in her book, she points out that the differences between the brains of males and females are actually quite small at birth and throughout childhood. Eliot focuses on socialization—on how we approach gender roles and how we treat boys and girls so wildly differently—as the chief contributing factor in the later differences between males and females in terms of their emotional, social, and verbal skills. Eliot also notes that although there are some early, sex-based differences in verbal abilities (girls are sometimes more verbal than boys, but not always), as well as some differences in activity levels (boys are sometimes more active than girls, but not always), there is not as much difference as we've been led to believe. In fact, there is more difference *between* girls in these traits and *between* boys in these traits than there is between the sexes. However, parents tend to support these gender-linked behaviors very early. For example, they may respond positively to baby girls' vocalizations while subtly ignoring their activity levels (and vice versa for boys).

In numerous disguised-gender studies, people describe identical behavior differently depending on whether they think a baby is a boy or a girl. A pink-attired sleeping baby will be called delicate and darling, while the same sleeping baby attired in blue will be called strong and dynamic. What? It's the *same* baby! But in a heavily gendered world such as ours, it's not the same baby at all. We actually attribute different (and sometimes opposite) emotional and empathic qualities to identical behaviors in boys and girls. We enforce gender so strongly and so incessantly that we don't even notice we're doing it; it's the air we breathe and the ground we walk on.[6]

Most of our valenced ideas about gender roles for males and females are socially created; they're not biologically or objectively true, and they can't be found in the brains of infants. But because so few people understand the difference between objective reality and socially constructed reality, these myths and falsehoods gain the status of concrete truth. Accordingly, many little girls are encouraged to become relatively inactive people who love to talk about emotions and social relationships (but hate math), while little boys are urged to stop crying at a certain age, even when they've been hurt deeply. Boys are given guns and trucks and told to *man up,* stop crying, there's nothing to be afraid of, stop being *girly,* stop talking about feelings, and basically stop being fully alive. When we enforce gender stereotypes, we actually reduce the intelligence, the emotional capacity, the empathic skills, and the very humanity of little boys and little girls. We also throw most of the emotional awareness tasks in heterosexual relationships onto women, which might seem helpful but which actually further reduces males' emotional skills.

Enforced gender stereotypes can certainly interfere with the emotional and social development of human beings. And yet we all have the capacity for emotional and empathic awareness. All of us—males, females, and everyone in between—can intentionally learn how to identify and work with emotions and empathy at any age and from any position on the gender continuum. Empathy is a human skill; it's not gender specific.

As we grow up, our brains do change, and adult women often have different emotional skills and neurological profiles from adult men. But the brain is a highly plastic organ, and it will change in response to any strong training. For instance, the brains of highly trained musicians or people who speak many languages look and behave differently from the brains of nonmusical people or speakers of only one language. But this doesn't mean that music and language are forbidden to you if you weren't trained early; your brain is plastic, and you can learn new things at any age. There may be some discernible differences in the brains of adult males and adult females, but the old myth about men being less emotional or less able to feel emotions has no basis in neurology. Even the idea that men have smaller corpora callosa than women (the corpus callosum carries information between the left and right hemispheres of the brain) was based on a study of just fourteen brains and has since been disconfirmed, as Eliot points out. But people hold onto this sexist idea, repeat it constantly, and write books and make whole careers around it, while males suffer silently (or act out) the emotions they clearly feel but aren't invited (or allowed) to understand.

Even so, males have always found ways to feel deeply, to become highly skilled in the social world, to create great art, to parent lovingly, to care for animals, to heal the sick, to fight for social justice, to love fully, to dance and sing and act, to communicate meaningfully, and to be profoundly emotive beings. So let me state this right out loud: males have all the human emotions, males can feel and understand all emotions, males have empathy, males can display empathy, and males are natural empaths. As such, there will be no gendering of emotions or empathy anywhere in this book. I enthusiastically welcome men and boys into the empathic community. (We'll talk more about the trouble we create for males from infancy forward when we look at empathy and child development in Chapter 9.)

Another group of people who are tragically and unfairly excluded from the empathic community are people on the autism spectrum, whom I and others[7] have identified as *hyperempathic* rather than unempathic. In some areas of empathy research, the multiple hypersensitivities that many autistic people experience are not clearly understood, which has led to the mistaken assumption that because many autistic people have difficulty deciphering social cues, they must therefore lack the capacity for empathy. (When I describe people as *autistic,* I'm using "identity first" language very intentionally; please see the endnote.) This deeply unempathic assumption creates continual misery for autistic people, such that many otherwise caring people will blithely refer to autistics as being cold and incapable of meaningful relationships or even love.[8] This is not only thoroughly and demonstrably wrong, but it's also insensitive, discriminatory, and ableist.[9] It also has terrible effects on the way autistic people are viewed, taught, portrayed, and treated in the larger community. Some researchers in the area of autism are becoming more awake to the humanity and dignity of autistic people, but there's still a very, very long way to go.

In our work as empaths, however, we'll enthusiastically welcome autistic people as fellow empaths—and often hyperempaths—who have unique sensitivities and immeasurable capacities for deep relationships, social interactions, and love. Let's state this right out loud: autistic people have all the human emotions—autistics can feel and understand all emotions, autistics have empathy, autistics can display empathy, and autistic people are natural empaths.

The deeply mistaken exclusion of boys, men, and autistic people from the world of fully realized empathy tells us that the study of empathy is a very active and tumultuous (and, in some cases, very backward) undertaking. Clearly, the story of empathy is still being written.

There is yet another category of humans who are excluded from the realm of empathy; these people are variously called psychopaths, sociopaths (though this term is considered dated), narcissists, borderlines, or antisocial personalities. There is a great deal of interplay among these definitions, and diagnostic criteria shift (as do the diagnostic titles). However, each condition includes assumptions of a pathological lack of empathy. As a survivor of predatory abuse (I'll explain what I mean by that, gently, at the end of this chapter), I've had a lifelong interest in the dark side of human nature: of criminals and victims, abusers and manipulators, and our many shifting conceptualizations of human evil. Right now, one approach is to attribute all human evil to a lack of empathy, but I find that explanation to be too pat and too simplistic. I'm also very concerned sociopolitically about the fact that early research on psychopathy was conducted on imprisoned people, who are a socially created category rather than a truly different type of person.[10] Although there are certainly people who victimize others intentionally, attributing this abusive and predatory tendency merely to a lack of empathy displays an incomplete understanding of empathy, emotions, the nature of conflict, a sociologically grounded approach to crime and social control methods, and the many ways in which empathy development in early childhood can go awry.[11]

As we move into a deeper study of empathy, beginning with a short history of the concept, we'll revisit abusers and predatory people not as ominously inhuman specimens with terrifying empathy deficits, but rather in a more empathic way altogether.

A SHORT HISTORY OF EMPATHY

Empathy and compassion have a long history in spiritual traditions. In Judaism, God is called the father of compassion, and in Islam, chief among Allah's attributes are mercy and compassion. In Christianity, Jesus had such compassion and empathy that he chose to be crucified in order to take the pains of the world into his body and cleanse humanity of its sins. In Buddhism, the bodhisattva is an enlightened being who, in boundless compassion and empathy, forgoes Nirvana until all beings have achieved enlightenment. In Hinduism, *daya,* or compassion, is one of the three central virtues, and in Jainism, compassion for all life is the central tenet of the faith and of the Jainist dietary tradition of veganism. Compassion and empathy are vital aspects of sacred traditions all across our planet and all throughout recorded history.

Our current Western idea of empathy arises from two places. In English, the word *empathy* comes from the Greek root *pathos,* which means "emotion, feeling, suffering, or pity" (it also comes from a German word, as we'll explore below). The English words *empathy* and *sympathy* are used interchangeably to refer to the sharing of or knowledge of emotions, whereas *apathy* relates to lack of emotions, and *antipathy* relates to antagonistic emotions. Some sources make a distinction between empathy (the ability to share an emotion viscerally) and sympathy (the ability to understand the emotions of others without actually feeling them yourself), but this distinction isn't concrete or stable. In some dictionaries, the definitions of empathy and sympathy are the exact opposite of the ones I just gave you. So, from this point forward, I'll be folding the contested word *sympathy* into our larger definition of empathy, and I won't focus on sympathy as a separate entity in this book.

In the research, these two seemingly separate categories of empathizing have now been renamed as *affective* (viscerally feeling) empathy and *cognitive* (objectively understanding) empathy. Although these new terms address the sympathy–empathy confusion very nicely, they create a distinction that is problematic (and we'll come back to that problem later in this chapter).

I was surprised to learn that the English word *empathy* was coined in 1909.[12] That's so recent! I was also surprised to learn that the word came into our language as a translation of the German word *Einfühlung* (pronounced EIN-fhoo-loong), which means "in feeling" or "feeling into" and which first appeared in print in German philosopher Robert Vischer's 1873 PhD dissertation on aesthetics.[13] Vischer used the word to describe both our capacity to enter into a piece of art or literature, to feel the emotions that the artist had intended, and our capacity to imbue a piece of art (or any object) with meaning and emotions. Einfühlung adds a wonderful dimension to empathy because it helps us view empathy not only as our interactional capacity to share emotions with others, but also as our ability to engage emotively with the world around us and with the nuances and intentions underlying art, music, literature, and symbolism. With the concept of Einfühlung, we can easily see that men—great artists, writers, musicians, thinkers, and lovers of aesthetics—are absolutely equal to women in their capacity to interact deeply and empathically with the world. The same is true for people on the autism spectrum.

You may have already noticed that when I explain the act of empathizing, I don't refer specifically to other *people*. Instead, I refer to *others*, because empathizing is not limited to human beings. The concept of Einfühlung really helps us encompass the larger aspects of the empathic experience, and it helps us include animals, art, literature, ideas, and symbols in the category of things we can empathize with. The concept of Einfühlung also helps us clearly identify people on the autism spectrum as empaths[14] who, in some cases, focus their intense sensitivities, empathy, and interactional capacities on things other than human beings.

There's a beautiful documentary from 2010 called *Loving Lampposts,* which filmmaker Todd Drezner made about his autistic son, Sam. In it, you can use your own Einfühlung capacity to watch Sam interact adoringly and completely with his beloved lampposts—he communicates with them wordlessly, interacts with them, and has full-bodied, aesthetic Einfühlung with those lampposts right in front of your eyes. It's clear that the lampposts soothe, calm, and ground Sam. Empathy is an active, interactional, and deeply emotional skill, but it is not—and never has been—restricted to human relationships.

The concept of Einfühlung really resonates with my experience (does this mean I'm having Einfühlung about Einfühlung?), because the people I know who are most empathic are often very deeply engaged with the nonhuman world. Nature, animals, art, music, movement and exercise, dance, drama, literature, ideas, concepts, symbolism, science, mathematics, philosophy, and spirituality resonate very profoundly for my fellow empaths—and their empathic abilities help them develop not just talent in their chosen interests, but also intensive *relationships* with their interests. For an empath, playing music, for instance, is not just a physical act of hitting the right notes in the right order with the right intonation; rather, the musical experience is a fully embodied, fully emotive interaction between the empath and the art form.

We'll return to this process of empathic embodiment and deep aesthetic engagement throughout this book, because for empaths, these full-bodied, sensual interactions with nonhuman entities can be vital healing activities. In a hectic world filled with the unmet (and often disowned) emotional needs of others, empaths can attain deep relaxation, restoration, and rejuvenation by focusing their full-bodied empathic abilities on art, nature, music, animals, intellectual pursuits, ideas, and interactions with other nonhuman entities. Nearly all current definitions of empathy focus on human interactions, but thankfully, the concept of Einfühlung will help us enormously as we learn how to become healthy and balanced empaths in a human social world that is often stunningly unempathic.

For empaths, interaction is food; it's oxygen; it's everything. Yet, if we mistakenly think that empathy can *only* occur in human relationships (and if we can't find enough good and deep relationships), then our empathic capacities can wither on the vine. When empathic people can't find deep and meaningful interactions, they can sometimes feel out of place in the social world. Unseen. Inappropriate. Unwanted. Too much.

If this form of social dislocation has been your experience, there is a cure—you can redirect your empathy toward healthy and delightful non-human entities, such as art, music, animals, literature, ideas, movement, dance, tactile activities, gardening, building, mathematics, physics—anything that engages you. A huge part of the art of empathy is to learn to behave empathically toward yourself and to honor your empathic nature, no matter what unempathic or counterempathic shenanigans are occurring in the human social world.

THE SIX ESSENTIAL ASPECTS OF EMPATHY

Empathy is an innate and accessible skill; however, because it operates in the often-hidden interactional world of nuance, gesture, and undercurrent, it can be a somewhat mysterious process. After many decades of helping people balance their empathic skills and increase their emotional awareness, I've separated the processes of empathy into six discrete (but interrelated), step-by-step aspects.

I've organized empathy in this way for two important reasons. First, I want you to understand empathy as a *process* that is accessible and malleable (no matter where you currently reside on the empathic continuum). That way, if you have issues with empathy, you'll be able to zero in on your specific area of concern. Second, I'll be using these six aspects throughout this book to explain the purpose of the empathic skills and practices I'll be teaching you and to help you learn how to identify your strengths and challenges (and those of your loved ones). I'll first quickly define my six aspects of empathy before I move into a deeper examination.

1. **Emotion Contagion:** Before empathy can take place, you need to sense that an emotion is occurring in another or that an emotion is expected of you. There is currently great debate about how Emotion Contagion occurs and how we realize that emotions are required from us, but it is agreed that the process of empathy depends on our capacity to feel and share emotions. *Empathy is first and foremost an emotional skill.*

2. **Empathic Accuracy:**[15] This is your ability to accurately identify and understand emotional states, thoughts, and intentions in yourself and others.

3. **Emotion Regulation:** To be an effective empath, you have to develop the ability to understand, regulate, and work with your own emotions; you have to be self-aware. When you can clearly identify and regulate your own emotions, you'll tend to be able to function skillfully in the presence of strong emotions (your own and others'), rather than being overtaken or knocked out of commission by them.

4. **Perspective Taking:** This skill helps you imaginatively put yourself in the place of others, see situations through their eyes, and accurately sense what they might be feeling and thinking so that you can understand what they might want or need.

5. **Concern for Others:** Empathy helps you connect with others, but the quality of your response depends on your ability to care about others as well. When you feel emotions with others, accurately identify those emotions, regulate them in yourself, and take the perspective of others, your sensitive concern will help you engage with them in a way that displays your care and compassion.

6. **Perceptive Engagement:** This skill allows you to make perceptive decisions based on your empathy and to respond—or act (if necessary)—in a way that works for others. Perceptive Engagement can be considered the pinnacle of empathic skill, because it combines your capacity to sense and accurately identify the emotions, thoughts, and intentions of others; to regulate your own emotions; to take the perspective of others; to focus on them with care and concern; and then to do something skillful based on your perceptions. Notably, in Perceptive Engagement, you'll often do something for another that would not work for you at all and that might not even be in your best interests. Perceptive Engagement is about meeting the needs of the other.

These six aspects of empathy build upon one another. Although Emotion Contagion tends to occur instinctively, the rest are more intentional. However, all of these aspects can be developed (or calmed down in the case of hyperempathy) with the empathic skills you'll learn in this book.

Let's look at each aspect in a bit more depth.

EMOTION CONTAGION

Emotion Contagion is central to an understanding of empathy, which always includes some form of transmission of emotion from one to another. There is currently a great deal of debate about how this transmission occurs. Is emotion transmitted primarily through the face? Is it moderated through a few specific visual structures in the brain? Is emotion copied in a more intentionally cognitive manner, such that I can only feel an emotion from you if I can understand it in myself? Or is there more to the story?

As I write this book in 2013, a great deal of our capacity to empathize is being attributed to a group of structures in the brain called *mirror neurons*. These structures are thought to activate movement-related areas in your brain when you view movement in someone else (for instance, if you see someone moving his or her arm, your brain will fire the same neurons you use when you move your own arm). The mirror-neuron hypothesis puts forth the idea that these structures do the same kind of thing in response to emotions—that is, when you see someone feeling happy or sad, for instance, your brain might fire the same neurons that you use when *you* feel happy or sad.

The hypothesis behind mirror neurons is that they help you empathize because you can actually feel the movement or the emotion of another in your own body—the idea is that you can empathize because you can actually *feel like* the other person. However, I don't find this to be a full enough explanation for empathy. Because this hypothesis focuses so much attention on visual cues, I'm concerned that it leaves out a great deal.

Emotion Contagion is so much more than simply mirroring emotion. To accurately pick up on the emotion of another, you also have to understand social contexts and the specific display rules[16] of your community. (Each family, community, and culture has a different set of rules about how emotions are displayed, which emotions are accepted, which emotions are denied, and how intensely group members can feel and display some or all emotions.) You also have to be able to identify moods and multiple gradations of emotion, hear vocal tone changes, watch for subtle body-language cues, understand social relationships, and read nuances, undercurrents, and gestural language—you even have to rely upon your sense of smell in many cases (most of us are not consciously aware of the many decisions we make based on our very sensitive noses). There's a great deal more to this contagion process than mirroring others[17]—you really have to understand the full context in which the emotion occurs in order to sense which emotion it is. Although this contextual sensitivity is a part of the second aspect of empathy—Empathic Accuracy—it's important to mention it here. Emotion Contagion can feel completely autonomic, as if it somehow happens to you without your involvement; but it is also something you learn how to do as a social being.[18]

In the academic realm, there's a great deal of debate about Emotion Contagion and its relationship to empathy. Some researchers argue that contagion, in and of itself, is *not* empathic—and, in fact, may be counterempathic. This idea was very surprising to me, because for many years, my definition of an empath was someone who felt the emotions of others strongly in his or her own body. And yet, I have to agree with this new approach. Let's look at the distinction.

In research performed by German psychologist Doris Bischof-Köhler,[19] infants and toddlers were presented with situations in which both the experimenter and the infant played with either teddy bears or spoons. In this study, the experimenter's teddy or spoon was rigged to break, thus causing the experimenter to act distressed and to cry. Bischof-Köhler carefully watched what happened next. If the child noticed the distress and cried alongside the distressed experimenter, Bischof-Köhler did not consider that response to be empathic. Rather, she called this example of contagion *self-centered*, because the child merely became wrapped up in his or her own distress. Only when the child offered some form of consolation (patting the experimenter, trying to fix the teddy or the spoon, or offering his or her own teddy or spoon to the distressed experimenter) did Bischof-Köhler consider the child to have developed true empathy.

This action-based definition of empathy is currently contested in empathy research, and some researchers want to roll back the definition to include *only* Emotion Contagion (in everyday English, the consoling actions that Bischof-Köhler wanted to see in her young subjects would be called *compassion* rather than empathy). I understand these reservations, because it's very helpful to make clear separations between the different aspects of empathy. However, for our uses as working empaths, I find this action component of empathy to be extremely important, and it's something we'll focus on throughout the rest of this book.

Here's why: If your experience of empathy is primarily contagion, such that you act as an emotional sponge and become overwhelmed by the emotions of others, you'll probably be unable to provide much support to them. You'll be like the children in the experiment who dissolved into the emotion of the experimenter and who could neither soothe themselves nor offer any support. In other words, you'll shut down. It may also be difficult for you to take the perspective of others if they are a continual source of emotional discomfort for you, and your ability to engage perceptively may therefore be reduced. Too much empathy is just as much trouble as too little. In fact, many workers in healthcare, counseling, emergency response, and criminal justice have to learn to reduce their Emotion Contagion in order to do their work.

If you experience strong contagion, hyperempathy, and emotional sponging that is very uncomfortable for you, you can learn to focus on increasing your ability to identify, understand, and work with your own emotional states and emotions in general (specifically, you can develop your skills in Empathic Accuracy and Emotion Regulation).

Emotions are *tools* for empaths, and learning to understand them, welcome them, and work with them skillfully is a central empathic activity. However, this empathic understanding is continually impeded in our everyday emotional training, to the extent that many people are afraid of emotions and actually try to avoid them altogether. We'll look very closely at why people are so afraid of emotions (or so dismissive toward them), because humankind's nearly universal problems with emotions truly impede empathy. Most of us have been trained to view and approach emotions in a way that makes contagion problematic—*not* because emotions are problematic in and of themselves, but because our training is so backward and unhelpful. We are actually trained to be emotionally avoidant and therefore empathically unskilled; accordingly, if our Emotion Contagion skills are naturally strong, we may experience a great deal of discomfort simply because we have no idea how to work with the emotions we feel and perceive.

If your current empathic condition is primarily one of uncomfortable contagion, I'll help you learn to identify and work with emotions *as tools* so that you can become grounded in and comfortable with them and the other five aspects of empathy. With this empathic emotional grounding, you'll be able to have a fuller and healthier experience of empathy, instead of being stuck in an uncomfortable and unworkable level of contagion. Conversely, if your current capacity for Emotion Contagion is very low, I'll teach you a new way to approach emotions and to clearly identify them as reliable responses to very specific situations and stimuli.

Why might your capacity for Emotion Contagion be low? There are many possible reasons, but the ones I've seen most often are (1) sensory hyperawareness that is overwhelming and leads a person to turn inward and reduce his or her receptivity as a form of protection (this is true for many people on the autism spectrum); (2) early-childhood experiences with depressed and low-affect caretakers who didn't give the child enough experience with a full range of emotions (we'll talk more about this in Chapter 9); and (3) early childhood experiences of (or extended periods of contact with) emotionally explosive or abusive people, such that the person learns to turn away from (or distrust) emotions as a survival tactic.

If you experienced any of these situations, this book will support you in retrieving and rebuilding your empathic capacities in a way that is understandable, accessible, and reliable for you. However, you may also benefit from the support of a trusted counselor or therapist. The capacity to experience the full range of emotions (inside yourself and with others) is your birthright, and you can do a great deal to retrieve this empathic capacity, no matter what kind of obstructions you experienced. And, of course, engaging with your artistic, literary, and philosophical Einfühlung capacities will help you explore emotional and empathic skills in intentional and self-expanding ways. We'll explore more about the specific healing effects of artistic expression in Chapters 5 and 6.

EMPATHIC ACCURACY

Empathic Accuracy is your empathic capacity to accurately identify emotions, thoughts, and intentions in yourself and others. This is an interior skill, an interactional skill, and an observational skill. The quality of your accuracy depends on your own internal emotional awareness and your capacity for emotional self-regulation.

Emotions are a world unto themselves—I call them a language. In order to learn the language of emotions, it's important to have a rich emotional vocabulary with plenty of words for differing intensities of emotions. In the Appendix, I provide you with an Emotional Vocabulary List so you can become sensitive to and accurate about differing emotional states. If you know which emotions you or others are feeling and if you can gauge the intensity of those emotions, your empathic work will be much more precise and skillful. But if you don't know which emotions are occurring or in what intensity, you'll continually miss important social cues about what people are thinking and feeling and what their intentions are. Emotional awareness and accuracy are crucial to skilled empathy.

It's also important that you know how to work with each emotion in yourself. If you don't, your accuracy could be compromised. For instance, you might accurately pick up the emotions or intentions of another through Emotion Contagion, but due to a preexisting problem with your own emotional regulation skills, you might get the entirely wrong idea about what's going on. For instance, let's imagine that you have sensed fear in another; however, due to an issue inside yourself, you might intensify that fear into anxiety or panic, and then imagine that you have picked up those emotions instead. Without realizing it, you may incorrectly attribute emotions, thoughts, intentions, and reactions to another based on your own difficulties with and reactions to that emotion (or that intensity of emotion).

The way to gauge your Empathic Accuracy is both very simple and infinitely hard: you ask people if what you're sensing from them is true. This is simple, because it's a very easy thing to ask, "Are you feeling (afraid, anxious, angry, sad, happy, ashamed) right now?" Yet it can be infinitely hard because people can be unaware of their own emotional states, embarrassed or confused by emotions, or unwilling to admit to what they're feeling (worry not—Chapter 8 illustrates a number of ways around this). For empaths, this lack of emotional transparency is a very sticky problem, because even though we're surrounded by emotions, we tend to grow up without any clear or workable understanding of them. In fact, many of the things we learn about emotions are so backward that it's amazing we can function at all.

For instance, the idea that there are negative or positive emotions is a completely unempathic and unhelpful fallacy. Our deeply unfortunate tendency to divide emotions into positive and negative categories has dreadful consequences in our everyday lives—many of us focus most of our attention on the supposedly positive emotions of happiness and joy, while ignoring, suppressing, trying to change, or running from the supposedly negative emotions (anger, hatred, fear, anxiety, sadness, grief, envy, jealousy, rage, depression, etc.). This misguided pathologizing of normal emotions actually makes us less able to work with emotions in intelligent ways and creates an empathic capacity that is stilted and incomplete. We'll look at this and three other serious impediments to emotional awareness in the next chapter.

Luckily, despite the problems in our emotional and empathic training, it's fairly easy to become more empathically accurate internally, because it's a simple process of tuning in to your interior life and learning to articulate your different emotional states. This can take a bit of practice if you've had bad training in one or more emotional categories (sadly, most of us have bad training in pretty much every emotion except happiness!), but it's actually fairly easy to become more accurate about your own emotions once you have an empathic understanding of what emotions are and what emotions do.

However, the relationship others have with their own emotions can make accuracy in interactions with them more difficult. In addition, many empathic people grow up without much confidence in their skills, because they've been told repeatedly, "I'm *not* mad! You're projecting!" Or "We don't talk about grief in this family." Or "Why would I be afraid? There's nothing to be afraid of." Or "I'm not laughing *at* you; I'm laughing *with* you." Emotional subterfuge, emotional bait-and-switch, emotional squelching, and straight-up emotional dishonesty are common everyday behaviors that can make Empathic Accuracy very hard to master.[20]

Another impediment to this accuracy is the unfortunate focus that's been placed on reading facial expressions and body language, as if they provide precise or reliable cues. Simply put, they don't. Frowns don't always signal anger, yawns don't always signal boredom (or fatigue), looking up and away doesn't always signal lying, looking down doesn't always signal insecurity, smiles don't always signal happiness, tears don't always signal sadness, fidgeting doesn't always signal nervousness, and crossed arms don't always signal anger. Faces and bodies are as individual as fingerprints, and though you can generalize about some things in regard to the bodies and faces of others, you can't really know what a gesture or expression means until you know another person for a while—or unless you ask.

Body language and facial expressions *can* provide a wonderful entrée into the empathic space of others, and we'll focus on ways to use these signals in our communication. However, our focus won't be on discovering secrets people think they're hiding or on becoming all-powerful body-language experts. Instead, we'll learn to use body language in a nonthreatening way to open conversations about emotions and empathy. And I mean that literally: "When you curve your body downward and sigh out loud, it seems to me that you're feeling discouraged, or maybe really tired, or both. Is that what's going on?" "When you use very short sentences and don't look at me when you speak, it seems that you're feeling impatient and frustrated with me. Is that true?" Body language and facial expressions are extremely important, but Empathic Accuracy is built, moment by moment, in empathic *interactions*. What others mean and what they're signaling are individual, and the key to understanding those signals cannot be found in a book. Instead, you have to get out and interact, make mistakes, be vulnerable and curious, and be deeply interested in the individual ways that others signal their emotional states.

Empathic Accuracy is developed in interactions—in honest, vulnerable, and curious empathic interactions inside yourself, as you learn to identify your own emotional states, and with others, as you learn the myriad ways that individuals signal their emotions and intentions. In this book, we'll look at many ways to develop and nurture those kinds of honest, vulnerable interactions.

EMOTION REGULATION

Emotion Regulation is a vitally important aspect of empathy. If you're good with contagion and you can accurately pick up on, identify, and feel the emotions of others, yet you have no internal capacity to *regulate* those emotions in yourself (to understand them, work with them, and get some perspective on them so that you can focus on the other person), you won't be able to empathize perceptively. You'll just be engulfed in emotional contagion, and you won't be able to engage or empathize with much skill (or possibly at all).

We'll explore numerous emotional regulation skills in this book. As an intrinsic aspect of those skills, we'll explore emotions empathically, so that you'll be able to approach each emotion as a tool that contains specific gifts and skills. Admittedly, this is a startling approach, because there are extensive problems in our understanding of the emotional realm, such that many people are deeply suspicious of—or even outright afraid of or offended by—actual emotions. But this is not a situation that can go unaddressed.

In my definition from Chapter 1, I wrote that an empath is someone who is aware of reading emotions, subtext, nuances *to a greater degree than is deemed normal.* In my work, this greater degree does not simply refer to a talent for Emotion Contagion and Empathic Accuracy; it also refers to an empathic understanding of emotions and how to work with them with skill and grace. Emotions are tools for empaths, and you have to know how to work with all of them—not just the allegedly "positive" ones. Emotional regulation skills are vital to empathy, and yet a major impediment to regulating emotions intelligently is that most of us have been trained to view emotions as annoyances to be avoided, rewards to be pursued, or problems to be eradicated. Intelligent, empathic Emotion Regulation isn't about controlling, eradicating, or chasing down emotions; rather, it's about working with them as vital, irreplaceable tools. When you can do that, all aspects of empathy become much, much easier.

PERSPECTIVE TAKING

Skilled empathy helps you take the perspective of others and to imagine what life feels like for them—how they feel, how they approach situations, what their intentions are, and how they'll respond to others and to circumstances. When you take the perspective of others, you often imagine the emotions that they might be feeling (or might soon feel in response to an action you might take), rather than directly sharing those emotions with them.

Let's return to the concepts of affective and cognitive empathy. As I noted a few pages back, some researchers make a sharp distinction between *affective* empathy (directly feeling the same or similar emotion in concurrence with another) and *cognitive* empathy (the capacity to understand the emotion of another without currently sharing it). Although this distinction is central to some areas of empathy theory, I don't find it to be valid in actual empathic practice.[21] Instead, I've focused on Emotion Contagion as the direct, affective dimension of empathy, and on Perspective Taking as the somewhat detached cognitive aspect. However, I don't see the two as distinct or separable abilities; rather, I see your capacity to take the perspective of others as totally dependent upon your ability to feel, share, and understand emotions. It is not likely that you would be able to skillfully take the perspective of others unless you also had the capacity to feel and understand emotions in the first place.

When you take the perspective of others, you essentially don their demeanor, attitudes, expectations, emotions, and intentions; you put yourself in their shoes so that you can see the world from their perspective and understand what they might do next (or what they might wish for). Skillful Perspective Taking certainly relies upon your ability to share emotions with others, but it also relies upon your Empathic Accuracy and your Emotion Regulation, so that you can work with anything that might trigger you and then quickly refocus yourself on what is happening with the other.

When you take the perspective of others, the point is not to ask yourself what you would do in their place; it's to try to understand what *they* would do. If your Empathic Accuracy and your Emotion Regulation are strong, you'll have the emotional range and depth needed to imagine attitudes, expectations, and intentions that may be very different from yours.

There's also a wonderful Einfühlung aspect to Perspective Taking—a feeling into, an aesthetic, literary capacity to embody characters and imbue them with life, hopes, dreams, wishes, and attitudes. When you skillfully take the perspective of others, you bring all parts of yourself to the process of trying to understand how they might feel and respond. *Skilled Perspective Taking helps you see things clearly from another's standpoint.*

CONCERN FOR OTHERS

Concern for Others is an empathic aspect that is both crucial and tricky. If you have too much concern, you may expend all of your time and energy on the needs of others, while essentially ignoring your own. On the other hand, if you have too little concern, your relationships may suffer, because others won't feel your interest, and they'll assume that you don't care about them. Interestingly, I find that some people who feel a great deal of concern shut down their empathy pretty early in life because they simply don't know how to meet all the needs they perceive. These people can appear to be deceptively low in empathy when, in truth, they may simply be low in empathic self-care skills.

For an empath, the other tends to be an endless source of fascination, frustration, confusion, joy, struggle, delight, exasperation, comfort, and discomfort (remember that *the other* also includes art, ideas, music, movement, literature, animals, etc.). In service to this empathic need for engagement, some of us focus all of our attention on the other and totally ignore our own needs until we burn out. I address empathic burnout throughout this book so that you can learn to balance your Concern for Others with healthy concern for yourself. The world needs empaths, but your health and well-being are equally important. If you burn out, not only is it very painful for you, but it's also a loss in the larger sense. If you burn out, there will be one less healthy empath in the world. *Self-care and Concern for Others should and must coexist.*

On the other side of this equation is a lack of concern for or a lack of interest in others. I've put forth the proposal that unconcerned behavior *may* actually be masking or obscuring hyperconcern or hyperempathy (or empathy that has not been supported). When I see obviously empathic people who exhibit very little Concern for Others, my suspicion is that they have burnt out already; I don't immediately think that they're *incapable* of empathy. If you scratch underneath the surface just a little, you'll find that some of the angriest, most anxious, most arrogant, and most antisocial people harbor a profound well of concern that they're either unable to manage or unwilling to acknowledge—or both.

It's very easy for a highly empathic person to burn out and retreat inward. I'd even go so far as calling that process an empathic tendency. In a world in which emotional awareness is often low to nonexistent, such that Empathic Accuracy is continually impeded and skilled Emotion Regulation is rare, being highly empathic can be a pretty grueling situation of uncontrolled Emotion Contagion. We'll tackle this situation head-on in this book, but just be aware: people (and animals) you might think of as uncaring and unempathic might actually be hyperempathic and burnt out. And the way you approach them can make it better or worse.

Most of us are gruff, cold, or angry toward those we've identified as uncaring, but I'll tell you, empath to empath, that a complete and constitutional lack of empathy is rare. It is hundreds of times more likely that seemingly uncaring others are burnt out or impaired in their emotional regulation skills than that they are pathologically unempathic. Therefore, approaching them somewhat neutrally is a more truly empathic thing to do. Too much coldness will only cement them in their isolation (and confirm their belief that others aren't worth their time), whereas too much warmth might feel threatening. When a person is in empathic burnout, they can be likened to real burn patients; their defenses are down, and their emotional pain receptors may be hyperactivated. Gentleness is called for.

This gentleness is especially necessary for those people who have been exiled from empathy—men and boys, people on the autism spectrum, and those who have been nearly tossed out of the human race altogether: psychopaths, sociopaths (a dated term in the United States), or those with antisocial, narcissistic, or personality disorders. I organized the six aspects of empathy, in part, to help myself think about and locate where allegedly unempathic people might have difficulties. Certainly, we can all have trouble with excessive Emotion Contagion abilities, and that's definitely where I place people on the autism spectrum—many of whom are hyperempaths. Empathic Accuracy is also a huge problem for many of us, in part due to our deeply unempathic and unhelpful emotional training, which confuses us about emotions. Emotion Regulation is another area in which many of us need help, because we'll often pick up an emotion, then react to it, then react to our reactions, and then become completely overwhelmed with emotions *about* emotions.

We can also fall down in the area of Perspective Taking if our skills in the first three aspects of empathy are impeded in some way. If our own capacity to receive, identify, and work with emotions is not strong, then we're not going to be able to develop a true and valid picture of others. We won't be able to take their perspectives skillfully, and we'll attribute thoughts, emotions, ideas, and intentions to them that might be *way* off base.

However, when I look at the ways we talk about those who seem to lack empathy—and when I look at what scares people the most—I rest my gaze on Concern for Others. Think about it: You can be an absolute clod in the empathic realm, taking in too much, being emotionally volatile, overreacting, being clumsy and emotionally imprecise, but if others know that you *care* about them, then a great deal of your empathic clumsiness will be forgiven. But if people sense that you don't care about them? Oh, no! That will shut everything down. If you don't seem to care about others, then every other aspect of your empathic skills will be discounted as unimportant at best and manipulative at worst. Concern for Others is a deal breaker: If you seem to have it, you can get away with almost anything, empathically speaking. But if you don't seem to have it, you'll be exiled.

It's interesting, then, to note which kinds of people are causally referred to as being absolutely antiempathic and psychopathic; certainly criminals are,[22] but so are bosses, ex-spouses, capitalists, and politicians. But, in fact, these people have to be able to read us and meet our needs in order to influence us skillfully and get their own needs met. There are many aspects of empathy working in all of these seemingly unempathic people; where they fall down is in their Concern for Others. Anyone who doesn't seem to have this concern gets exiled from our empathic community—we display a distinct lack of empathy for people who don't demonstrate their Concern for Others!

Concern for Others is vital and life affirming, but it can be a very difficult aspect of empathy, especially when those in your life are suffering, repeating painful behaviors, or mismanaging their emotions and their lives. Because Concern for Others can be very problematic, we'll explore ways to maintain (or restore) your concern without throwing yourself away and to temper your concern without completely abandoning your connections to others.

PERCEPTIVE ENGAGEMENT

In empathy research, the aspect that I'm renaming Perceptive Engagement is often called *targeted helping*[23] or *consolation*. In general, empathy researchers focus a great deal of attention on empathy as an active and obvious response to pain or need. However, this focus unnecessarily reduces our understanding of the totality of empathic responses. Empathic responses are just as likely in situations of joy, laughter, and a *lack* of need as they are in troubling or consolation-requiring situations. Empathy is first and foremost an emotional skill, and skilled empaths work with all emotions, not just the painful ones. It's just as empathic to laugh and joke with someone as it is to offer them a shoulder to cry on. Empathy is about *perceptive* emotional interaction and engagement; it's not restricted only to consolation.

In renaming this aspect of empathy, I also chose the word *engagement* carefully. Many empathy researchers focus primarily on action as a sign of empathy, which makes sense in a testing environment, where you have to chart observable, action-based behaviors. In the real world of empathic interactions, however, this focus on action can be very misleading. In many situations, it's actually more empathic *not* to act or not to notice the pain of others (if they're signaling that they want to be left alone) than it is to make a great show of being outwardly consoling. When you engage with others in a truly perceptive way, the choices you make are not about what you would like or what would work for you (or what would make you look most empathic!); instead, they're about the needs of the other. And sometimes others need to be unseen, untouched, and undisturbed. Sometimes the most empathic response possible is to do nothing, to look away, and to ignore people (if that's what would comfort them the most).

And yet action-based research can tell us very useful things about the development of empathy. In a wonderful experiment[24] done with toddlers, University of California–Berkeley psychology researcher Alison Gopnik placed an adult and a toddler at a table with two bowls of food between them. One bowl contained Goldfish crackers (which the vast majority of children love) and the other contained raw broccoli (which the vast majority of children decidedly do *not* love). To determine whether the toddlers had developed targeted helping skills, Gopnik asked the adult to mime strong distaste for the crackers and strong, yummy love for the broccoli—and then to ask the child to share some food.

At a certain stage in their development, toddlers will offer crackers to the adult, perhaps, because in their experience, the crackers are delicious, and therefore everyone should want some. Although offering the crackers is very generous (since the children love the crackers), it is not *perceptive*. Gopnik would call the giving of crackers a selfish and egocentric act and not a fully empathic one, because it is only when the child understands that the adult has entirely different needs that he or she can be seen as being empathically aware. I was fascinated to see that in Gopnik's study, the age at which children offered broccoli to the experimenter was at around eighteen months, which suggests that babies develop the capacity for the most advanced aspect of our six-part empathy model even before they can speak full sentences.

In Perceptive Engagement, you listen and watch carefully for what another wants and needs; then, to the extent that you are able, you interact based upon those wants and needs (or, sometimes, you don't interact at all, if that's what would work best for the other). Perceptive Engagement is the culmination of the previous five aspects of the empathic process. To engage perceptively, you have to be able to share emotions, accurately identify them, regulate them in yourself, take the perspective of others, be concerned enough to want to engage helpfully, and, finally, engage from an unselfish position of empathic knowledge of the other.

That sounds like an incredibly complicated process, but we've all done it since early childhood, and we continue to do it every day—at home, at work, with animals, in e-mails, at the store, when we drive, when we walk down the street, and when we interact with art, literature, and music. We're in constant empathic contact with each other and with the nonhuman world, and it's important to remember this. We humans are an actively empathic species, and though our empathy is often problematic, hyperactive, or seemingly absent, empathy is the nonverbal language we all speak fluently.

EMPATHY FOR YOURSELF

Did you notice something missing in my six aspects of empathy? There's an important factor I didn't include. You may find this omission rather startling, but hear me out. This missing aspect might be called self-care, self-love, self-empathy, or something along those lines. To be a happy, healthy, and effective empath, you have to take care of yourself first—in essence, you have to be able to put on your own oxygen mask before you help other passengers with theirs. And obviously, developing and nurturing empathy for yourself is what this entire book is about. I want to help you develop self-awareness, self-care, and self-love as central features of your life. These are absolutely vital things.

Yet I have to be honest with you. You can perform effectively as an empath even if you're self-abandoning and even if you're filled with self-loathing. Some of the most amazing and hugely empathic social justice workers the world has ever known have been self-abandoning people who were running from the deep trouble in their own souls. Their homes, their love lives, and their family lives were often chaotic or nonexistent (and many of them burned out). The process of empathizing skillfully does not require that you take good care of yourself. Of course, you'll burn out if you don't take care of yourself, and your empathic work won't be social activism as much as it will be martyrdom. But you *can* empathize pretty effectively, even if you have very little empathy for yourself. In fact, most of us have performed skillful empathy from a self-abandoning position, and many burnt-out empaths have turned away from empathy precisely because it can lead to martyrdom.

This is a central reason that empathy is such a difficult subject—and why it can be in such short supply. To be good with empathy, especially in Perspective Taking, Concern for Others, and Perceptive Engagement, you must have empathy for *the other*. Empathy is not about you. If you have a healthy inner life, healthy relationships, and clear-eyed emotional awareness, empathy can be fun, engaging, and delightful—*especially* when it's not about you. You can learn so much when you empathize, particularly when you empathize with people who are nothing like you. However, if your inner life is unstable, if your childhood was chaotic or traumatic, if your caregivers were inconsistent or neglectful and didn't support your empathy development, if your personal life isn't supportive, if your self-care and emotional awareness are negligible, or if your human social interactions are unsatisfying, empathy can drain the lifeblood out of you. But even so, you'll still be able to empathize, because it's an innate skill that tends to operate whether or not you ask it to, and it's a skill we all possess to a greater or lesser degree.

So as you move forward to build skills, awareness, support, and multiple foundations under and around you, know that all of these will make your experience of empathy more rewarding and more fun. But even on your worst day, or even in the worst of circumstances, know that you're already an empath, and that these six aspects are already a part of your life. What we're doing in this book is making sure that your innate empathy is a beneficial and workable part of your whole life.

With the foundation of these six aspects of empathy, you can move forward into a deeper engagement with the process of becoming an accurate, emotionally well-regulated, self-aware, self-respecting, perceptive, happy, and healthy empath. And I'm telling you that it's not only possible to do this but also actually achievable. If you have difficulty getting into sync with others, I'll teach you simple ways to empathize more gracefully. If you overidentify with others, I'll show you many different emotional and social awareness tools that will help you create effective boundaries to regulate your own emotions. If your empathy has been more like uncontrolled martyrdom than intentional activism, and even if you developed empathic burnout a long time ago, empathy is an innate feature of human nature and human intelligence, which means you can retrieve it. But this time, you'll be able to engage with your empathy in a way that will work for you.

Throughout this book, I'll refer to these six aspects of empathy as we delve into your emotional life, your home life, your communication skills, your work life, and so forth. These six aspects will help you gain a tangible understanding of your empathic abilities so that you can address your specific empathic strengths and challenges.

WHEN ALL SIX ASPECTS ARE CHALLENGED

In Chapter 1, I shared my empathic observation of Joseph and Iris so that you could experience a felt sense of empathy and see the world through a kind of empath-cam. I chose that situation carefully, and most important, I chose the time period carefully, so that you could feel how empathy works for me *now*. As I wrote in that chapter, it hasn't always been like this for me. In my childhood, the world of emotions, empathy, and interactions was a very painful place indeed.

When I was a little hyperempathic child, I felt every emotion in every room. I compare myself to a malfunctioning radio, because I picked up all emotional frequencies from every direction—yet I couldn't home in on specific ones, and it all felt like static. I experienced a constant sense of emotional overload (unless I was alone with one calm human or in the presence of animals), and I felt fundamentally unsafe in the human social world. Being in a crowd, at school, or at a party was excruciating. There was even a joke in my family that parties didn't really start until little Karla dashed around the house, threw up in response to all the commotion, and had to be put to bed. Yeah, that's awful! I wish things had been different, but an empath wasn't even a *thing* when I was little, so my family gets some leeway for their ignorance and insensitivity. At least they used humor; they could have punished me instead. I'm glad I grew up in a funny ignorant family instead of a cruel ignorant one.

I grew up the fourth of five children in what is a fairly normally dysfunctional family. My mother was a brilliant woman who was not able to go to college; she was also a brilliant painter with five children and an unfortunate perfectionist streak that prevented her from being able to fully live her artistic life. She was a childhood trauma survivor and had trouble with a number of emotions (though she could be an absolute champion in the face of abuse). Mom could be emotionally erratic, but she was not emotionally loud or obvious; her emotions were deeply felt, but they were usually only expressed in undertones. For instance, when she was angry, she never swore or expressed it outright; instead, her body would heat up, and she'd avoid eye contact, or she'd move more quickly and avoid talking about what bothered her. My father was also a brilliant man who wasn't able to complete college and a wonderful writer who published two children's books but primarily worked as an insurance adjustor. Dad was emotionally very steady and rather unaffected. He didn't display most emotions openly, but unlike Mom, he didn't actually feel them very strongly either. If I had an extreme emotion to deal with, I simply didn't go to Dad; Mom could help to a certain extent, but Dad seemed entirely perplexed by extreme emotions.

Extreme emotions were a central feature of my childhood, because we lived across the street from a child molester (*Empath alert:* I will not go into detail; I respect your sensitivity). From the age of about thirty months until I was four years old, I was molested by the dad across the street, who also molested many of the little girls in my neighborhood. Although my childhood was filled with normal kid stuff, it was also filled with extreme fear and anxiety about what would happen next. I learned to rely heavily upon rage and intense (often violent) physical activity to help me deal with what was happening to me, to my little sister (who is sixteen months younger than I am), and to the other little girls in our neighborhood. This ongoing abuse was discovered and stopped when our elder sister (who was twelve at the time) found out and told our parents. The police interviewed us, and we eventually went to the district attorney. But the other girls were too ashamed to talk about what had happened (and their parents were unwilling to believe us), so the case was dropped. After the case was dropped, no one ever spoke openly of the situation again, and we continued to live in a neighborhood filled with toxic secrets for another seven years. The molestation stopped, but things didn't get much better.

I was an *intense* kid—fiercely angry, wildly active (I liked to run fast and throw myself off of high things)—and I was filled with a sense of terror that I tried to cover in any way I could. I had a stutter and multiple learning disabilities, and I had so many nightmares that a family friend created a monster catcher for me out of an old radio that he painted and decorated. (I could turn the dial to whatever level of monster I wanted to be protected from, and I always turned it all the way up to eleven!) At that time, my hyperempathy was both a survival tool and a burden. I had learned to ramp up my empathic skills and read my molester's moods carefully so that I could give him what he wanted and avoid excessive harm (though what he wanted was directly harmful, so my relationship with my own empathy became deeply conflicted and entwined with hazardous levels of self-abandonment). But I couldn't turn off my intense empathic skills, because I didn't know how I had turned them on. My hyperempathic skills became involuntary, unmanageable survival mechanisms in a human emotional world that was pretty much incomprehensible to me.

Here's why: Even when you put aside actual instances of abuse, the following are normal everyday behaviors among humans—lying about our feelings; avoiding sensitive subjects that are glaringly obvious; leaving important words unsaid; pretending to like things we don't like; pretending we're not feeling an emotion that we're *clearly* feeling; using language to hide, obscure, and skirt crucial issues; attacking people who frighten us without ever realizing we are full of fear (most people think they're angry when they do this; they're not); stopping all movement toward change without ever realizing we're full of anger and grief (most people think they're being careful when they do this; they are, but they don't often know why); and claiming that we're being rational when huge, steamy clouds of emotion are pouring out of us. My experience of human interaction was one of noise, static, emotional absurdity, and continual bewilderment. Humans were emotionally *exhausting*, and they made me feel confused, afraid, unsafe, angry, and desperately lonely.

Thank goodness, my home and my neighborhood were filled with cats and dogs. They gathered around me and provided safe, emotionally honest relationships in which I could hone my empathy in understandable interactions. My wonderful dog and cat friends never lied about their emotions, and they never confused me about what they were feeling. If they were crabby, they'd growl. If they were afraid, they'd become hyperalert or they'd cower or snap. If they were happy, they'd smile and waggle. If they trusted me, they'd cuddle and give lots of affection. If they were tired, they'd nap. If they were in pain, they'd whine and ask for help or withdraw and get very quiet. There was no lying, no subterfuge, no pretense, no blaming, and no projecting. No animal ever told me that it wasn't polite to point out an emotion. No animal ever laughed at me for feeling fear or sadness or anger or anything else. No animal ever tried to victimize me. And no animal ever blamed me for things they did to hurt me. Animals were my sanctuary, and they made it possible for me to survive the overwhelming emotional realities of my childhood. When people ask me jokingly, "Were you raised by wolves?" I proudly say, "*Yes*, house wolves and housecats."

As I look back at my situation in regard to my six aspects of empathy, I can see that my hyperempathy in childhood consisted of extreme Emotion Contagion and an adult's level of Empathic Accuracy (about the darkness inside the human soul), combined with no Emotion Regulation to speak of. I used perpetual activity to moderate my intense emotional receptivity, and I used anger and anxiety to create emergency boundaries—either I'd lash out with anger if I felt too emotionally vulnerable, or I'd dash around or fidget anxiously if too much input came at me. Although all of these emergency tactics worked to get me away from people, none of them was very effective in helping me regulate my emotions. As a result, my ability to perform skilled Perspective Taking with humans wasn't great, unless I was in imminent danger, and my Concern for Others (and myself) was often negligible. People were overwhelming for me, and I really didn't have the internal resources or the interest to offer any sort of Perceptive Engagement. I often just raged or ran—or both.

If you were to observe me as a child, you would never have thought, "Say, there goes a very empathic child!" No, you would have thought that I didn't care about people at all and that I was a little hellion to boot. In a different family, my arc as an empath might have turned out very badly indeed, but my mother (with the help of that wonderful neurologist I wrote about in Chapter 1) protected me from a lot of people who wanted to punish and control me. To the extent that she could, she provided a safe place for me to grow up. Mom identified my hypersensitivities as what she termed *plus* disabilities, and she did what she could to surround me with love, music, art, animals, books, laughter, physical activity, and lots of freedom.

I contrast the scene that I wrote for you about Joseph and Iris to so many scenes in my childhood, in which my social, emotional, and empathic awareness was excruciatingly difficult for me to tolerate, moderate, organize, or even comprehend. With Joseph and Iris, I chose a scene in which the emotional situations were rather delicate and large, obvious actions weren't required from me. I also chose that scene to give you a sense of all six aspects of empathy working together for me now, in a way that's comfortable, understandable, manageable, and accessible to my conscious awareness.

AN EMPATH IS SOMEONE WHO IS AWARE

I'm going to return to my definition of an empath, but this time I'll emphasize my sentence a bit differently:

> An empath is someone *who is aware* that he or she reads emotions,
> nuances, subtexts, undercurrents, intentions, thoughts, social space,
> interactions, relational behaviors, body language, and gestural
> language to a greater degree than is deemed normal.

As a little girl, I wasn't aware of what I was reading or why; I wasn't aware that I could perceive things others couldn't or that my abilities were greater than normal. I was just struggling to keep my head above water as wave after wave of emotions and social information hit me full force, while other people stood by, comfortable, seemingly uncomprehending, and more upset by *my* behavior than by the truckloads of emotions careening all over the joint. *What?* Until I gained awareness of what an empath was, I really wasn't able to make heads or tails of the human world.

It took me about a decade to discover a preliminary definition for *empath* (from an episode of the original *Star Trek* TV show,[25] of all places), and it took about another five years to get on top of my hypersensitivity and hyper-reactivity. I've spent my life since then studying emotions and social interactions empathically, helping hyperempathic people learn how to work with their sensitivities, and helping fellow trauma survivors heal. I also wrote an entire book on reframing emotions empathically (*The Language of Emotions: What Your Feelings Are Trying to Tell You*) to help people at every level of empathic ability learn how to work with emotions skillfully and how to view emotions as absolutely essential aspects of cognition and social functioning.

I've told you my story so that you'll know there's hope for you if you're a hyperempath, no matter what kind of early training you had. There's also hope for you if you've experienced empathic burnout. And there's hope for you if your current level of empathic awareness is pretty low. The empathic world of emotions and interactions *is* a hidden world, but it's a tangible, knowable, and marvelous world that babies as young as eighteen months can access. You can access it, too.

I'm glad you're willing to do so, because we need more healthy empaths in this world. Empathy and the extensive sociability it makes possible helped early bands of hairless, clawless, small-toothed hominids become the dominant mammalian species on Earth. Now that we've reached a population of approximately seven billion souls with wildly differing notions of what's true and what's important, empathy has become a crucial element in helping us learn how to live with one another. Empathy is what made us such a successful species in the first place, and now, empathy is what will help us address our many conflicts so that we can survive and flourish.

CHAPTER 3

An Empath's Guide to Empathy

Developing Your Social and Emotional Intelligence

THE FIRST STEP in the process of becoming a happy and healthy empath is to realize that there *is* such a thing as an empath. You can now check off that step! *Bing.* Easy, right? The second step is to separate empathy into manageable pieces. *Bing*—we did that by identifying empathy's six essential aspects. Your next steps are to gather specific skills and create a series of supports around yourself so you can become more able to identify and effectively address what you're picking up (or what you're missing, if your empathy levels are currently low). That's what this book is for.

From this point forward, we'll work from the inside out. We'll start by creating a supportive structure of self-care and mindfulness skills so that you can work with your empathic sensitivity (or relative insensitivity) in new ways. Then we'll look at ways to bring healthy empathy to yourself, your home, your family and friends, your love relationships, your communication skills, your work, and your approach to social justice. In essence, we'll work to create a support structure that can function as a wonderful container—a terrarium, perhaps—for your sensitive self: a container, a framework, and a clear-eyed standpoint from which you can become a comfortable, happy, and healthy empath.

Before you learn these specific skills (in Chapter 5), I'll introduce some concepts that can make empathy and emotions more comprehensible and more comfortable. The first is Howard Gardner's concept of *multiple intelligences.* The second is Richard J. Davidson's *emotional styles* framework. And the third is my empathic approach to emotions as tools that contribute specific skills and abilities that help you function in every area of your life—from basic cognition and self-awareness to your most skillful and perceptive empathic interactions.

YOUR SEVEN INTELLIGENCES[26]

When your empathic abilities are strong, you tend to *get* people and animals and their needs in the way some intellectual geniuses *get* mathematics or physics or in the way artistic geniuses *get* color, shape, and perspective. Empathy is one of the multiple kinds of intelligence we humans have. However, many of us grew up in a world in which there was not any idea about multiple intelligences. It was only in 1983 that Harvard psychologist Howard Gardner's work on multiple intelligences became known. Gardner identified more than just the *logical* intelligence that most people focused on at the time—which is the intelligence that allows us to do math and science, identify patterns, and use logic and deductive reasoning. Logical intelligence is the form that can most easily be measured on an IQ test; for decades, it was the only aptitude that was openly called *intelligence.*

Gardner saw intelligence differently, and he eventually put a name to many other forms of intelligence in addition to logical intelligence. It's important to point out that some educators and researchers have strong criticisms of the implications of Gardner's work. However, I'm not proposing any sort of teaching style or any reframing of IQ tests here. Instead, I'm using Gardner's work to explore the idea of intelligence as a larger, more full-bodied constellation of talents and abilities than the merely logical one that many of us grew up with (and which is still the basis for formal designations of IQ). I'm also focusing on Gardner's unique approach to social and emotional awareness as a distinct form of intelligence.

Gardner identified many areas of skill, talent, and ability beyond the logical, mathematical, and reasoning capacities that are the focus of most IQ tests. (Note: I'm not including every form of intelligence Gardner identified, because his categories are still in flux.) In Gardner's framework, four of these extra intelligences are *linguistic* intelligence, which enables you to write, communicate, and learn languages skillfully; *musical* intelligence, which enables you to identify tone/pitch/rhythm, appreciate music, compose it, and perform musically; *bodily–kinesthetic* intelligence, which enables you to use your body with great skill (think of dancers, athletes, and gymnasts); and *spatial* intelligence, or the ability to recognize patterns in space and to use space in novel ways. Architects, builders, sculptors, geometricians, and most visual artists would be high in spatial intelligence.

The other two intelligences Gardner identified are *interpersonal* intelligence, which allows you to understand the intentions, motivations, and desires of others, and *intrapersonal* intelligence, which gives you the ability to understand *your own* motivations, intentions, and desires. These last two are incredibly important forms of intelligence that help you pilot through the social world. Because empathy is first and foremost an emotional skill, it's important to focus on these interpersonal and intrapersonal areas of intelligence if you want to understand and develop your empathic skills.

With the ground of Gardner's work to stand on, we can refer to intelligence as a rich constellation of talents, abilities, and traits and not simply those skills you use on IQ tests. However, here's the problem for empaths: When most of us were growing up, the only kinds of intelligence that mattered were the logical and spatial kinds on those IQ tests. Even today, social and emotional intelligence are not considered true aspects of intelligence, except in Gardner's work. Maybe our musical and artistic intelligences were accessed in school, and probably our bodily, sports-focused abilities were too, but P.E. and art were probably not an equal focus of our school day. When I went to school, P.E. and art were not seen as essential to learning, and now, with all the budgetary problems and the testing focus facing schools, P.E. and art are even less likely to be a large part of the school day. Therefore, schools don't tend to access the full richness of our many different kinds of intelligence.

However, it is important to note that our interpersonal and intrapersonal intelligences are not a part of our formal schooling at all. I think I took a citizenship class once, but I can't really remember it. What I do remember, in school and out of it, is that behavioral and social skills were often taught on the fly. We learned how to act by watching others or by being praised or shamed, but there wasn't any actual instruction. No one said, "Here's what anger does, and here's how it's different from fear and sadness." No one said, "When other people are feeling these specific emotions, here are some ideas for how to respond." No one explained complex social behaviors to us: "Watch how that tall girl drops her body when she's around boys; it looks as if she's trying to project a version of femininity that is actually detrimental to who she is as a person." Or, "Look at that gang of boys; it looks as if they're not dangerous, because their body language is loose, and they're making nonthreatening eye contact with out-group members. They're probably a friendly gang and not a mean gang." (These days, however, now that bullying has become such a problem in schools, some social skills courses, conflict-mediation workshops, and empathy curricula are being offered in schools.)

We learned how to work with emotions and how to understand people through osmosis or on the fly or by the seat of our pants. We didn't receive direct instruction about our relationships or our emotions, unless we made some huge social mistake, such as openly displaying unwanted emotions or unwittingly trampling over someone's obvious social cues. We were taught reading, writing, math, and perhaps languages; we were taught science, history, and P.E.; and some of us were taught art and music. But in regard to our emotions, our interpersonal skills, our intrapersonal skills, and our empathic skills, we were just supposed to figure it all out somehow.

As children, we were expected to come into school with our interpersonal and intrapersonal intelligences already fully matured. We were expected to have our emotions, our social awareness, and our understanding of others under our belts already. We got demerits or gold stars for our behavior, but we didn't learn *how* to identify our emotions or work with them skillfully in ourselves and others. So if we were angry or sad or afraid at school, we had to keep it hidden or risk being made the center of attention. If we openly cried or expressed our angers or envies, we were often sent to the principal or the school counselor, or we'd go to detention or stay after school. Our emotions would take us out of the normal school day, out of the classroom, and out of the way. If we acted out our fear or our sadness, other kids might see us as weaklings and make us targets, or we might become the teacher's pet, which is often the same thing as being a target. Other kids would learn, "Don't express most emotions, or you'll be isolated, punished, or publicly shamed."

What I saw growing up—and what I still see—is that we're asked to grow to maturity while keeping two of the most important aspects of our intelligence—our intrapersonal and interpersonal intelligences—under wraps, in the shadows, out of the way, and off the radar. As adults, we tend to need therapists, counselors, and psychiatrists to help us access not only our emotions, but also these two intelligences, even though they belong to us and are essential to pretty much everything we do. It's not surprising, then, that we don't know what emotions are or what they do. It's also not surprising that we're left to figure out emotions for ourselves. And it's not surprising that empathy, which is first and foremost an emotional skill, is such a difficult thing for so many of us to figure out.

Gardner's multiple intelligences give us an excellent foundation for focusing on the intelligence that's inherent in emotional awareness and social skills, but I also want to add another model, which I discovered more recently.

In neuroscientist Richard J. Davidson's work on emotional styles, I found something wonderful—Davidson's assertion that even if your emotional or social training has been poor, many aspects of your emotional and social functioning remain malleable and flexible throughout your lifetime. With proper support, awareness, and retraining, you can modify your social and emotional skills, become more empathically aware, and actually change the way your brain responds to the world.

YOUR EMOTIONAL STYLE

In his book, *The Emotional Life of Your Brain,* neuroscientist and professor of psychology and psychiatry Richard Davidson (with science writer Sharon Begley) identified six dimensions of personality and behavior that can be linked to specific neurological processes. Davidson's work is captivating to me because he moves away from the old psychological and pop-psych personality models (which I find very limiting and dubious) and instead describes human temperament in terms of six dimensions that exist in each of us at differing levels and that can be observed in the brain.

These six dimensions are very useful, not only because they're based on actual neurological processes, but also because, in most cases, there's something you can *do* about them. In many personality typing models, you're just one kind of person, and that's where you stay. You're an introvert or an extrovert; you're rational or intuitive; you're a 9 or a 2 on the enneagram; you're a Scorpio or a Taurus; you're a highly sensitive person, or you're not. I realize that the entire point of personality typing is to separate people into categories, and in some stages of personal growth and awareness, these categories can be very helpful ways to identify yourself and others. They can even be avenues to understanding and empathizing with people. However, I eventually tired of them, and I now find them to be restrictive rather than liberating. I speak to you as a person whose mother was an astrologer, who was once interested in Myers Briggs personality types, who once thought of herself as a highly sensitive person, and who spent a great many years looking at all sorts of ways to categorize and separate people into types, elements, or archetypes. It's a thing we do—typing and categorizing and labeling people, sometimes as a path to empathy, but other times as a way to reduce our empathy for *those people* (whoever they are). At this point in my life, however, I'm no longer interested in personality typing, and I prefer to experience people as unique and unrepeatable beings, because honestly, there are only two types of people: those who separate people into types, and those who don't. That's a joke—but not really.

As I searched for a supportive framework to add to Gardner's theory about multiple kinds of intelligence, I read through and discarded dozens of models, because each focused on personality types, polar opposites (where you're one thing or the other, but never all things), and behaviors or temperaments that were written in stone. These models didn't have the necessary fluidity to take into account the uniqueness of every person and the often-startling ways that people can change over the course of their lives. Davidson's work was a wonderful surprise, because it is grounded not only in neuroscience and actual research but also in the understanding that people can and do change. It's also wonderful to see the nuance Davidson brings to his six dimensions, because he doesn't support polarization—that is, he doesn't suggest that being all the way to one end of any of these dimensions is preferred. Instead, he suggests that moderation in all of these dimensions is a really good idea. So, even though he's created a categorization model, it doesn't put people into straitjackets. Wonderful!

These are Davidson's six dimensions of emotional style:

Resilience is your capacity to recover from setbacks. In this dimension, perhaps you bounce back easily, or perhaps you take a long time to regain your equilibrium. In the dimension of Resilience, Davidson identifies people as fast to recover or slow to recover, and he offers skills to help people balance their recovery rates, because, depending on the situation, both fast *and* slow recovery rates can be either useful or problematic. If you recover too slowly, you can remain uncomfortably engaged in difficult situations for extended periods of time, but if you recover too quickly, you can speed right past situations that could help you develop better emotional and empathic awareness. This dimension is connected to your capacity for Emotion Contagion, Empathic Accuracy, Emotion Regulation, and Perspective Taking in our empathic frame.

Outlook is your overall approach to life, which Davidson identifies on a continuum from positive to negative. In my empathic approach to emotions, I explore the problem of using terms like *positive* and *negative* in regard to emotions. *All* emotions are necessary, and relegating specific emotions to the dustbin of alleged negativity can create a great deal of trouble. However, Davidson points out that a negative outlook can be very useful and purposeful in some situations, whereas an unrelentingly positive outlook can be completely inappropriate and dysfunctional—that is, overly positive people can have problems with planning, learning from mistakes, and delaying gratification. Davidson also has some helpful suggestions for creating appropriate balance in your outlook. The Outlook dimension is connected to your Empathic Accuracy and Emotion Regulation.

Social Intuition is your ability to read people and the signals they send. This dimension relates to a combination of Emotion Contagion, Empathic Accuracy, and Perspective Taking. It asks: How well can you decipher the signals you receive? Davidson measures this skill on a continuum from socially intuitive to puzzled. Although you'd think that being all the way to the socially intuitive end would be great, Davidson points out that, as many of us know, being hyperempathic can be too stimulating and overwhelming. He suggests ways to work toward balance in this dimension. For socially puzzled people, for example, Davidson suggests studying people, interactions, and faces intently in order to develop better Emotion Contagion, Empathic Accuracy, and Perspective Taking.

Self-awareness is your internal, intrapersonal capacity to identify your own emotions, sensations, and inner thoughts. In our frame, your capacity for Emotion Regulation and your ability to identify Emotion Contagion correctly through Empathic Accuracy exist in this area. Davidson measures this dimension on a continuum from self-aware to self-opaque, the latter of which means that your inner self is pretty mysterious to you. Again, though you might think that being on the self-aware end of the spectrum is the golden position, being too aware of what's going on inside you—your heart rate, your pain sensitivity, your digestion, your transitory emotional states, your temperature, your hormonal shifts—can be exhausting! Balance in this dimension is crucial to your ability to focus on others, rather than being uncomfortably hyperfocused on yourself.

Sensitivity to Context is your capacity to understand the usually unspoken and hidden rules of social interaction so that you can respond in a socially sensitive way. This skill is very dependent on all six aspects of your empathic capacity, and it's a skill I illustrated very intentionally in the empath-cam scene with Joseph and Iris. Almost none of the social rules or signals that Joseph or Iris displayed were openly discussed; instead, their signals primarily existed in undercurrent, subtext, gestural language, and nuance. Reading those signals required Joseph, Iris, and me to have strong Sensitivity to Context. Davidson identifies this skill on a continuum from tuned in to tuned out. I would characterize both Joseph and Iris as being on the tuned-in side of this continuum. However, as all of us know, the skill of tuning out context is invaluable when we're surrounded by conversations we shouldn't hear, conflicts we don't want to be a part of, and people we don't want to interact with. Davidson also suggests that being too tuned in can mean that people might lose their own sense of self in deference to the multiple inputs that are a part of each social context they encounter.

Attention is your capacity to focus yourself or to screen out unrelated emotional, social, or sensory input. In this dimension, Davidson has identified a continuum that ranges from focused to unfocused. He discusses ways to reduce hyperfocus and to increase focusing capacity in people who are unfocused.

These six dimensions of emotional style are malleable—some more so than others. Davidson explains each in terms of the neurological structures that underlie each dimension. He also makes specific suggestions for how to manage, reduce, increase, or temper each dimension so that you can live more comfortably. (See Appendix B for a description of Davidson's suggestions.) Davidson's focus is primarily on Buddhist meditation practices (he developed his theory of the six dimensions after performing extensive functional magnetic resonance imaging observations on mindfulness meditators); on cognitive behavioral therapy; and, in some cases where change isn't currently possible, on creating environments in which specific emotional styles can be accommodated rather than changed.

Davidson's work is theoretical. Although he has more raw data to back up his six dimensions of emotional styles than Gardner has to back up his multiple intelligences, I want to be clear that Davidson is working in a new area and is bringing a very specific frame to his observations. Because this work is new, it can and will change over the next few decades. I'm including it not as a concrete set of facts, but as a useful set of ideas and approaches.

I'm drawn to the emotional styles frame, as well as to Davidson's assertion that the brain can change and that people can modify ingrained patterns, because I've experienced this change myself—and I've helped many other people experience it. I didn't have Davidson's framework underneath me as I struggled to become more resilient; to ground my outlook in the present, rather than on the horrors of my past; to balance my extreme Social Intuition, Sensitivity to Context, and Self-awareness; and to manage my ADHD-like lack of focus, which I combined with hyperfocus when it suited me. In my work as an empathic healer, however, I created mindfulness practices to address each dimension (you'll learn these practices in Chapter 5), and I've watched thousands of people use these practices to make significant and lasting changes in their social, emotional, and internal functioning.

It is vitally important to realize something as you move deeper into the art of empathy: *you can change.* If your empathy is way off the charts, to the extent that it's making you miserable, you can modify and work with it intentionally, and you can change. If your capacity for empathy is currently low or if you hit empathic burnout quite a while ago, you can address your areas of difficulty (now that we have these frameworks), and you can change. And if your experience of your own or others' emotions is very uncomfortable, you can approach emotions in new ways so that you can access their wisdom and their gifts, and you can change.

EMPATHIC MINDFULNESS MEDITATIONS FOR KINETIC SCULPTURES

I want to make these next points carefully and with respect to people whose neurology and physiology are different from mine: Davidson's approach, which I outline in Appendix B, relies in most cases upon various stillness meditation practices. These forms of meditation are very helpful for many people; however, they don't work for everybody. In my particular case, they actually make things worse. My mother became a yoga teacher when I was ten years old, so I was introduced to stillness meditations very early, but sitting was never my path. I'm a kinetic sculpture, and I learn through movement. Extended imposed stillness is not supportive for me. Specific kinds of meditations work for specific people, and they don't work for others. For instance, people with anxiety disorders may experience increased anxiety and even panic attacks during stillness meditations.[27] If stillness practices work wonders for you, then by all means, keep doing them. Just know that there are other ways to achieve similar outcomes.

The simple empathic mindfulness techniques I developed more than three decades ago were my way to achieve the kind of grounded focus, integration, and relaxation (in real life and in everyday situations) that people seek in extended stillness practices. Many very empathic people often do not have the time to sit on a cushion or wait for a long meditative retreat when situations become intense. Instead, empaths and sensitive people need to work on their feet in each moment to understand, reframe, ground, refocus, respond to, and shift their perspectives. I find that I need to be able to access my inner resources and my mindfulness immediately, and that's what these empathic mindfulness skills allow me to do.

This book contains many empathic mindfulness techniques that you can use in the moment, on the fly, with your eyes open, and with your thoughts and emotions fully engaged. I certainly want you to read Davidson's book, and if his forms of meditation and therapy work for you and your body, then by all means, focus on those. But I also want you to know that there are many ways to become more mindful. If you're an emotionally aware kinetic sculpture who simply doesn't respond to stillness meditations, that's cool. I've got your back.

Now that we've looked at the working theories of Howard Gardner and Richard Davidson, I'd like to introduce you to my empathic theory of emotions. Since empathy is first and foremost an emotional skill, let's look empathically at the exquisite world of emotions themselves. And let's add a new category of genius to the kinds of intelligences we can have.

DEVELOPING EMOTIONAL GENIUS

Understanding emotions has been a lifelong process for me. From my early days as an emotionally inundated hyperempath, I struggled to make sense of my own intense emotions and of the intense and confusing emotions that ruled my neighborhood after the case against my neighbor was dropped. With the help of my wonderful animal friends, I found a place to explore emotions in safety—out on the lawn with my cat and dog friends, I could relax and think aloud about what I saw in the land of emotions. For instance, I watched anger in people who expressed it as rage, and I studied what they were trying to accomplish. I also watched people, like my mother, who were never openly angry; I contrasted their behavior with the behavior of the rage-filled people I knew. How did life work for them? What did their anger do for them? What did it prevent them from doing?

I watched people who expressed lots of fear and anxiety and contrasted them with people like my father, who never seemed to feel much of either emotion. I studied how people lived and the things they were able to accomplish in their relationship with these emotions. I also watched neighbors who were seemingly always depressed, and I contrasted them with people who always seemed to be upbeat. I studied how people's lives worked or didn't work in relation to depression and happiness. For me, emotions were the most interesting parts of human nature; but in this special area of interest, I was pretty much alone.

People never seemed to want to talk about emotions at all. It was almost as if they were ashamed of emotions and couldn't bear to hear anything about them. This was very strange to me, and it took me almost two decades to acquire a functional, empathic understanding of emotions and their purpose—*not* because it takes decades to understand emotions, but because our ways of approaching, thinking about, and dealing with emotions are so backward and unhelpful. Even today, in the second decade of the twenty-first century, people who come across my work are startled by the absolute newness of it (it is still the only work anywhere that covers all of the emotions in terms of what they do and how to work with them) and by the absolute "Well, duh!" aspect of what anyone should have known.

Emotions were not well understood when I was young. Although a great deal of work is now being done in emotion research, emotions are still an area of massive confusion in numerous academic fields. If you'd like to read about the process that I underwent in my quest to understand emotions empathically, my book *The Language of Emotions* is a chronicle of that decades-long work. In this book, however, we'll move forward without too much preamble, except for an introduction to the most helpful definition of emotions that I've found so far, plus a discussion of four key problems that lead directly to emotional confusion.

ACTION-REQUIRING NEUROLOGICAL PROGRAMS

In his work as a neuroscientist of emotion, Antonio Damasio has been able to study people who have lost their ability to feel some or all emotions. If you have been trained to think of emotions as mostly problematic, you might think of these people as lucky. Many of us imagine that without emotions, people would be completely rational, like a computer or like the hyperlogical and seemingly unemotional *Star Trek* character Mr. Spock. However, nothing could be further from the truth. What Damasio discovered as he worked with many emotion-impaired patients throughout his career is that each emotion has a specific role in the maintenance of essential social and cognitive functions. If you take emotions away from people, they don't become smarter; instead, they become less able to function independently, they lose many of their interactional skills, and they often require direct assistance to care for and protect themselves.

For instance, Damasio wrote about a male patient[28] with brain damage that severely impaired his emotions. Although this patient was still able to think, speak, and drive, he had a fascinating inability to make simple decisions. Damasio described giving this patient two possible dates for an upcoming appointment and then watching in frustration-tinged fascination as the man spent nearly thirty minutes listing all of the possible differences between the two appointment dates (weather, driving conditions, other appointments—he was exhaustive). Finally, Damasio spoke up and suggested one of the two dates. The man agreed willingly and easily—nothing in his meticulous list seemed to matter to him in the least—and then he left.

This patient's logical, linguistic, and sequencing abilities were intact. His memory was intact. He could easily orient to day and time. But he couldn't make any decisions about his preferences, and he couldn't respond appropriately to the boredom and *hurry-up* signals Damasio was sending. He was as smart and as logical as anyone needs to be, but without his emotions, he couldn't make decisions. Damasio eventually realized that decision making is the emotional process of attaching value and meaning to data. This patient knew all of the facts, but he didn't know how he *felt* about any of them, and he was unable to make even a simple decision without assistance. Emotions are intimately involved in our cognitive processes, and without them, facts just pile on top of each other without meaning or value. Emotions help us understand what's important and what isn't, and they help us attend empathically to the signals and needs of others.

Even the allegedly "negative" emotions are intrinsic to our functioning—even shame, even fear. Damasio wrote about another patient,[29] a young woman who had a head trauma in early childhood that interfered with her ability to feel shame, guilt, or embarrassment. Although you might think that this would be a wonderfully freeing state, it was a disaster. Without the ability to feel ashamed or embarrassed, this young woman was a social hurricane, unable (and unwilling) to behave in ways that worked for others and, eventually, for herself. She was insensitive, unapologetic, unreliable, self-endangering, other-endangering, and so disruptive that she landed in multiple treatment facilities as a teen. Eventually, as a young adult, she had to be conserved because she was so socially disabled. She was intelligent, she came from a good family, and she had plenty of therapy and support. But without her shame, guilt, and embarrassment, she couldn't function socially, feel concern, empathize effectively, maintain relationships, complete schooling, keep a job, amend her behaviors, apologize for her misdeeds, or live independently. Without her shame, she couldn't live as a fully functional member of the social world.

Damasio wrote of another woman[30] with a very rare disease that caused calcium deposits to collect in, and essentially disable, her amygdala—a small, almond-shaped region of the brain that's involved in processing fear. This intelligent woman, an artist and mother, was able to feel and identify all other emotions except fear. She couldn't even draw a fearful face, though she could draw facial expressions of other emotions. She was a happy, outgoing person who had no social impediments, but she couldn't tell instinctively whether people or situations were safe. She had to learn the hard way, and she reported that many people she had trusted had gone on to take advantage of her. Without access to her fear, this woman was not completely safe in the world; she didn't have the instincts or the intuition she needed to identify people and situations that might have harmed her. We've been trained to think of fear as a negative emotion, but without it, people are actually quite vulnerable.

Patients like these helped Damasio see through the confusing mists that obscure our understanding of emotions and helped him identify the *purpose* of emotions. These patients and their disabilities helped Damasio create a working definition for emotions that brings them into clear focus: emotions are *action-requiring neurological programs*. They're not positive or negative, glorious or shameful, right or wrong; they're action-requiring neurological programs.

With this definition in place, we can approach emotions empathically—not as problems to be eradicated, but as action-requiring programs that are essential for the maintenance of our whole and healthy lives. Understanding emotions as action-requiring neurological programs helps us observe them more intelligently and more functionally. Because if an emotion requires an action, the next obvious question is (1) *Which* action? And then, the question after that is, (2) What happens when I perform that action?

The answers to these questions are (1) The action you perform depends upon which emotion has arisen, and (2) When you perform the correct action, that emotion should recede naturally. This action-requiring approach helps us reframe not just emotions but also the conditions we usually blame on emotions, such as repetitive anxiety or depression, or problems with anger, fear, or envy (and so on). Instead of looking at emotions as problems in and of themselves, we can—with this action-focused approach—become more empathically intelligent about them.

WHICH ACTIONS ARE REQUIRED?

Let's look a bit more closely at Damasio's assertion that emotions are action-requiring neurological programs by focusing on the requirements of specific emotions. I'll go into more detail in the next chapter, but for now, let's look at five emotions and their related actions (the following is based on an essay that originated on my website[31]).

Fear requires that you take action to orient to change and novelty or to avoid possible physical hazards. *Anger* requires that you take action to protect or restore your sense of self or your standpoint (or the selves and standpoints of others, if your anger is related to social justice). *Shame* requires that you take action to avoid embarrassing or offending yourself or others (*if* the shame is authentic to you; it's important to first identify whether the shame has been applied as a control mechanism from the outside). *Sadness* requires that you take action to let go of something that isn't working anyway. *Grief* requires that you actively mourn something or someone that is lost irretrievably. And so forth.

Each emotion represents a unique action-requiring neurological program that, as Damasio explains, has evolved over millions of years to help humans become a successful social species. In the following excerpt from his book *Self Comes to Mind: Constructing the Conscious Brain,* my explanations of Damasio's terms are in brackets:

> Emotions are present even in cultures that lack names for the emotions. . . . The universality of emotional expressions reveals the degree to which the emotional action program is unlearned and automated. The execution of the same emotion can vary from occasion to occasion but not enough to make it unrecognizable to the subject or to others. It varies as much as the interpretation of [George] Gershwin's song *Summertime* can change with different interpreters or even with the same interpreter on different occasions, yet it is still perfectly identifiable because the general contour of the behavior has been maintained. . . .
>
> The fact that emotions are unlearned, automated, and predictably stable across action programs [emotional responses] betrays their origins in natural selection and in the resulting genomic instructions [human genetic inheritance]. These instructions have been highly conserved across evolution and result in the brain's being assembled in a particular, dependable way, such that certain neuron circuits can process emotionally competent stimuli [anything that evokes an emotion] and lead emotion-triggering brain regions to construct a full-fledged emotional response.

*Emotions and their underlying phenomena are so essential for the
maintenance of life and for subsequent maturation of the individual
that they are reliably deployed in early development.* [All normally
developing human infants are born with specific emotions intact,
and all develop further emotional responses at dependable stages.]
(123–124, *emphasis mine*)

Emotions are essential for the maintenance of life. That powerful statement
stands in stark contrast to what most of us were taught about emotions—even
in otherwise supportive meditative practices, in which we're often taught to
disengage from our emotions or to breathe them away as if they are impediments to consciousness. Sadly, in most places you look, many of our emotions
are treated as signs of pathology in and of themselves. We've received endless
instructions about how *not* to have the allegedly negative ones or how to
have the allegedly positive ones all day long. But that's not helpful, because it
teaches us to treat emotions as problems, when they're actually essential and
highly evolved aspects of consciousness, cognition, social skill, empathy, and
human nature.

It's so helpful to understand emotions as action-requiring neurological
programs, because it means that you get to decide which action (out of dozens) you want to take. This gives you intentionality and agency in regard to
your emotions; you become a person who can act intelligently when your
emotions arise, rather than being their puppet or their puppet-master. This
concept also lifts away the blotch of pathology that has been smeared onto
emotions for so many centuries. Emotions are necessary, evolved, and reliable.

When a snake crosses your path, your *fear program* starts so that you can
orient yourself to change, novelty, and possible hazards. You take action to
avoid the snake, or you pick him up gently and get him out of harm's way, or
any number of other responses. Then your fear recedes.

When your brother calls you a jerk, your *anger program* starts so that you
can address challenges to your sense of self and your standpoint. You can
take action to repair the damage: you could yell, but that might just start a
war; you could ignore the slur, if that's the best idea; you could lean into the
relationship and gently ask him to explain his behavior, if you want to protect
his sense of self and move the relationship to a new place; or you could laugh
and defuse the intensity. Whichever action you take will complete the program—though fighting back will require a new and stronger anger response

that could get you into trouble. (We'll explore this in the section on repression and expression of emotions in this chapter, and in "How Much Emotion Is Too Much?" in Chapter 4.)

When you move toward a bad habit or you're about to say something really insensitive, your *shame program* starts so that you can avoid offending or embarrassing yourself or others (note that this example involves healthy and authentic shame). Shame also brings its own actions—it fills you with heat, flushes your face, and stops you in your tracks, because you're about to do something potentially injurious. Your job is to check in, think about your next move, and hopefully stop yourself from doing it. If you don't, your shame program may intensify or other emotions may arise, depending on your relationship to shame. You might start to feel depression, apathy ("I don't care; I do what I want!"), fear, and so forth. Each emotion has its own action-requiring program, and though there's a tremendous amount of nuance and individual distinctions in how each of our emotions works and interacts, they are reliable and "perfectly identifiable," as Damasio states.

FOUR IDEAS THAT ENSURE EMOTIONAL CONFUSION

Damasio's groundbreaking reframing of emotions as action-requiring neurological programs is wonderfully helpful, but there's so much trouble in the emotional realm that I want to clear away four ideas that create endless emotional confusion. Before we can empathically explore the specific actions that your emotions require (in Chapter 4), we need to take a look at some commonly accepted ideas that actually prevent you from being able to approach emotions intelligently.

THE PROBLEM WITH VALENCING

Valencing is a way to separate things into specific categories. Emotions are valenced in two ways: they're categorized as either positive *or* negative, or they're framed as either prosocial *or* antisocial. So, instead of being viewed as a constellation of important, action-requiring programs that are reliable parts of your cognitive abilities, emotions are often separated into categories that have come to mean good versus bad, wanted versus unwanted, or nice versus mean.

Here's the problem: If you believe that emotions are either positive *or* negative, you'll tend to focus on the allegedly positive ones and avoid the allegedly negative ones. As such, you won't develop a full range of emotional or empathic skills. You might be able to work skillfully with the emotions you identify as positive, but you might be clueless about the ones you iden-tify as negative. Likewise, if you believe that emotions are either prosocial *or* antisocial, you'll think that only a few emotions are acceptable in your relationships. Therefore, when supposedly antisocial emotions arise, you may become shocked or destabilized, and you may view yourself and others in ways that actually reduce your social and emotional intelligence. You may think, for instance, that people are trustworthy *only* when they display emo-tions that you approve of, but that people who display emotions you don't like should be shamed, changed, or avoided altogether.

If you valence emotions, you'll also lose awareness of and access to a great number of the skills your emotions bring to you. If you look at the five emo-tions I described earlier (fear, anger, shame, sadness, and grief), you'll notice that they would all be valenced into negative or antisocial categories. They would be typecast as emotions that cause trouble, don't feel good, and don't look good to others. However, without them, you would have no instincts or intuition *(fear)*, no capacity to set boundaries or protect your (or others') stand-point or sense of self *(anger)*, no capacity to manage your behavior *(shame)*, no capacity to let things go when it's time *(sadness)*, and no capacity to mourn when irretrievable loss has occurred *(grief)*. When any of these emotions are necessary—when any of these actions are required—then each of these emo-tions is the most positive emotion possible. When *any* emotion is necessary and appropriate, it's *always* positive (if you really need to use that word).

If you had inserted one of the allegedly positive emotions, such as happi-ness, into the place of these five emotions, you'd see something very negative indeed, because happiness was not required in the situations I described. Happiness is a very specific emotion that arises to help you look forward to the future with delight and amusement, and it's wonderful! But so are anger, fear, shame, grief, sadness, jealousy, envy, and so forth. All emotions are won-derful and necessary when you need them, and all emotions can be a problem if they arise at the wrong time.

For instance, if you're at a funeral, happiness is completely inappropriate. You need your grief to help you mourn your losses. At a funeral, grief is the positive and prosocial emotion, and happiness is negative and antisocial. Of course, emotions move and change all the time, and they certainly do so during a funeral, so it's normal to cry, and then laugh, and then smile, and then cry again. However, pasting an unchangeably happy smile on your face during a funeral is not prosocial.

Or let's look at fear: if a car is veering directly toward you on the freeway, happiness would probably lead to injury, because you need the lightning-fast instincts and intuitive actions of fear to get yourself to safety. In a situation of immediate physical danger in which fear is required to save your life, happiness is a ridiculous emotion—it's completely inappropriate.

So instead of valencing emotions into simple-minded either/or categories, the empathic approach is to observe all emotions as reliable and evolutionarily evolved responses that are uniquely *appropriate* to specific situations. When you stop valencing, you'll learn to empathically respond to what's actually going on, and you'll learn to observe emotions calmly and perceptively, without demonizing them or glorifying them. This calm and unvalenced approach will make your experience of Emotion Contagion infinitely more comfortable, which means that you'll have an easier time understanding and working with every other aspect of your empathy.

When you can understand emotions as action-requiring neurological programs, you can ask whether each program is *appropriate* for its situation. If it is, you can support the emotion and take suitable action. If it's not, you can help yourself or others take a look at why that program got activated or why that emotion is so prominent that it steps into situations where another emotion would be more appropriate. (We'll explore situations in which emotions are confused or seemingly inappropriate later in this chapter, and in Chapter 4.)

In this empathic approach to emotions, you'll learn to welcome all of your emotions—and the emotions of others—as valid and legitimate action-requiring aspects of social skills, empathy, and intelligence, because *all emotions are necessary.* Unvalencing emotions is a crucial first step in addressing Emotion Contagion, increasing your Empathic Accuracy, and gaining extensive Emotion Regulation skills—all of which will help you skillfully perform all six aspects of empathy. Befriending and welcoming your emotions—all of them, valence free—makes becoming a healthy, happy, and intentional empath significantly easier.

THE PROBLEM WITH EXPRESSION AND REPRESSION

When an emotion arises and requires an action, many of us fall into a simple binary world in which we can only *express* the emotion outwardly or *repress* it inwardly. It's as if we have an on/off switch with no middle ground. This situation is almost a form of valencing in itself, in that we're given two simpleminded choices that actually obscure our intelligence and reduce our options when emotions arise. And of course, this, in turn, reduces our emotional regulation skills and our empathic awareness.

In many instances, expression and repression are fine. If you're happy, sometimes it's awesome to express it—*Yay!* And other times, it's a really good idea to repress your happiness if it's not shared (say, when you're happy that you didn't get picked for a team at work, but you don't want to offend everyone). Expression and repression aren't problems in and of themselves. They're fine in many instances. They're only problems when they're the *only* choices you have.

For instance, when an intense or socially unacceptable emotion arises and requires an action from you, both expression *and* repression can be deeply problematic. Let's say that you're at a party, and a friend does something deeply offensive in public. Let's say that he makes a sarcastic joke about your clothing that's funny but also really cruel. Now, because your self and your standpoint have been offended (and shockingly so), your anger will need to arise, and it will probably be accompanied by some shame and maybe even fear. This is an intensely embarrassing attack that came out of nowhere! If you *express* your intense anger, you might score some points against your friend, but you might also injure him and come off looking like a jerk yourself—like you're so uncool that you can't even take a joke. Also, you might not know how your friend will respond to a counterattack (your shame and fear might have arisen specifically to alert you to this). Your friend could become even meaner, and then the whole evening would be ruined for everyone.

So, if you know that expression can be dangerous, you might take the other option in our restricted either/or scenario. Let's say you *repress* your anger and your shame and your fear. You might laugh and pretend not to be offended, or you might make an even uglier joke about your own clothing. Ha-ha, you're a good sport—you can take a joke! But when you repress an emotion, you interfere with the basic operation of your emotional and neurological functioning. In this instance, your anger arose for a specific reason. It required that you perform a specific action to restore your *voice* (your capacity to express yourself, your opinions, your ideas, and your morals), your standpoint, and your sense of self. You chose not to, which was probably a good idea, socially speaking, because exploding at your friend might have ruined the party for everyone. But by merely repressing your appropriate anger, you've interfered with its natural progression, and because you didn't perform any appropriate action, your anger will remain activated. You might paste a smile on your face and go get a drink and a snack, but for the rest of the night, you'll repeat the situation in your head, and you'll think of what you *should* have said. Your anger won't relieve itself; in fact, it might become more intense, your fear might increase, your shame might become hyperactivated, and *yow!* Repressing your emotions when they're intense and immediate can really cause trouble inside you.

Luckily, there is another option. There's a middle path between expression and repression. I call it *channeling your emotions*—by that, I mean completing the actions your emotions require so that they can recede naturally and gracefully. In the situation above, expression and repression were both problematic. Your anger was very intense, and it was accompanied by two other strong emotions. As we all know, that can be a powder-keg situation. But if you have access to an empathic view of the gifts your emotions contain (these gifts are listed in the next chapter)—if you know anger as the *Honorable Sentry* and fear as *Intuition and Action,* and if you know that shame is about *Restoring Integrity*—then you can take actions with all three of these emotions that are respectful toward yourself, toward your mouthy friend, toward onlookers, and toward your own emotions.

I don't have a simple, step-by-step process for dealing with the situation above, and I am really suspicious of people who do. Interaction is so incredibly situation specific, and your responses usually need to shift in each second. However, I do have a simple approach, which is this: listen to your emotions and work with each of them empathically, interact with others honestly, and then you'll know what to do.

If you make a mistake, you can apologize, and then you can try something different. The trick to this isn't any kind of trick at all: you simply listen to your emotions and pay attention to others and to their responses. This empathic and interactive approach will actually give you untold resources, because your emotions have evolved over millions of years to help you become a socially successful member of an intensely social species. Emotions are millions of years older than spoken language, and simply put, they're smarter than words, they're deeper than any technique, and they can help you in ways you cannot imagine (especially if all you've ever done with emotions is express or repress them).

So let me put myself into the situation above. Let's say that my friend said something cruel about my clothing in front of other people. I feel the power of anger filling me, and there is some fear activating me as well—this tells me that, sure, my boundaries have been crossed, but there could also be some hazard here. My shame also arises, and I know that its function is to help me moderate my behavior. I'm pretty good friends with shame, so I listen carefully to its warning. With the power that anger gives me, I stand up a little straighter, I ground myself (we'll learn this practice in Chapter 5), and I make eye contact with my mouthy friend. I know that I could attack him if I need to, but my fear and shame are warning me: Don't. There's further danger here.

I also know that if I *don't* say something (if I repress my anger), I'll be telling all of the people surrounding us that I can be attacked without any repercussions. My shame and fear tell me that this is not a good approach to my social survival, so I ask myself the questions for anger (which are from the list in the next chapter): *What must be protected, and what must be restored?* Certainly, my fashion sense isn't that important, but this direct attack cannot go unaddressed. Ignoring this situation would leave me vulnerable, but equally important, it would train my friend to be obnoxious and verbally abusive without consequence, which would severely reduce his social viability. Anger is the *Honorable Sentry*, and if you channel it honorably, it will protect everyone—not just you.

However, I know from past experience that people who attack others have trouble with their own anger and shame, as well as trouble with their own boundaries. Therefore, one thing that needs to be protected in this situation is my mouthy friend's already damaged sense of self. Wow, that's a tremendous amount of social information that my emotions brought to me.

Okay, anger helps me feel empowered and energized, which means I have a third option: I have the strength that I need to be vulnerable without too much danger. I lean over and say something very direct and slightly humorous, but nonthreatening, like, "Whoa, I like your sense of humor, but man, that stings! Why you gotta *be* like that?" I tell him that I see the fun and that I appreciate him, but that he went too far. When I channel my anger appropriately, I have the strength that I need to say, "Hey, that hurt" in a way that isn't brutal. I don't pretend to be invulnerable, because that's not a position of strength—that's just a lie. No one is invulnerable.

When I can complete the action my anger requires, which is to reset my boundaries honorably, then my anger will recede naturally. In this situation, my shame will also recede, because I managed my behavior respectfully and acted appropriately to protect my friend and myself from excessive social harm. My fear will recede as well, because I oriented myself effectively in regard to possible dangers and hazards.

Where we go from here is completely individual. My friend might hear me and apologize, and this might set him on a path of wondering why he finds it so easy to be cruel. Or he might escalate and get more pointed, at which time I could identify the new emotions that arise and work with each of them to figure out what the heck to do next. But whatever he decides, we'll be in a new place, and I'll have new information about who my friend is in the presence of honesty and vulnerability. By responding empathically to the true emotions that arose, I helped my friend understand exactly who I am and exactly how his behavior affected me. What he does with that information is up to him, but his subsequent behavior will show me true and pertinent things about who he really is.

With anger, the problem of expression (which often damages others) and repression (which often damages us) is a function of how we've all been trained to use anger as strength *over* others instead of strength *within* ourselves. When emotions have been thrown onto the trash heap of negative and antisocial valencing, we're almost forced to take a moral stance for or against the emotions instead of learning how to work with them intelligently. This happens with a great many emotions, but it's most obvious in regard to anger. If anger is about cruelty, then you have to take a moral stand: will you express anger and be cruel when people deserve it, or will you repress all anger and never defend yourself? These simpleminded either/or options flow naturally and tragically from simpleminded either/or valancing and either/or expression and repression.

Had I used *only* emotional expression of my anger in an attempt to dishonor my friend or had I used *only* emotional repression to essentially dishonor myself, our interaction would have been very different, and my friend would have learned very different things about me. When I only know how to repress or express my emotions when a difficult or socially uncomfortable emotion arises, people will become acquainted with whatever emotional training I've ingested in my life. They won't meet me as an individual; they won't meet my true self, my hopes, my dreams, my preferences, my intelligence, my humor, my challenges, and my strengths—no. When my emotional skills are poor, people will meet my emotional reactivity and my problems with whichever emotion has arisen, but they won't meet me.

In a situation in which I have only two rigid choices about how to work with my emotions, a fully empathic exchange is very unlikely, because I'm not even being empathic with my own emotions. But when I can *channel* my emotions and interact with more suppleness and authenticity, people can meet and interact with me as a unique individual—and if they feel able to, they can interact in a more authentic and empathic way with me as well. When I can work with my emotions honestly and in diverse ways, empathic exchanges are far more likely, because they're a natural outgrowth of emotional honesty and availability. Remember that *empathy is first and foremost an emotional skill.* Empathy is also honed in honest, emotionally awake interactions that help you develop deeper and more accurate empathy for yourself and others.

As I said earlier, emotional expression and repression aren't bad in and of themselves; they're actually fine in many situations! When a snake crosses your path, *express* your fear and jump and yell a little! Or when someone trips on the sidewalk and you think it's funny, *repress* your laughter so you won't hurt the person's feelings. When you drop your phone, *express* your shock and anger by swearing. When you feel like crying but you know that the person with you cannot handle it, *repress* your tears until you're in a safer place. Expression and repression are excellent options in many instances, but this third path—this middle path of *channeling* your emotions—gives you infinite options when repression isn't healthy and expression isn't wise.

There are, of course, situations in which your emotions will be out of place or strangely repetitive or dysfunctional in some way. We'll look at those situations in Chapter 4 in the section "How Much Emotion Is Too Much?" As I like to say: *Emotions are always true, but they're not always right.* We'll learn some simple ways to tell the difference between the two. Learning to channel your emotions will help you manage Emotion Contagion and increase your Empathic Accuracy and Emotion Regulation, which will help you in all areas of empathic awareness and engagement.

THE PROBLEM OF NUANCE

Emotions arise in many different intensities and gradations, but our simplistic emotional training doesn't help us identify or understand emotional nuance. Understanding nuance is a critical part of understanding emotions, but we don't tend to have much training in it, especially if we're taught that emotions should be valenced into very rigid categories. For instance, *all* anger is negative and antisocial; therefore, you should repress and avoid *all* of it! Or *all* happiness is positive and prosocial; therefore, you should express happiness all of the time in every possible situation, *yay!* But emotions don't work that way. Emotions arise at many different levels of intensity, from the subtlest nuanced attitudes to obvious moods to the most fervent outward expressions. Identifying emotions when they're at the mood level or the very intense level can be quite easy; however, if you only focus on those two intensities of emotion, you can overlook massive amounts of vital emotional information.

Emotions are action-requiring neurological programs, and, as such, they bring you specific gifts and skills that you can identify, even when you're not in an obvious mood state. Emotions are intrinsic aspects of your most basic cognitive abilities and your intelligence, and I can tell right away whether you're good with anger, fear, shame, or a dozen other emotions just by asking questions about your everyday social skills. I even created a short quiz to help people gauge their current relationship with their own emotions.[32]

Take a look at these eleven questions. Even if you can already identify which emotion-based gifts and skills I'm looking for, try to answer them honestly.

1. I feel heard and respected in my interpersonal relationships.
2. I'm comfortable speaking up for myself, even during conflicts.

3. I tend to remain calm and focused in emergencies.
4. I tend to know when new situations and new relationships are going to work out.

5. I can relax and calm myself, and I have reliable self-soothing skills.
6. I'm able to change my mind when I discover better information and ideas.

7. I have a fairly easy time changing problem behaviors or old habits.
8. When I make a social blunder, I'm able to apologize and correct myself.

9. I'm comfortable talking about my talents and my achievements.

10. I'm good at asking for what I want in regard to money, possessions, and recognition.

11. I have good time-management skills, and I follow through on my plans and commitments.

Questions 1 and 2: The Gifts of Anger. If you don't understand that emotions can be reliably identified as everyday skills and capacities that underlie your more obvious mood states, you might not even connect questions 1 and 2 to the gifts of anger. These gifts help you set and maintain effective interpersonal boundaries. At its subtlest level, anger helps you uphold mutual respect and keep open the lines of communication in your relationships. Sadly, most of us can only identify anger when it gets to the level of a mood. And since most of us were never taught how to take effective actions with our anger, we don't know how to access the skills and gifts that anger brings us.

Questions 3 and 4: The Gifts of Fear. If you have no understanding of emotional nuance, you might think that the gifts in questions 3 and 4 relate to being focused and intuitive—and you'd be right. However, you'd miss the fact that those are the gifts of fear, which help you orient effectively to change, novelty, or possible physical hazards. If you and your fear are working nicely together, you'll calmly and instinctually identify hazards and safety, though you may have no idea that you're working with fear, because you won't feel obviously afraid. However, all emotions exist at this subtle gift-and-skill level, and identifying them at this soft and flowing stage makes working with their more intense variations much easier.

Questions 5 and 6: The Gifts of Sadness. These questions may seem to relate to calmness, self-soothing behaviors, and flexibility, but they're actually the gifts of sadness, which help you identify things that aren't working so that you can let go and make room for things that *do* work. It's interesting to note that all relaxation techniques (and many meditation practices) intentionally evoke the relaxing and softening gifts of sadness, though this is not usually stated or even understood. I laugh when I see heavily valenced, emotion-pathologizing relaxation techniques that teach you to breathe away pesky emotions (including sadness) by intentionally relaxing yourself with the gifts of sadness. Ha!

Questions 7 and 8: The Gifts of Shame. These questions may seem to relate to behavioral maturity (and they do), but they're also the gifts of shame, which help you monitor and modify your behavior. (*Note:* I make a very strong distinction between guilt and shame, and I don't actually classify guilt as an emotion at all.[33]) When your shame is working gracefully, you won't feel it. For instance, you'll floss because you like clean teeth (and not because you've been shamed into obsessive dental hygiene), you'll avoid larceny and abusiveness because they don't feel right (and not because you've been shamed or terrorized out of them), and you'll manage your intense emotions skillfully because you respect the basic human rights of others. As I wrote earlier, many of us have a problematic relationship with shame because it was applied to us as punishment when we were young. However, as we saw in Damasio's story about the shameless young woman, shame is absolutely crucial for your social viability. Without your shame, you cannot live independently or safely.

If you and your shame do not work well together, the skill called Burning Contracts in Chapter 5 will help you reclaim and return your shame (or any other problematic emotion) to its proper functioning.

Question 9: The Gifts of Contentment. This question may seem to relate to a healthy sense of self-regard, and it does, but it also relates to the gifts of contentment. Contentment is a little bit like happiness, but it brings its own set of gifts to you. Whereas happiness helps you look outward with amusement and delight, contentment helps you turn toward yourself with pride and satisfaction, so you can say, "Hey, good job!" Contentment arises when you've worked hard and well, and it relates to your healthy self-image. This means that it has a close connection to your healthy anger and especially to your healthy shame—and I bet you won't hear that anyplace else, but hear me out.

When you set clear boundaries, behave honorably, and act conscientiously (actions that your healthy anger and shame will help you take), your contentment will arise naturally as a kind of reward—"Good job!" Contentment arises to tell you when you've done good work—not only in your accomplishments but also in your treatment of yourself and others. If you attend to your anger and your shame honorably, you'll naturally feel content and proud of yourself, because you'll have done good work inside yourself and in relation to the people in your life.

If you don't work well with your anger and shame, and if your shame is primarily inauthentic and self-tormenting, your contentment might not arise reliably, and your self-regard and self-image might be pretty low. Accordingly, when you have a problem with self-esteem, you'll often look for ways to increase contentment and happiness first, so that you can feel better about yourself. But it doesn't work that way, because contentment arises for specific reasons, and you can't take a shortcut to get there. If you have low self-regard, contentment is probably the emotion you'd like to feel, but working on your boundaries (the gifts of anger) and your behavior (the gifts of shame) will actually help your contentment arise naturally. Interestingly, too much self-esteem and contentment can be problematic and can actually be a factor in bullying. We'll look more closely at bullying in Chapter 9.

Question 10: The Gifts of Envy. This question may seem to relate to your capacity for self-preservation and financial and social viability—and it does. But these are also the gifts of envy, which help you create and maintain stable connections to security, material and financial resources, and appropriate social recognition. Envy is related to the emotion of jealousy, though the two have distinct differences: envy helps you function effectively in the area of security, resources, and recognition, whereas jealousy helps you create and maintain stable connections to loyalty, mate retention, and love.

Envy and jealousy are possibly the most hated emotions in the entire emotional realm, but they are absolutely crucial to your social survival. As we explore relationship skills in Chapter 7, childhood rivalries in Chapter 9, and workplace relationships in Chapter 10, we'll look at how healthy envy and healthy jealousy can help you become more effective in your relationships.

Question 11: The Gifts of Anxiety. This question may seem to relate to being a good planner, and it does, because that's one of the gifts anxiety brings to you. People are often surprised to learn that anxiety contains specific gifts, because anxiety is usually described in terms of disorder or disease. However, at its most subtle gift level, anxiety (which is related to fear) helps you plan for the future and complete important tasks. I call anxiety your *procrastination alert system;* a bonus with anxiety is that if you're feeling it, then there's probably nothing to fear in the present moment. If there's a problem in your immediate environment, fear will help you orient to change, novelty, or possible hazards. But if you're feeling anxiety, it relates to the future, and its presence usually means that things in the present moment are pretty stable.

As we all know, anxiety can become problematic if it isn't attended to, and it can become uncomfortably repetitive. We'll look at a specific practice for anxiety (Conscious Questioning) in Chapter 5.

All emotions bring you specific gifts, and all emotions exist in a continuum of different intensities. As the questions in my short emotion quiz demonstrate, your emotions actually contribute vital skills that support your basic cognition and social functioning. If you can learn to identify the subtle presentations of your emotions, these skills will be available to you in every waking moment; you won't have to wait until a mood overtakes you. It's important to develop an awareness of emotions at many different and subtle levels so that you can become more skilled with these basic tools of social intelligence and empathic awareness.

To help you develop a larger, more nuanced range of emotional awareness, I include the "Emotional Vocabulary List" in Appendix A to give you many vocabulary words for specific emotions at three different levels of intensity. In the list, I refer to the subtle, gift-level presentation of emotions as their *soft* states. I call their more obvious presentations *mood* states. When they're highly activated, I call that their *intense* states.

To help you understand what I mean, let me put anxiety into the mix and run it through the three states. In its *soft* state, anxiety simply helps you be aware of what you need to bring for an upcoming trip, for instance. You don't feel obviously anxious; you're just connected to anxiety's capacity to help you prepare yourself for the future and to complete your tasks intelligently.

In its *mood* state, your anxiety is more insistent. You feel more of a sense of a time crunch, and you might experience intense focus and energy. You might orient toward the future and bring a great deal of laser focus to what you need to do; you might even ignore things in the room that are not related to the tasks you need to complete. You feel more activated in this state, and you might be a bit snappy if anyone gets in your way. This is a very task-oriented emotion, and it has things to do! In this state, you feel a little bit riled up, but not uncomfortably so, and you're able to identify that you're working with the gifts of anxiety. In their mood states, your emotions are usually obvious to you and others.

In its *intense* state, your anxiety is in a kind of feedback loop, which can be initiated by many things. Internally, it could be generated by an increase in adrenaline, cortisol, heart rate, or other physical conditions unrelated to task completion. When you feel those ramped-up intensities, you might think, "Oh, I have a ton of work to do on a tight deadline!!" Externally, this intense level of anxiety could be initiated by a sudden, overwhelmingly close deadline or by a flurry of things that need to be handled but are actually impossible for one person to do. In situations like this, your anxiety might set itself into a tizzy of activation. It might spin out and take you from room to room, completing three tasks badly and four not at all. You might orient so strongly to one thing that you miss other things in the room, and you might trip or walk into a wall. Or your focus might get so overwhelmed that you can't see or find that check you just put down on the table, *dagnabbit!!* At this point, Conscious Questioning (in Chapter 5) will be invaluable.

Notice that all three levels of activation involve the exact same emotion—anxiety. But also notice that when we talk about anxiety, we usually only talk about its intense state, and we usually categorize anxiety as a thoroughly negative emotion. That's understandable, because if you only know anxiety in its intense form, then the act of valencing is actually sort of logical: An emotion that walks you into walls and makes you lose checks is not helpful! It's negative! But that's not all that anxiety does, and it's important to remember that all emotions exist at many different levels of activation and nuance, and all emotions are necessary.

Increasing your emotional vocabulary and extending your emotional awareness to include nuance will help you become more articulate, more knowledgeable, and more empathic about emotions—in yourself and in others. It will also help you increase your Emotion Contagion, Empathic Accuracy, Emotion Regulation, and Perspective Taking skills. Increasing your emotional awareness increases your empathic awareness.

THE PROBLEM OF QUANTITY

Emotions don't arise one at a time in a kind of military precision. Instead, they usually arise in pairs, groups, or clusters. In many cases, such as the party situation I described earlier, we saw that fear and shame arose alongside anger when our mouthy friend insulted our clothing. These three emotions arose together because we needed all three of them. We needed *anger* to address the direct affront to our sense of self, we needed *fear* so that we could be awake and intuitive about possible hazards, and we needed *shame* to help us moderate our behavior so that the situation wouldn't spiral out of control. All three of these emotions were necessary in that situation.

Emotions arise because they're necessary, and in many situations, multiple emotions are needed. Emotions are action-requiring programs, and you can easily have more than one program running at any given time. Emotions are a collection of interrelated skills, abilities, and aptitudes, so it's natural for them to arise in pairs or groups. It's also natural for them to follow one another swiftly after you complete the distinct actions required by each one.

Vocabulary may be a problem here: In the English language, we have almost no words that meld emotions in the way they actually work in real life. Some friends and I were talking recently about finding a word for the kind of happiness that makes you cry, perhaps when something is so beautiful and also so touching that you become overtaken by joy and sadness and happiness (and sometimes grief) all at once. The closest we could come was *bittersweet*, but that's not an emotion—it's a flavor!

To find emotion-melding words, we actually had to go outside the English language. In the German language, for instance, a wonderful melded-emotion word is *schadenfreude*, which means "feeling joy about the misfortune of another." In schadenfreude, which I sometimes call *savage glee*, there's anger, happiness, joy, a distinct lack of shame, envy, jealousy, and a sense of righteous exultation when you see someone receive what you deem to be a much-deserved comeuppance. Usually, there's a lot of history behind those combined emotions—the person who is suddenly brought so low may have been lording over you for quite some time or may have received many undeserved accolades while your own work went unacknowledged. When that many emotions arise in a cluster, there's a tremendous amount of social information that can be gleaned empathically. It's a continual source of fascination for me that the English language doesn't identify clustered emotions. Besides the word *nostalgia* (which is present-day sadness or longing for past happiness) the only other word I could think of is *gloating*, which is a little bit like schadenfreude. In schadenfreude, the other person has lost, but you haven't necessarily won. But when you gloat, you win or prevail over someone, and you gloatingly express your savage glee, apply shame to your opponent, and kick her when she's down. *Ouch!*

The English word *ambivalence* describes the state of feeling more than one emotion—and if you're a wordsmith, you'll notice the word *valence* right inside *ambivalence*. Ambivalence means that you're feeling an allegedly negative emotion and an allegedly positive emotion together, and you're confused because you can't possibly decide which of the two emotions is true (hint: they're *both* true!). We actually do have a word in our language that tells us that two emotions are *way* too many and that confusion is the correct response. Wow, English language, wow!

I'm interested in our limited emotional vocabulary in another way—I notice that people use the word *emotional* to mean just about anything. "You're so emotional" can mean that you're angry, anxious, sad, or fearful, or perhaps that your emotions change a lot (as they should). "Let's not get emotional" can mean almost anything, but it's usually a way to shame you out of a behavior or a position that doesn't work for the other person. "Emotions ran high" can mean that people fought in anger, that they cried, or that they responded in many different ways, such as laughing, shouting, booing, or walking out in disgust. The word *emotional* can mean everything and nothing, mainly because many people don't have strong emotional vocabularies. Sadly, this also means they don't have strong emotional awareness, which also means their empathic skills are likely very limited. Luckily, the work we're doing now will help with all of these problems.

Understanding emotions individually is a great first step in increasing your empathic skills. But out in the real world, emotions don't always arise individually. For instance, I wrote earlier about the connection between anger, shame, and contentment. If you want to feel more contentment, you actually need to make sure that you're working well with the gifts of anger and the gifts of shame. If you don't know that emotions are strongly interrelated, you might waste your time trying to evoke an individual emotion, such as contentment (which can't arise healthfully until you actually do something commendable), without understanding that other emotions need to be involved.

Another problem that arises when you don't know that emotions work together is one that happens regularly with anger, which many people misidentify as an allegedly secondhand emotion. Anger is sort of the whipping boy of the emotional realm (okay, all emotions, except possibly happiness, are the whipping boy at some point), and I notice that people hold a great deal of entrenched misconceptions about anger. The secondhand mistake is a case in point, and it's a very easy mistake to make if you don't understand how emotions work together and how anger, in particular, will arise to protect you and your other emotions (especially sadness and fear).

Think about this in terms of the self-protective gifts that anger brings you: In many cases, honestly expressing your sadness or fear is actually socially dangerous. Openly displaying sadness (and tears) can cause you to lose face; likewise, openly displaying fear can make others think you're a coward. Neither of these displays is good for your standpoint or your self-image. In these instances, your anger will be activated, not because it's a dishonest or secondhand emotion, but because it's *necessary.*

We've all had the experience of feeling sadness—of feeling as if we're going to cry—and then suddenly getting angry and cranky at someone instead. Or with fear, we've all had someone jump out and scare the wits out of us, and right after we jump back, we snap angrily, "Cut it out!" In these situations, the "real" emotions are being protected by expressive outbursts of anger. That's anger's job; it's a protective emotion. It's not a secondhand emotion when it jumps in front of the supposedly real emotions you're feeling. Anger is real, too. Anger is doing its job. It's protecting your voice, your sense of self, and your standpoint.

You can clearly observe the ignorance-producing effects of emotional valencing when you look at another secondhand emotion that might arise in these two situations. In both situations, happiness can also jump out in front of your "real" emotions: If you're about to cry but it's not safe, you might smile or laugh instead. And if someone jumps out and scares the heck out of you, you might laugh after you jump back. In both instances, the smiling and laughing will cover your sadness and your fear, and yet no one calls happiness a secondhand emotion. In fact, if you laugh when someone scares you, you'll be seen as a good sport. Yet it's the exact same mechanism, with one emotion jumping out to protect you when displaying the so-called real emotions might be socially unwise. However, when anger is involved, it's suddenly a big problem. Valencing makes us blind to the actual functions of individual emotions, so thank goodness we don't have to rely on valencing in our empathic work!

Problems can arise when emotions step out in front of the seemingly real ones. Empathically speaking, when I see someone who uses anger (or happiness, sadness, fear, or any other emotion) in front of pretty much every other emotion they have, then yes, I want to ask about what's going on. You don't want to see the same emotion arising in every possible situation, because that's not how emotions work in an emotionally flexible person. But having just one emotion is a pretty rare situation. For most of us, emotions arise in pairs, groups, and clusters. Your job as an empathically aware person is to understand which actions are required and then complete those actions to the best of your ability.

When you can successfully complete the actions that your emotions require, new and different emotions will arise—some in the subtle form of gifts and skills, some as identifiable moods, and some as intensely activated calls to immediate action. In many cases, more than one emotion will be active at any given time. That's natural; that's how emotions work. And knowing how emotions work will help you develop all aspects of your emotional and empathic skills.

As we move forward in emotional awareness, we'll unvalance emotions, learn how to channel them, understand them at many different levels of activation, and know that it is perfectly normal for them to arise in pairs, groups, or clusters. In the next chapter, we'll look at emotions in terms of the gifts they bring you and the actions they require. We'll also explore a group of emotionally supportive and pertinent questions to ask when each of your emotions is activated.

CHAPTER 4

The Empath's Guide to Emotions

Why Emotions Arise

THIS BOOK IS about empathy, which is honed in interactions with others. But your first interaction is intrapersonal—it's between you and your own emotions. Your emotional awareness is a key aspect of your capacity to accurately identify and work with the emotions, thoughts, and intentions of others. As I pointed out in Chapter 1, the emotional sphere is where many people lose their empathic abilities. Our emotional training is often insufficient and confusing (and even backward), and subsequently, our emotional understanding tends to be low. Often, when a troubling emotion appears, we may shut down our Emotion Contagion, our Concern for Others, and our Perspective Taking simply because we have no idea how to work with the emotion at hand. We might shut down because we've learned to valence the emotion as negative and unwanted, or we might shut down because we don't have any emotional regulation skills for that emotion. If we haven't learned how emotions work and why they arise, our reactions to them can lead us into the empathic badlands.

THE SIXTEEN CATEGORIES OF EMOTIONS

Now that we've looked at four problems that lead us into emotional confusion and empathic trouble, let's bring emotions into the light of day and observe them empathically and intelligently. In this book, I organize emotions into sixteen categories,[34] but this does not mean that I'm ignoring nuance. In the "Emotional Vocabulary List" in Appendix A, I provide vocabulary words for many different intensities[35] of most of these sixteen emotions. So, if you're looking at anger below, and you're wondering about frustration, peevishness, rage, or other intensities of anger, know that I'm including those in the overall category of anger. When I look at emotions empathically, I look at what they do—how they behave and what their purpose is. Therefore, I include frustration, peevishness, and rage in the area of anger, which is the emotion that helps you set boundaries around your voice, standpoint, and sense of self.

I don't mean to oversimplify emotions and get us into another area of trouble. I'm organizing emotions into sixteen distinct categories so that we can more easily get a handle on them and develop emotional awareness. Otherwise, we might focus too much of our attention on nuance and vocabulary and miss the big picture—which is that emotions are reliable, action-requiring neurological programs that form the foundation of our social, emotional, and empathic skills.

Emotions are your tools; they're your empathic entrée into understanding yourself and others more deeply. These sixteen emotional categories will give you a working vocabulary and a working set of tools to begin understanding emotions empathically—as nuanced and reliable action-requiring responses to very specific stimuli. Emotions bring you multiple skills, abilities, gifts, and capacities. They motivate you, and they help you learn, decide, behave, interact, and relate to yourself and others.

ANGER: *The Honorable Sentry*

Gifts: Honor ~ Conviction ~ Healthy self-esteem ~ Proper boundaries ~ Healthy detachment ~ Protection of yourself and others

Action Required: Anger arises to address challenges to your voice, standpoint, position, interpersonal boundaries, or self-image. Your task is to restore your interpersonal boundaries without violating the boundaries of others. This is the sacred practice for anger, which I very intentionally call the *Honorable* Sentry.

The Internal Questions: What must be protected? What must be restored?

APATHY AND BOREDOM: *The Mask for Anger*

Gifts: Detachment ~ Boundary setting ~ Separation ~ Taking a time-out

Action Required: Apathy is a protective mask for anger, and it arises in situations when you cannot or probably should not express your anger openly. Apathy can give you an excellent time-out, as long as you don't let it take you completely out of commission. The questions for apathy often unmask your legitimate anger (and other emotions), so be ready to work with those subsequent emotions as well.

The Internal Questions: What is being avoided? What must be made conscious?

GUILT AND SHAME: *Restoring Integrity*

Gifts: Atonement ~ Integrity ~ Self-respect ~ Behavioral change

Action Required: Shame arises to help you moderate your behavior and make sure that you don't hurt, embarrass, destabilize, or dehumanize yourself or others. Shame is a tricky emotion, because most of us learned about shame by *being* shamed. The healing practice for shame is to root out inauthentic and applied shame and to encourage authentic, appropriate, and healthy shame (and remorse) in yourself and others.

The Internal Questions: Who has been hurt? What must be made right?

HATRED: *The Profound Mirror*

Gifts: Intense awareness ~ Piercing vision ~ Sudden evolution ~ Shadow work

Action Required: Hatred is a very powerful emotion that arises in the presence of shadow material (things you cannot accept in yourself and demonize in others). Shadow work helps you reintegrate and detoxify this material so that it no longer activates your hatred program. There are two shadow-work practices in the next chapter—Burning Contracts and Conscious Complaining—plus another shadow practice called Ethical Empathic Gossip in Chapter 10. I've also included a list of excellent books on shadow work in the Further Resources section.

The Internal Questions: What has fallen into my shadow? What must be reintegrated?

FEAR: *Intuition and Action*

Gifts: Intuition ~ Instinct ~ Focus ~ Clarity ~ Attentiveness ~ Vigor ~ Readiness

Action Required: Fear arises to orient you to change, novelty, or possible physical hazards. Fear focuses on the present moment and your immediate surroundings.

The Internal Question: What action should be taken?

WORRY AND ANXIETY: *Focus and Completion*

Gifts: Foresight ~ Focus ~ Conscience ~ Procrastination alert! ~ Task completion

Action Required: Worry and anxiety arise to help you organize, plan for, and complete your tasks. Both are related to fear, but they arise to help you orient to *possible upcoming* change, novelty, or hazard. *Bonus:* If you feel anxiety or worry, you'll know that there is probably nothing to fear in the present moment.

The Internal Questions: What triggered this feeling? What really needs to get done?

CONFUSION: *The Mask for Fear*

Gifts: Diffused awareness ~ Innocence ~ Malleability ~ Taking a time-out

Action Required: Confusion is a mask for fear and anxiety, and it arises when you're overwhelmed by change, novelty, or too many tasks. Confusion can be a lovely vacation from overwhelm.

The Internal Questions: What is my intention? What action should be taken?

JEALOUSY: *Relational Radar*

Gifts: Commitment ~ Security ~ Connection ~ Loyalty ~ Fairness

Action Required: Jealousy arises in response to challenges that may destabilize your connection to love, mate retention, or loyalty. These challenges may come from external sources, from an internal lack of self-worth, or both.

The Internal Questions: What has been betrayed? What must be healed and restored?

ENVY: *Interactional Radar*

Gifts: Fairness ~ Security ~ Access to resources ~ Proper recognition ~ Self-preservation

Action Required: Envy arises in response to challenges that may destabilize your connection to material security, resources, or recognition. These challenges may come from external sources, from an internal lack of self-regard, or both.

The Internal Questions: What has been betrayed? What must be made right?

PANIC AND TERROR: *Frozen Fire*

Gifts: Sudden energy ~ Fixed attention ~ Absolute stillness ~ Healing from trauma

Action Required: Panic and terror arise when your physical life is directly and immediately threatened. You have three choices: fight, flee, or freeze.

The Internal Questions: (during the emergency): Just listen to your body—don't think; just react. Your instinctual body is a survival expert, and it will keep you safe.

The Internal Questions: (for post-traumatic stress disorder [PTSD]): What has been frozen in time? What healing action must be taken? In cases of PTSD, the somatic work of Peter Levine (which is referenced in the Further Resources section) is invaluable.

SADNESS: *The Water Bearer*

Gifts: Release ~ Fluidity ~ Grounding ~ Relaxation ~ Rejuvenation

Action Required: Sadness arises when it's time to let go of something that isn't working anyway. If you can truly let go, relaxation and rejuvenation will surely follow.

The Internal Questions: What must be released? What must be rejuvenated?

GRIEF: *The Deep River of the Soul*

Gifts: Complete immersion in the river of life, death, and eternity

Action Required: Grief arises when something has been lost irretrievably or when someone has died. Grief and sadness are intimately related, but with sadness, you still have a choice about letting go. Grief arises when the loss is completely out of your hands, and you need to mourn.

The Internal Questions: What must be mourned? What must be released completely?

SITUATIONAL DEPRESSION: *Ingenious Stagnation*

Gifts: The Ingenious Stop Sign of the Soul

Action Required: Situational depression arises when some aspect of your life is already unworkable or dysfunctional; depression stops you for a vital reason.

The Internal Questions: Where has my energy gone? Why was it sent away?

Important note: Situational depression refers specifically to a low mood that tracks to something you can affect with changes to your lifestyle or behavior. There are many other forms of depression, many of which require therapeutic or medical intervention. If your depression is cyclical or if it doesn't respond to healing changes you make, please seek counseling or therapeutic support.

HAPPINESS: *Anticipation and Possibility*

Gifts: Delight ~ Amusement ~ Hope ~ Wonder ~ Playfulness ~ Invigoration

Action Required: Happiness arises to help you look forward to the future with hope and delight.

The Internal Statement: Thank you for this lively celebration!

CONTENTMENT: *Pleasure and Appreciation*

Gifts: Enjoyment ⁓ Satisfaction ⁓ Self-respect ⁓ Pride ⁓ Confidence ⁓ Fulfillment

Action Required: Contentment arises to help you look toward yourself with pride and satisfaction.

The Internal Statement: Thank you for renewing my faith in myself!

JOY: *Affinity and Communion*

Gifts: Expansion ⁓ Communion ⁓ Inspiration ⁓ Splendor ⁓ Radiance ⁓ Bliss

Action Required: Joy arises to help you feel a blissful sense of expansiveness and connection to others, to ideas, or to experiences.

The Internal Statement: Thank you for this radiant moment!

Be aware: Extreme joy (exhilaration) is a state to approach with care, especially if it cycles with depression or sadness. Repetitive exhilaration or flights of giddy mania may be a sign of emotional dysregulation. Please take care of yourself and reach out for help if necessary.

Emotions form the basis of many of your cognitive and social abilities, yet, as we all know, emotions can also be very problematic. In the next section, which originated on my blog,[36] we'll take an empathic look at emotions that are out of kilter.

HOW MUCH EMOTION IS TOO MUCH?

All emotions are necessary, important, and valuable. Although some very intense emotions (such as hatred and panic) need to be handled with care, in most normal situations, you can understand and work with your emotions on your own. However, there are times when you'll need assistance with your emotions. The way to know when you need help is simple: when your emotions repeat incessantly and do not resolve, or when they overwhelm you or the people in your life, it's time to find out what's going on.

When things are going well, all of your emotions (even very intense ones) will respond and resolve when you pay attention to them and perform whatever corrective actions they require. But sometimes emotions become destabilized, and this action-requiring construct will help you understand what's going on: If you are dealing with an emotion that repeats continually and will not resolve itself, no matter how many times you try to perform the correct action for that emotion, that's *too much*. It's a clear sign that you could use some help. Let's look at two specific emotions (fear and anger) so you'll know what too much emotion actually looks like.

UNDERSTANDING THE PURPOSE OF FEAR

Your fear arises when you need to orient to change, novelty, or possible physical hazards. The actions that fear requires are uncountable, because fear is the emotion of instinct and intuition. When your fear signals you, you might need to hold your breath, freeze, run, laugh, recoil, move forward, orient yourself, strike out quickly to avoid an incoming hazard, leap sideways, be still, lower your head and studiously ignore something, or any of a hundred other actions. When you and your instincts choose the right action, you'll complete the actions that your fear required, and your mood-state fear will recede naturally.

Your fear should never disappear completely, because fear brings you the gifts and instincts needed to prepare for any eventuality. However, you shouldn't be in a fear *mood state* every minute of every day (this would be rough on your health). If everything in your environment knocks your fear from its flowing, nearly imperceptible, intuitive state into its full-on, adrenaline-pumping, action-requiring state, then something is going on. In this situation, you may have a physical condition or a past trauma that needs to be addressed. Cognitive behavioral therapy can be very helpful for hyperactivated fear conditions, as can certain antidepressants and beta blockers. Somatic therapy is also wonderful for resolving the residual activation that can be associated with traumas.

It's really important to address hyperactivated fear, because fear's job is to keep you aware and safe. If your fear is hyperactivated, you'll orient to everything, whether or not you need to, and every change will feel like a threat or a physical hazard. You don't want to be feeling that way all day long (unless you're in a war, and then I take it back). But even for very competent warriors, feeling mood-state fear all the time is hard on the body. PTSD is a very real possibility when you live at the mood-state level of fear for long stretches of time.

The point with fear (and every other emotion) is that it has a very specific purpose. Fear needs you to take action—to orient to change, novelty, and possible hazards. When you properly identify the change or hazard and when you take an action to ensure your safety (or the safety of others, if your fear was evoked on their behalf), then fear's work is done. When you complete the correct action, your fear will revert to its flowing state, and you won't consciously feel afraid. Your fear will still be there, but it won't be in a mood state, and it won't require any overt actions from you. You will have completed the actions that your fear required. Excellent!

The problem with emotions is almost never about the emotion itself—even when the emotion is *way* out of kilter. The fact that people can get into trouble with repetitive fear doesn't mean that fear is negative. Fear is irreplaceable—it brings you instincts and intuition, and it will literally save your life. You want fear! But you want fear to be in its proper place, doing its proper work, with the proper intensity.

For instance, if a child's ball rolls into your field of vision, you want fear to help you notice it, orient to it, and then realize it's not a threat. Excellent, fear, thank you! If a car suddenly swerves toward you, you want your fear to orient you, make a series of split-second decisions and maneuvers (that you don't even have to think about, thanks to fear), and get your car out of harm's way. Whew! Adrenaline rush! Excellent, fear, thank you!

UNDERSTANDING THE PURPOSE OF ANGER

From its healthy, flowing state (where it quietly maintains your self-image and your standpoint), your anger is evoked into its mood state when you sense threats to your self-image, your standpoint, your voice, or your position (I call these, collectively, your *boundaries*). When someone tries to disrespect you, your anger should come forward to protect your boundaries honorably. With that anger, you can set the person straight (or laugh, or raise your eyebrows, or deepen your voice, or any of a hundred nonviolent but self-strengthening, boundary-setting actions). Then your anger will recede, and your boundary will be reset. *Bing*. It's done. No one gets hurt.

I call anger the Honorable Sentry because when you understand the importance of boundaries, you will honor those boundaries in other people. Your anger will not be a weapon; it will be a tool. In a healthy conflict, you *both* should be protected by healthy anger, and you *both* should be restored. Anger is the *Honorable* Sentry.

If you ignore or repress your anger, you're teaching people that it's totally okay to be unkind and insensitive, and you're helping them become less skilled, less socially aware, and less valuable in the social world. You're not doing them any favors; you're actually dishonoring them. The healthy action for anger is to take hold of its strength so you can address any boundary violations honestly and without cruelty. This healthy action helps your relationships deepen and flourish; therefore, you shouldn't repress your anger (in a pantomime of politeness) as a matter of course.

Now, let's switch things around and say you feel anger *all the time.* Politics inflame you, advertising inflames you, other people's behavior inflames you, and you wake up every morning with your fists raised, yelling, "Why, there oughtta be a law!" You also lash out at people regularly, sometimes without meaning to. In this situation, you have *too much* anger, and it's being activated by absolutely everything in your environment. This is a very precarious situation for your social viability. If you ratchet up your anger every time it appears and you attack persistently, you're teaching people that you are (1) not a safe person to be around, (2) not emotionally skilled, and (3) not empathically aware. You might think that your anger outbursts make you look strong, like some action figure. But if you're using your anger to destroy the boundaries and the self-image of others, you haven't learned the true strength and purpose of anger. Sorry. Learning how to channel your anger will help you create and define an honorable and healthy sense of self—for everyone.

Too much of any emotion—even joy—is not healthy for you, for your social viability, for your cognitive skills, or for your physical health. But with continual anger, there's the possibility of damaging your cardiovascular system as well. There's work you can do on your own, such as asking yourself why you're so completely boundary impaired that absolutely everything gets to you. However, you might also need some help from a counselor or your doctor, because repetitive anger that never resolves is simply not good for you.

If your anger goes to DEFCON 1 every time it appears (or even every other time it appears), you may have a rage disorder. Repetitive rage can also be a sign of untreated major depression, so don't fool around with repetitive rage; instead, reach out for help. But remember, it's not the anger that isn't good for you; you absolutely need your anger. (You can get into a repetitive state with any number of emotions, including depression, fear, joy, sadness, or shame, and each will destabilize you in its own particular way.) The problem in a rage disorder isn't that the anger exists; the problem is that the anger is stuck in a feedback loop that needs to be resolved so the anger can get back to its regular job.

What I notice about raging people is that their boundaries are totally permeable—absolutely everything gets to them. Therefore, their anger, which exists to help them strengthen their boundaries, is continually required (remember that emotions are always true, though they're not always right). The anger is responding appropriately to the actual circumstances in their lives. Their anger constantly, regularly, and dependably arises (this anger is true), but because they don't understand how to complete the actions that anger requests of them, their anger becomes trapped in a feedback loop (this anger is not actually right). We all require healthy boundaries and healthy anger, but in the case of a rage disorder, this feedback problem must be dealt with first.

Emotions are very powerful, and their nature is to move quickly, address an issue succinctly, and then move on. All of your emotions have important jobs to do, and you need all of them. But if something behavioral, chemical, or neurological is impeding or inflating your emotions, you can easily tumble into confusion, exhaustion, and disorder. If this happens, your job as the partner of your emotions is to reach out for help—from a friend, a counselor, or your health provider—so that you can bring balance back to your emotional life.

If you have an emotion that's hyperactivated, that appears in seemingly inappropriate situations, or that won't resolve, then that emotion is out of kilter. Your job isn't to crush or suppress the emotion, or breathe it out and pretend to be feeling something else. No, your job is to find out what's going on so that your emotion can get back to its regular work!

THE ANSWER IS PRETTY SIMPLE, REALLY

So, the answer to the question *How much emotion is too much?* is the same for any of the emotions: If an emotion appears constantly or repetitively, and you can't get it to resolve, then that's too much. That emotion is out of balance, and you need to attend to it so it can get back to its regular work.

Emotions are very powerful, and a repetitive emotional state can throw your chemistry out of whack. Attending to a destabilized emotion may require therapy, mindfulness practices, antidepressants (in cases of repetitive rage, anxiety, or depression), antianxiety meds, or a change in your lifestyle so you can work your way back to health. You can also rely on your Einfühlung capacity to make a full-bodied empathic study of the emotion that got out of balance in you—and wow, this will tell you amazing things about yourself, your current home and work environments, your social life, your childhood emotional training, and your beliefs about the world.

Your emotional awareness is crucial to your ability to empathize with others, to take their perspective, and to have concern for them. Think about it: if you have a problem with one or more emotions, you probably won't be able to be fully present when that emotion arises in others. For instance, if you have an unaddressed feedback loop in your own anger program and someone near you gets angry, *your* anger will probably start looping. Anger is an awesome emotion, but when it's in a feedback loop, it's too much—and it will probably impede your ability to perform Perspective Taking or do anything other than rant or shake internally with rage. That's not helpful! You definitely want to have the capacity to use rage when you need to, but it should be a choice and not an involuntary, repetitive reflex. The situation is the same with fear, sadness, joy, envy, anxiety, or any other emotion: if you have a problem with your own emotions, your empathic capacities will be reduced when that emotion is present in others.

In our six aspects of empathy, Empathic Accuracy and Emotion Regulation are the stepping-stones that help you make the journey from the fairly involuntary act of Emotion Contagion to the culminating and intentional act of Perceptive Engagement. So, if you have one or more emotions that are problematic for you, take care of yourself and get them back into balance within your entire emotional realm. Emotions are irreplaceable, necessary, and powerful aspects of your cognitive skills, but if they're out of kilter, every single one of them can be too much!

IS IT A FEELING OR AN EMOTION?[37]

It's important to understand the distinct difference between emotions and feelings. This understanding will help you become more empathically accurate and aware of your emotions.

Someone once asked me about the difference between an emotion and a feeling. My answer was that emotion is a *thing*, and feeling is an *action*. One's a noun; the other's a verb. Although I didn't really understand why the distinction was important, I did think about it a great deal. I really wondered what the confusion was about—I mean, you have an emotion, you feel it, you identify it, and then, you know exactly how to work with it. Right?

Oh, yeah. It's not that simple for many people.

So I went back to the books, and after rereading Damasio's books (*Descartes' Error, The Feeling of What Happens,* and *Looking for Spinoza*), some books on the sociology of emotion (*How Emotions Work,* by Jack Katz), and some books on the neurology of emotion (*The Emotional Brain,* by Joseph LeDoux, and *On Being Certain,* by Robert Burton), I finally figured out what's up.

IT'S THE DIFFERENCE BETWEEN HAVING AND KNOWING

An *emotion* is a physiological experience or neurological program that gives you information about the world, and a *feeling* is your conscious awareness of the emotion itself. I hadn't really understood why the distinction was such a big deal, because I don't experience a huge gap between emotion and feeling. I mean, if there's an emotion going on, I feel it, and because I've organized emotions into sixteen distinct categories, it's easy for me to identify which one it is. But this isn't true for everyone. Many people are honestly unaware that they're experiencing an emotion. For them, the emotion and the capacity to feel it are not strongly connected, and they don't even realize that (for instance) they're fearful or angry or depressed. They *have* the emotion, but they don't *know* about it. The emotion is certainly there, and their behavior displays the emotion (to others at least), but they aren't *feeling* it properly. Their emotional state has to become an obvious mood—or it has to become very persistent—before they can realize, "Oh, I guess I've been really sad about my dad, or afraid about money, or angry about work." Their Empathic Accuracy is low and, therefore, so are their Emotion Regulation skills.

My hypothesis is that this detachment between emotions and feelings (in a neurologically intact person, that is) stems from the constant, repetitive, and relentlessly antiemotion training we get, most of which I wrote about when I described the four problems that ensure emotional confusion in the previous chapter. I think that people aren't aware of their emotions because they've been trained since birth to valence, repress, suppress, ignore, or demonize them. Or they swing to the opposite pole and express their emotions explosively. As we've all seen, repression and expression can both be very troubling, because in many cases, they actually make you less able to understand your own emotions. Luckily, if you can stop repressing or exploding with your emotions—if you can instead learn to simply *feel* them—then you can develop better Empathic Accuracy and stronger Emotional Regulation skills. In turn, you'll become more skillful in all aspects of empathy. Identifying and naming your emotions is an important first step in learning how to feel them skillfully.

FEELING, NAMING, AND KNOWING

Matthew Lieberman,[38] a psychological researcher at the University of California–Los Angeles, has done some interesting work on the ways that verbal identification of emotions can help you address and alleviate emotional pain. In his and other studies, there's a suggestion that simply naming your intense emotions can help your brain calm down so you can restore your resilience in the face of challenging situations.

I've found this to be true, especially for overwhelmed hyperempaths who have very permeable boundaries and problems with excessive Emotion Contagion. Naming emotions helps hyperempaths begin to articulate and organize emotions so that they can begin to feel more grounded and focused in the presence of strong emotions. On the other side of the equation, people with low emotional awareness and low empathy also benefit from learning to identify and name emotions. I've noticed in my four decades of practice and teaching that learning to identify emotions does three things:

1. It helps you learn to feel and identify your emotions, which helps you calm and focus yourself and develop Emotion Regulation skills.
2. It helps you understand when, why, and how your emotions arise so you can become more emotionally aware and increase your Empathic Accuracy.
3. It recruits your verbal skills to support and consult with your emotions so you can learn from them and take constructive, emotionally appropriate actions.

In my work, I don't set up a hierarchy in which your verbal and rational intelligence is somehow smarter than your emotions. As I wrote earlier, emotions are millions of years older than language, and if there were a hierarchy, I would have to give the higher position to emotions. But I don't do hierarchies. In my empathic work, we rely on your verbal and rational skills to *support* your emotional awareness. Emotions are neurological signalers of what's going on in your world. Emotions are simply data; *you* are the interpreter of those data. How you interpret and work with your emotions determines whether your outcomes are healthy and workable. Research is continually showing how vital emotions are to your thought and decision-making processes, and if you can learn to feel emotions *intelligently,* then you'll widen the boundaries of your intelligence to include your social, emotional, and empathic skills.

As you learn how to feel more intelligently, a few simple flowcharts may help you understand the pathway that emotions take and where the act of feeling occurs in the process.

THE PATHWAY FROM EMOTION TO FEELING

Let's look at the simplest healthy pathway from emotion to action. (My flowcharts are simplified, and there's clearly a great deal more complexity involved when emotional disorders are present. But these broad strokes are worth understanding.)

Emotion → Feeling → Naming → Acting on
the information the emotion provides

Let's put sadness into this flowchart. It would go like this: I *have* an emotion; I *feel* that it is sadness; I *name* the sadness; and I *take the action* my sadness requires (which might be sighing, slowing down, letting go of tension, or crying, among many other sadness-based actions).

But something is missing. I didn't include the situations and stimuli that induce emotions; let's not leave those out. Emotional stimuli can be anything that *evokes* an emotion, including your own thoughts. Emotions tell you that something requires an action; that something can include your own thoughts. Notice that I'm using the word *evoke* here.[39] Emotions are not created out of thin air, and they're not created by your thoughts; emotions have evolved over millions of years to help you understand and respond to the world. Emotions exist within you, and they are *evoked,* not created, by specific stimuli. So let's include those stimuli:

Emotionally evocative stimulus → Emotion → Feeling →
Naming → Acting on the information the emotion provides

But something is still missing—you may misperceive the stimulus! For instance, you may see a coiled-up rope and experience fear as if you were seeing a snake. Or, if your emotion is evoked by your thoughts about something (for instance, you might think that your neighbor is intentionally being noisy to annoy you), you can misperceive reality. Your thoughts might not be right, especially if you don't regularly stop to question them. If you act on an emotion that was evoked by stimuli that aren't valid, you might do something misguided or injurious (like race away from a coiled rope or yell at your neighbor). Remember that *emotions are always true,* because they're always responding to emotionally evocative stimuli, *but they're not always right,* because the stimuli may not be valid.

Stimuli can also be unrelated to emotion and yet evoke an emotion anyway. For instance, if your heart rate or your adrenaline rises, your body may respond as if a fearful stimulus were present. Similarly, if you're smiling or frowning, your body may respond as if you were happy or angry. In some instances, it could be that your anger and depression are being evoked by the fact that you're slumping and frowning, without being aware that you are! Emotions give you valuable information about *something* that's going on, but it's up to you to figure out what that something might be.

That's why I created a process that allows you to turn toward your emotions and question them, to identify the stimulus, and (I hope) figure out what's really going on. So here's the complete process:

Emotionally evocative stimulus → **Emotion** → **Feeling** → **Naming** → *Questioning the emotion* → **Acting on the information the emotion provides OR** → *Deciding not to act* **because the stimulus is invalid**

I know this seems like a long pathway, but you can actually do it in a split second once you get your empathic skills under you. It's not hard. It's actually much harder in the long run to sleepwalk through your life, being pushed around by emotions that you can't identify or understand.

In our examples above, we worked with some pretty simple emotions. Now, let's put the intense emotion of rage into our flowchart to see how this process might work in a troubling real-life situation in which you might explode with rage (note that the stimulus and actions in these flowcharts are rage specific):

Something threatens your sense of self, standpoint, or voice → **Anger is evoked** → **You don't stop to name the anger; instead,**

> you add assumptions and accusations on top of it → More
> anger is evoked (this time, by *you*), and the anger morphs
> into rage → You attack → The other person backs down or
> attacks back → Rinse and repeat → Welcome to Hell!

Okay, we all know that flowchart! It's active on the Internet (and in the U.S. Senate and Congress) pretty much every day. But let's look at rage again, this time with cognitively moderated pauses and intentional emotional skills. (Please note that I'm not describing a rage disorder in either of these flow-charts. In a rage disorder, the stimulus is often untreated depression, other neurochemical factors, or possibly PTSD. The rage we're looking at here is common, garden-variety rage.)

> Something threatens your sense of self, standpoint, or voice →
> Anger is evoked → You calm and focus yourself and feel the anger
> → You name the anger and note its exact intensity, which gives you
> a moment to organize yourself → You ask yourself the questions
> for anger (*What must be protected? What must be restored?*) → You
> discover what the issue is, set clear boundaries without violence,
> and restore your sense of self without offending the humanity of
> the other person → Anger program ends → Congratulations!

Did you notice that there was no need to go to rage in the second flow-chart? When you understand that you're having an emotion, that you can feel it skillfully, that you can identify it, and that there are specific things you can do to examine the stimulus, then you don't have to throw yourself into the raging rapids every time an emotion appears.

When you have Emotion Regulation skills, you have options—and free-dom and breathing room—no matter what is going on around you.

So an emotion does this: it gives you information about an emotionally relevant stimulus, and it tells you what you've perceived and what you're experiencing. Your job as the partner of your emotions is to *feel* the emotion, *name* it, *ask* the correct questions, and *act* in a way that is both emotional *and* rational. I'm saying it's doable—not to mention vital for your mental health, the quality of your empathy, the quality of your relationships, and the health of your community. When you can work with your emotions empathically, your Emotion Contagion capacities will become much more understandable and manageable. This process will also support your Empathic Accuracy and your Emotion Regulation skills, which will increase your empathic abilities in healthy and workable ways.

When you know how to feel your emotions, empathic awareness becomes easy (and fun and enlightening). More important, when you know how to feel your emotions, name them, and take the necessary, cognitively moderated pauses that will help you understand whether the stimulus (or your reaction) is valid, then your big, intense, and potentially dangerous emotions will become less toxic, and so will you.

As we move forward into learning empathic mindfulness skills and empathic communication techniques, it's important to remember that the quality of your empathy relies upon the depth of your intrapersonal awareness. To become more empathically skilled, your primary empathic interaction needs to be internal—between you and your emotions (especially if you are currently dealing with any troublesome ones). In the next chapter, you'll learn the empathic mindfulness skills that I developed to help you work with emotions and your empathic abilities at a moment's notice. All of these skills will help you bring balance to your life—but again, if you're dealing with an emotion that's too much, please reach out for support from a friend, counselor, therapist, or doctor.

CHAPTER 5

The Art of Empathy

Gathering Your Tools

EMPATHY IS DEVELOPED (and flourishes) in healthy interactions. What I notice in people who are somewhat overwhelmed or overstimulated by their empathy is that they haven't found a balance between interpersonal interactions and intrapersonal self-care. Many empaths spend so much time on the needs of others that their personal needs get pushed aside or disregarded. This is not necessarily a sign of poorly developed empathic skills, because in many of the six aspects of empathy, *it's not about you.* It can honestly be tricky to balance your life in response to a skill that asks you to put the needs and perspectives of others before your own.

In people who experience empathic burnout (or caregiver burnout, which is a similar situation), I notice the presence of a type of either/or dichotomy: "*Either* I can take care of everyone else and get drained, *or* I can take care of myself and be selfish, but I can't do both." But I challenge that rigid idea and in this book, I provide options that restore flexibility. Empathic self-care can and does coexist with strong empathic skills. As we all know, it doesn't have to, but in our quest to be happy and healthy empaths, self-care is a must.

As we learn these empathic mindfulness practices, I'll explain each not only in terms of its purpose, but also in relation to our six aspects of empathy. I'll also relate my practices to Richard Davidson's six dimensions of emotional style. I want you to understand the intention behind each of these practices so that you can pick and choose among them, depending on your individual strengths and challenges.

THE FIVE EMPATHIC MINDFULNESS SKILLS

Each of my empathic mindfulness skills is an emotion-aware and emotion-honoring practice, and each relies upon the gifts and abilities that your emotions contribute to you. This is a distinct departure from many meditative practices, where observing and then completely releasing emotions (often called *extinction*) is a central activity. As I look at emotion-releasing practices, I see that most of the four problems that lead to emotional confusion are active. Certainly, there's the belief that most emotions are negative—otherwise, why else would you try to release or extinguish them? Releasing an emotion is not toxic in and of itself, because when an emotion is in a feedback loop, then certainly, you want to be able to calm yourself and calm that emotional activation. But merely observing and extinguishing an emotion is a repressive technique that undermines the action-requiring neurological program that's trying to occur. Repression can be a wonderful emergency skill if you're feeling an emotion that isn't socially safe to express (or that's stuck in a feedback loop), but in most other instances, repression will impede your emotional intelligence. It won't help you understand the emotion that has arisen; it won't help you recognize emotional nuance; and it won't help you identify why your emotions arise, how they interrelate, or which actions they require.

In my work, I've taken apart meditative practices in order to understand their underlying purpose, and I've added to them an awareness of the purpose of emotions. In my version of a mindfulness meditation that welcomes your emotions (rather than treating them as problems in and of themselves), you'll calm yourself and work with your breathing, you'll focus yourself and become aware of your responses, you'll observe your emotions without valencing them, and then you'll turn toward your emotions and ask them what they're doing. You'll work as a partner and a friend to your emotions, and you'll use your Einfühlung capacity to enter into a deep empathic relationship with your own emotions.

But you'll be doing all of this calmly, with skills, and with support. This isn't going to be a bad acting class; I'm not asking you to *become* your strong emotions or to go on an emotional bender. That's not empathic, nor is it mindful. That kind of either/or thinking is a function of one of the central problems that create emotional confusion—that is, you can either *repress* and extinguish an emotion or *express* it and go on a rampage. But these are not your only choices. Remember the process of channeling. There is a middle path, and these empathic mindfulness skills will help you learn how to enter that path and become emotionally adept—and therefore empathically skilled.

As I explain these skills, I'll intersperse pieces that I wrote about them in *The Language of Emotions.*[40] However, I'm continually tinkering with these skills to make them simpler and more focused; therefore, these descriptions will relate specifically to developing your empathic skills.

GETTING GROUNDED

Grounding is a simple breathing and focusing practice that helps you connect to your body and focus yourself in an intentional and calming way. Intentional body awareness supports your intrapersonal skills and helps you become more aware of yourself and your unique responses. Self-awareness is a primary empathic skill, because you have to know how you feel so that you can regulate your own emotions and identify differences between yourself and others (this really helps with Perspective Taking). However, as Richard Davidson points out, there is such a thing as being *too* self-aware. Some people are so aware of tiny shifts in their emotions, sensations, and sensory inputs that they become overly self-focused or even overwhelmed. For these people, empathy can be hindered, because they have too much going on internally to be able to effectively take the perspective of others. My grounding practice helps in both instances.

Grounding, which helps you feel calm, centered, focused, relaxed, and awake, helps you turn your focus inward in a simple and calming way. In Getting Grounded, you don't have to be isolated, immobile, or merely observational; you can be out in the world and interacting freely. Grounding is a highly portable skill that helps you focus internally as you center and calm yourself. You can ground yourself in a few seconds and restore your focus, even during tense interactions, or you can turn grounding into a luxurious and solitary meditative practice whenever you have the time.

Let's look at the specific emotional skills involved in grounding and focusing yourself.

THE GROUNDING PROCESS: *Welcoming the Gifts of Sadness*

Take a deep breath and fill up your chest and your belly so that you feel a little bit of tension—not too much, just a little. Hold your breath for a count of three. As you breathe out, let your body slump a little bit and relax yourself intentionally.

Let your muscles go slack, drop your head if that feels good, and just loll. Breathe normally for a few breaths as you maintain this state of simple relaxation.

Now, breathe in again, expand your chest and your belly until you feel a little bit of tension, hold for a count of three—and then breathe out with a sigh as you let go. You're a ragdoll. Let it go.

Now, breathe normally and check in with yourself. If you feel a bit softer and calmer, and maybe even a little bit tired, thank the emotion that helped you release some of your tension and restore some of your flow: thank your sadness. That's what the soft form of healthy, flowing sadness feels like, and that's what it does—it helps you let go of something that isn't working anyway, and it helps you bring ease and flow back to your system. In this short exercise, I created something that didn't work—I created a bit of tension by having you breathe in an uncomfortable way, and then I had you evoke the gifts of sadness to let go of that tension. You didn't need that tension; it wasn't working anyway. Sadness to the rescue!

|||||||||||||||||||||||||||||||

Each of your emotions has this soft, free-flowing state that brings you specific gifts and skills. Knowing this will help you access your emotions intentionally when you need the gifts they provide. It's important to realize that you don't have to cry or move into a sad mood in order to access the softening, relaxing, rejuvenating gifts of sadness; you can just relax and let go. Sadness is about releasing things and relaxing into yourself—and you can do that intentionally by working with your sadness as a skill.

Take a moment to notice how aware you are of your body. Sadness brings you back to yourself and makes you more aware of your interior state. Sadness brings flow back to you, it calms you, and it helps you release uncomfortable things you've been grasping onto—like tension, fatigue, or disappointments. It's necessary to let go regularly, *before* everything piles up into identifiable emotional distress, pain, or misery, and sadness is the emotion that helps you let go. Other emotions do other things, and they're necessary in other situations. But when you need to let go, refresh yourself, and regain your flexibility, you need the relaxing gifts of sadness.

Whenever you need to, you can consciously welcome your sadness and restore a sense of flow to yourself by breathing in and gathering any tension, and then breathing out gently as you yawn or sigh. It's that simple. To channel your sadness, just relax and let go of things that aren't working anyway.

|||||||||||||||||||||||||||||||||||||||||||||||||||||||||||||||||||||||||||||||||||||||||||||||||||||||||

THE FOCUSING PROCESS: *Welcoming the Gifts of Fear*

Now let's work at a very subtle level with an emotion that helps you focus yourself. Return to that sadness-resourced sense of relaxation and inner focus, and find a quiet place where you can perform a simple listening exercise.

When you've found your quiet place, lean your body forward a little bit and try to hear the quietest sound in your area. Keep your shoulders down and away from your ears (good posture helps your hearing). You can also open your mouth a little (relaxing your jaw creates more space in your ears) and gently move your head around as you pinpoint the quietest sound and filter out the more obvious ones. Keep your eyes open, but rely upon your ears for this exercise.

When you've located this quiet sound, hold still for a moment. Stand where you are and try to locate the sound with your eyes; then move toward it, recalibrating as you near the sound. Time may seem to slow down somewhat, your skin may feel more sensitive (almost as if it's sensing the air around you), and your mind may clear itself of anything that isn't related to your quiet sound. When you pinpoint that sound, thank the emotion that helped you find it. Thank your fear.

|||||||||||||||||||||||||||||||

Healthy, free-flowing fear helps you access your sensory skills, your instincts, and your intuition. When you need it to, your fear focuses all of your senses, scans your environment, and increases your ability to respond effectively to novel or changing situations. When your fear arises at this soft, subtle level, you'll feel focused, centered, capable, and agile; you won't feel agitated or obviously fearful. This soft focusing ability is one of the gifts of fear.

If you can access this subtle, curious form of fear when you're confused or upset, you can access the information you need to calmly figure out what's going on. You don't need to *feel* afraid in order to access the gifts that your fear brings you, just as you don't need to cry to access the gifts of sadness. This soft level of fear helps you focus on your instinctual knowledge as it connects you to your surroundings. This focus helps you stand upright, lean forward a bit, and bring your instincts and your intuition to the present moment.

Whereas the gifts of sadness focus you inward on what you need to release in order to relax, the gifts of fear bring you a forward, listening, sensing capacity that will help you interact with your environment and other people. If you can rely on fear's calm, listening, sensing stance, you will be able to read people and situations empathically. It's a wonderful emotion—but, then, all of them are! They're like an amazing toolkit, full of magic, which is why it's so bizarre that we've been taught to distrust our emotions.

What Grounding Will Do For You. Getting Grounded is an intrapersonal skill that supports the following aspects of empathy:

> Emotion Contagion—grounding can help you calm yourself when you're in the presence of intense emotions
> Empathic Accuracy—grounding can help you focus yourself so that you can identify emotions and your empathic perceptions more accurately
> Emotion Regulation—grounding and focusing can give you the internal stability you need to organize and work with your emotions intentionally
> All of these aspects will give you an excellent foundation for clearer Perspective Taking, Concern for Others, and Perceptive Engagement

In regard to your emotional style, grounding supports your Resilience by giving you the internal resources you need to recover quickly when you need to and to slow down and take your time when it's important to stay present with difficult issues. Grounding also supports your Outlook by helping you down-regulate from any kind of intense emotional activation, so that you can focus more calmly on your situation. It will also help you increase your Self-awareness, as you learn to manage your arousal and relaxation and become more able to tune in to yourself; develop fluid Sensitivity to Context, so you can tune in to others by focusing outward or tune out by intentionally turning your focus inward; and increase the precision of your Attention.

||||||||||||||||||||||||||||||||||||||||||||||||||||||||||||||||||||||||||

HOW TO GROUND YOURSELF

To ground yourself, you intentionally relax yourself and imagine breathing any tension downward, as if you're gathering tension and exhaling it down through your abdomen and into your pelvis, thighs, calves, and feet—and then into the ground. Next, when you're settled and calmer, you return to the subtle attention and focus you used when you listened for that quiet sound and welcomed the gifts of fear. That's it; that's the practice. When you're able to release tension intentionally, connect to the ground, and refocus yourself, you're done. The subtle gifts of sadness and fear belong to you, they work nicely together, and they're easy to access. That's it!

IIIIIIIIIIIIIIIIIIIIIIIIIIII

If you've learned any martial arts, you'll recognize grounding as a process of connecting your *chi*—or your life force—with the earth so that you can be more stable and resourced. Before martial artists are allowed to jump and kick, they must first learn to stabilize and ground themselves so they can become aware of their posture, their balance, and their center of gravity. Getting Grounded provides this same stability to sensitive and empathic people, who can become physically destabilized when there are too many emotions flying around, when they're in the presence of conflict, or when they're feeling tense.

If you empathically think back to disquieting situations in your own life, you'll probably recall that your body became rigid, that you may have lost your focus and your ability to relax yourself, and that you may have disconnected from the experience and become preoccupied, inattentive, or spaced out. Sometimes, those responses are fine, but if they're your *only* responses during trouble, you won't be able to develop strong empathic or interactive skills. If the troubles and difficulties of human interaction regularly unground, unfocus, and destabilize you, this simple grounding and focusing process will help you begin to develop Emotional Regulation skills. The simple acts of breathing intentionally and imagining yourself connecting to the earth as you let go of tension—and then reengaging with your soft focusing abilities—will help you reconnect to your emotional and physical center of gravity and to the intelligence inherent in your emotions. It seems very simple, I know, but that's the point. Empaths need skills that are easily accessible, emotion honoring, simple, and totally portable.

If you prefer longer meditations, you can extend this grounding practice. You can breathe into each area of your body separately as you gather and release tension from every part of yourself. Or you can enhance this grounding practice with mindfulness practices from other traditions. But if you have only a few minutes each day to check in, this practice will help you connect with yourself, release tensions, and refocus yourself intentionally and swiftly.

You can also engage in activities that are grounding in and of themselves, such as exercise, swimming, hot baths, massage, good sex, playing with animals, being with loved ones, playing with children, eating delicious food, doing art, playing music, viewing art, being in nature, reading, doing math or science, organizing your physical space, or any of a hundred healing and grounding activities. If something brings you a sense of delicious relaxation and healing focus, it's a grounding practice. Simple.

As you observe your life empathically, ask yourself how many relaxing, delightful, and grounding activities exist in your normal day or week. If you can think of very few naturally grounding activities, you might want to make this simple grounding practice a regular part of your life for a while. Then see whether you can find time for intentional relaxation (we'll talk more about finding that time in the next chapter). If you want to be a healthy and happy empath, relaxation and grounding are vital skills.

DEFINING YOUR BOUNDARIES

People talk a great deal about setting boundaries, but the concept is sort of hazy. Often, when people talk about setting boundaries, they mean that you should tell people "no" and take more time for yourself. However, if you have very permeable interpersonal boundaries, this kind of verbal boundary setting can be pretty ineffectual. I work with a lot of empathic people who've tried every form of assertive communication skill, but when someone really needs them—*boom!*—their hyperempathic tendencies kick in automatically, and they lose their resolve.

Learning to define your boundaries certainly involves communication skills, but I've found that you can't start there. In fact, I'd say that boundary definition is more of a behavioral and developmental process, in which you actually have to retrain yourself and learn to identify yourself as a distinct individual with distinct emotions, ideas, preferences, and requirements. This, in turn, makes you more able to understand others as distinct individuals. In fact, new research is connecting the capacity for self-identification with the development of empathic skills. Doris Bischof-Köhler, who created the teddy bear and spoon experiment I wrote about in Chapter 2, added a second phase to her experiment, which tested whether the children who could empathize also had the ability to identify themselves in a mirror. Mirror self-recognition tests indicate the point at which infants develop the ability to identify themselves in a mirror. Before this stage, infants may think that the baby in the mirror is someone else or that there's a baby behind the mirror somewhere. Mirror self-recognition abilities suggest that infants have developed the concept of a self.

In her experiments, Bischof-Köhler found that although some of the non-self-recognizing infants could empathize skillfully, *all* of the self-recognizers could. This would suggest that self-awareness is connected to the capacity to comprehend the selfhood of others (and their distinction from you)—and, therefore, to a capacity for skillful Perspective Taking and Perceptive Engagement. This is why I call Defining Boundaries a developmental process. You have to know who *you* are and where you begin and end before you can empathize skillfully; you first have to be able to identify and define your own boundaries.

Luckily, your boundaries already exist. You can sense them when people stare at you from behind, and you can feel their exact dimensions when you're in a crowded elevator. In the metaphysical community, this tangible sense of your personal space and your boundaries is called the *aura*, while in the neurological field, this personal space is now understood to be a part of your *proprioceptive* system. This system of neural and muscular networks in your brain and body actually maps your position in relation to everything around you. Your proprioceptive system works in every second to help you stand, balance, move, and understand your body's relationship to its environment. (For more information on your proprioceptive system, see the excellent book *The Body Has a Mind of Its Own*, by science writers Sandra and Matthew Blakeslee.)

Your proprioceptors map your body and your environment so that you can interact competently in the physical world. Your proprioceptors map your home, your car, your tools, your workplace, and all aspects of your physical habitat. If your proprioceptive system doesn't work well, you'll be pretty clumsy—you'll drop things, trip over your own feet, or walk into walls. Thus, this system is an important part of your basic physical awareness.

Your proprioceptors also map a specific area around your body that is called your *peripersonal* space. This space extends all around you and out to the reach of your arms and legs—about eighteen to thirty inches in front of and behind you, on both sides of you, above you, and below you. It is the exact dimension that most aura readers consider to be the size of a healthy aura. In the rest of this book, I'll focus on this area as your peripersonal boundary; however, if you require this area to be an aura, go ahead and trade the word *aura* for *boundary;* I now see them as one and the same thing. This peripersonal space is the area that you control and define, and you can use it to actually teach yourself how to set effective interpersonal boundaries.

If you can't yet wrap your mind around the idea of peripersonal space, no problem. Your proprioceptors are already brilliant at mapping territory, including imaginal territory, such as your avatar in a video game or the imaginal walls you create when you're pretending to be a mime. If you can't yet sense this boundary, you can use your imaginal skills as a kind of placeholder. (I use the word *imaginal* intentionally, and I contrast it with the word *imaginary*, which means pretend or unreal.) Your imaginal skills are both unreal and real in very important ways—they're creative skills that recruit your empathic, emotive, and artistic abilities to help you engage with ideas, concepts, and structures that may not be visible or tangible (such as your avatar or your mimed walls), yet they have their own kind of reality. Your real-but-unseen proprioceptive system is ready and able to help you create an imaginal boundary that will actually become tangible to you.

Learning to develop a tangible sense of your personal boundaries is very important if you're currently dealing with low empathic awareness, because this practice will help you develop better Empathic Accuracy and Emotion Regulation skills. You have to know where you begin and end so that you can scan through your body and your environment to properly identify emotional stimuli. On the other hand, this skill is also important if you're a hyperempath who experiences a great deal of Emotion Contagion. Defining your boundaries will help you develop a clear self/other distinction so that you can begin to identify the differences between your own emotions and the emotions of others. Defining your boundaries will help you develop better emotional hygiene.

This self/other distinction is a source of confusion for many people who want to develop their empathy. I see people who intentionally try to de-self and become one with others emotionally so that they can empathize, and these people would strongly question my suggestion that people with low empathy should learn to define their interpersonal boundaries. I understand their confusion. When people have low empathic skills, such that they aren't aware of emotions or can't understand *why* people would feel this or that emotion ("*I* don't feel it, so why should you?"), teaching them to set boundaries seems counterintuitive. Aren't their boundaries too rigid already? I say "no," and I see the situation of empathic insensitivity as a kind of analog to hyperempathy.

In a hyperempath, the *self* is not distinct, whereas in a low-empathy person, the *other* is not distinct. In both cases, there is boundary impairment combined with an inability to skillfully balance the needs of the self with the needs of the other. In both cases, learning to identify and work with the already-existing peripersonal space helps people identify self and other tangibly: "My clearly defined boundaries tell me where *I* begin and end, and now I understand where *you* begin and end." Clearly defined boundaries lead to clearer empathic awareness, no matter how empathically receptive you currently are.

In our distracted and emotionally confused culture, most of us don't see ourselves as distinct individuals with clear boundaries, and this truly impedes our ability to empathize skillfully. Luckily, this second empathic skill directly and imaginally addresses this problem. Empaths need safe space and privacy, and this skill helps you create both of them quickly, easily, and intentionally.

What Defining Your Boundaries Will Do for You. Boundary Definition is an intrapersonal skill that addresses these aspects of empathy:

Emotion Contagion—defining your boundaries helps you
   understand where you begin and end so that you can identify
   where emotions originate, and this, of course, increases your
   Empathic Accuracy
Emotion Regulation—defining your boundaries gives you a
   portable private space where you can work with your emotions
   in each moment
Perspective Taking—knowing where you begin and end helps you
   develop clearer self/other awareness
Perceptive Engagement—clear empathy is about the other, and
   knowing yourself more clearly allows you to meet the needs of
   others perceptively while also caring for yourself respectfully

In terms of the six dimensions of emotional style, the combination of this skill and your Getting Grounded practice is a full emotional-style healing that will help you develop a calm, focused, intuitive, sensitive, well-defined, and self-aware personal space in which you can address each dimension of your emotional style, from your Resilience and Outlook, to your Social Intuition and Self-awareness, to your Sensitivity to Context and your Attention.

||||||||||||||||||||||||||||||||||||||||||||||||||||||||||||||||||||||||||||||||||||||

HOW TO DEFINE YOUR BOUNDARIES

Please seat yourself comfortably and ground and focus yourself, if you can. (If not, it's okay.) Now stand up and reach your arms straight out to either side of you (if you cannot use your arms in this way, please use your imagination).

Imagine that your fingertips are touching the edges of a lighted oval-shaped bubble that encompasses your private, personal space. Reach your arms out in front of you and then raise them above your head. Feel how far the edges of your peripersonal boundary are from your body. Your boundary should be an arm's length away from you at all points—in front of you, behind you, on either side of you, above you, and even underneath you. When you can imagine this oval-shaped area all the way around you, drop your arms and let them relax.

Close your eyes if you need to as you imagine that the outer edges of this oval, which is around and above you and even underneath the floor, is now lit up in a bright neon color. Choose a very bright, lively color. (If you can't visualize, imagine a clear sound or a distinct movement at this distance from your body or draw a circle on the floor if you need to.) Make your boundary quite obvious in whatever way you can. This is all you need to do to define your peripersonal boundary; it's a very simple exercise. Just feel or imagine yourself standing inside this oval-shaped bubble, as if you're a yolk standing firmly inside the protective eggshell of your own boundary.

As you sense your boundary around yourself, return to your calm focus if you can, and ask yourself: "Do I claim this much room in the world?" As you connect with your brightly lit boundary, ask yourself whether it's normal to feel completely in control of this area around your body. For most of us, the answer is absolutely not! For most of us, our personal boundary is our skin itself; we don't live as distinct people who have enough room to live and breathe freely.

Remember this as you work with your boundary. You may feel frustrated at first, because you may not know, psychologically speaking, how to maintain proper boundaries or how to take your own place in the world. Don't feel alone in this—it's a situation we all face. Nevertheless, you *have* your peripersonal space, and you have a right to it. In fact, it's the area your brain already identifies as yours, even if you didn't realize that it existed before today. Now that you know it exists, get acquainted with your peripersonal boundaries. Get a feeling of having some space in the world, of knowing where you begin and end, and of having some privacy.

Now, thank the emotions that help you create your personal boundaries. Thank your free-flowing soft anger and your authentic, appropriate, and soft shame. Anger helps you claim your voice, standpoint, and territory and respond to any boundary violations coming from the exterior world. Shame—anger's close friend and partner—helps you moderate your voice and standpoint so that you don't unnecessarily hurt yourself or others. Healthy, authentic shame helps you avoid any boundary violations that may come from *you*.

||||||||||||||||||||||||||||||

Isn't it funny? The gifts of fear help you focus yourself, while sadness grounds you, and anger and shame help you set respectful boundaries. People generally avoid these emotions—yet look at what that would mean: if you kick fear out the door, you lose your focus and your intuition; if you avoid sadness, you won't be able to let go, ground yourself, or relax; and if you throw anger and shame onto the trash heap, you lose your ability to set and maintain effective boundaries! As we can all see, trouble with boundaries, intuition, grounding, and relaxation—and endless trouble with emotions—are normal, everyday problems for most people. But they don't have to be. You can set effective boundaries and reframe your approach to emotions. You can take a moment to sense your calm listening state and thank your fear. You can feel your grounding and thank your sadness. You can connect with the feeling of being safe and protected inside your own peripersonal space—you can light up the edges of your boundary again—and thank your healthy anger and shame. If you understand what they do and how they work, emotions can improve your life in amazing ways.

||||||||||||||||||||||||||||||||||||||||||||||||||||||||||||||||||||||||||||||||||||||||

BREATHING WITH YOUR BOUNDARIES

Here's a simple exercise to help you become more aware of your peripersonal boundaries right now: Ground and focus yourself if you can. Sit comfortably and imagine your boundary at that arm's-length distance and imagine that its edges are brightly lit or very distinctive. Choose an intense color for the edges, such as lime green or electric blue; your boundary should be exceedingly noticeable to you. (If you can't visualize, try to imagine a noticeable sensation or movement at the edges of your boundary.) Take a deep breath and imagine your boundary expanding a few inches in all directions (just as your torso does when you inhale). As you exhale, imagine your personal boundary resuming its healthy arm's-length distance from your body at all points. Feel your brightly lit boundary all around you, above you, and under the floor. Breathe in again and feel the edges of your boundary expand slightly in all directions. Breathe out and allow your boundary to resume its correct distance from your body. You're done! You can breathe with your boundary as often as you like—it's a simple, healing way to help your proprioceptive network connect viscerally with your new sense of your peripersonal boundaries.

Some quick pointers: You can use your imaginal skills as a placeholder for your personal boundaries if you can't envision or feel them just yet. For instance, you can fill your entire peripersonal space with your favorite natural environment by imagining yourself surrounded at arm's length by a shoreline, mountain, or desert scene. (Again, you don't have to *see* this scene; you can hear it, feel it, or even smell it if you can't visualize.) You can use this nature scene to calm the area around your body, which will help you inhabit your peripersonal space psychologically. If you can imagine yourself enveloped in your favorite mountain or oceanside scene, then you can use your Einfühlung skills to surround yourself with a healing sense of peacefulness. Also, you can imagine lighting up your boundary and breathing with it every day; soon it will be able to help you define yourself in health-building ways.

BURNING CONTRACTS

Burning Contracts is one of my favorite empathic mindfulness skills, because it teaches you how to channel your emotions intentionally. It's a practice in which your emotions can help you understand more about yourself, your behaviors, your decisions, your interactions, and your expectations. Burning Contracts also makes use of your Einfühlung capacity to feel your way into the crux of an issue and then use your imaginal skills to bring full-bodied resolution to ideas, behaviors, and situations that confuse, trouble, or torment you. Your imaginal skills can help you access issues from your past and from the wordless depths of your inner life. They can also help you question fundamental aspects of your identity without losing yourself in the process.

When I work with overwhelmed hyperempaths, I rely on contract burning a great deal, because if hyperempaths don't have any skills, their ungrounded, unfocused, and boundary-impaired bodies often run on a troubling kind of autopilot. When I was living this particular form of empathic nightmare, I called myself a *runaway healer,* and I likened myself to a truck heading downhill with no brakes: "Let me fix you! I know I can fix you!!!" Even though I intellectually knew better, I found myself powerfully drawn to emotionally unstable people and frankly unsafe situations, where I performed heavy empathic labor (unpaid and unacknowledged) and teetered continually on the edge of burnout. I wasn't happy, and I wasn't healthy. In many cases, I wasn't even valued—yet still, I magically found places where my empathic abilities had to kick into overdrive.

Conventional forms of therapy and meditation didn't touch this tendency in me, and they don't tend to touch other hyperempaths either, because empathic runaway healing behavior isn't something that can be talked away, thought away, breathed away, or chanted away. Empathic abilities are crucial for social functioning, they're powerfully preverbal, and they're evolutionarily very ancient—which means they can't just be talked to, argued with, or soothed away. Instead, you need to meet them where they are, work in their territory with their language, and engage with them in ways they can understand—which means you need to work emotively, empathically, and imaginally. Burning Contracts helps you do that.

The empathic practice of contract burning supports your equilibrium by allowing you to separate yourself from behaviors and attitudes that destabilize you and to treat them as contractual obligations that you entered into for some purpose but can now choose to end. This practice helps you envision your behaviors and attitudes as *tendencies* rather than concrete certainties. When you're grounded, focused, and well defined, you can approach your behaviors not as life sentences but as inclinations that you can now choose to support or release, depending on your intentions.

For instance, if you have trouble with certain emotions like anger or anxiety and if you lose your empathy when others are feeling those emotions, you can observe and then burn your behavioral contracts with those emotions and restore your emotional flexibility. If you're unhappy with distracted or addicted behaviors in yourself or if you lose all of your perspective-taking skills when someone else displays those behaviors, you can burn your contracts with those particular behaviors and begin to make separations from them. If you're unable to function skillfully in certain relationships, you can study, learn about, and burn your contracts with those relationships—not to end them, but to reorganize the behaviors that control your interactions with others. This empathic process of contract burning helps you meet each of your behaviors, attitudes, and stances from a grounded position of present-day choice and personal autonomy. It also gives you a way to channel emotions intentionally and to become more aware of the gifts and challenges that live inside each of your reactions, stances, behaviors, and emotions.

What Burning Contracts Will Do for You. This intrapersonal skill addresses all six aspects of empathy:

> Emotion Contagion—you can bring forward, observe, and burn
> your contracts with any emotion that troubles or confuses you,
> which will increase your Empathic Accuracy and your Emotion
> Regulation skills
>
> Perspective Taking—you can disentangle yourself from concrete
> expectations of how things are supposed to be, so that you
> can see the world from other perspectives and restore your
> Concern for Others
>
> Perceptive Engagement—you can free yourself from unworkable
> behaviors so you can then learn how to be perceptive and
> flexible enough to meet the needs of others skillfully

In terms of the six dimensions of your emotional style, Burning Contracts addresses and supports all of these as well, because you can burn your contracts with any area of these dimensions that don't work for you. Whether it's Resilience (from slow to recover to fast to recover), Outlook (from negative to positive), Social Intuition (from socially intuitive to puzzled), Self-awareness (from self-aware to self-opaque), Sensitivity to Context (from tuned in to tuned out), or Attention (from unfocused to focused), Burning Contracts will help you observe, become aware of, understand the purpose for, and reorganize any aspect of your emotional style that troubles you.

|||||||||||||||||||||||||||||||||||||||||||||||||||||||||||||||||||||||||||||

HOW TO BURN CONTRACTS

To burn a contract with an idea, behavior, stance, or relationship, begin by focusing and grounding yourself. Illuminate your boundary with a very bright color (if you can) and breathe normally. Imagine unrolling a large piece of blank parchment paper right in front of you. (If you can't visualize, use your hands to actually unroll this imaginary parchment.) Some people like to imagine that this parchment is rolled out flat on a table, but I like to imagine mine in front of my body, as if it were a whiteboard or a movie screen. This parchment should have a calming feeling to it. It shouldn't be bright or jazzy; it should be a gentle color that can absorb whatever you place onto it. Keep this roll of parchment *inside* your personal boundary for now, as this will help you develop more awareness of your peripersonal space.

With your parchment in front of you, you can use your Einfühlung skills to empathically project, envision, write, speak, or just think your distress onto it. You can project your emotional expectations—how you're supposed to feel and express yourself—onto the parchment. You can project your intellectual stances—how you're supposed to think, what you're supposed to think, how you're supposed to be intelligent. You can project physical rules—how your body is supposed to look and perform for others. You can project spiritual expectations—how you're supposed to meditate, pray, or behave in relation to spirituality or religion. Or, you can project entire relationships—images of yourself, your partner, and the ways you relate to one another—right onto the parchment. When you can get these behaviors, relationships, and ideas out in front of you, you can begin to observe and individuate from them. In this protected space, you can see yourself not as a victim of your behaviors or the situations in your life, but as an upright individual who *decides* to act, relate, react, or behave in certain ways and who can now decide to behave differently.

If this imaginal visualization process doesn't connect for you, please feel free to use an actual piece of paper and write or draw out these same rules, expectations, stances, and behaviors in words, sketches, or even big scribbles. What we're doing is creating a way for you to express yourself emotionally and imaginally in a safe, ceremonial way. We're also helping you become aware of situations that may only exist right now in behaviors and beliefs—they may not be fully conscious yet. This process brings your emotional and empathic awareness to situations, ideas, and behaviors you're already experiencing and struggling with in real life. This is an imaginal Einfühlung process, but it's also absolutely real.

As these behaviors, beliefs, and postures move out in front of you, you may feel emotions rising up inside you. This is absolutely fantastic. It means that your emotions are awake to the process and will contribute the exact gifts and skills you need to address these issues. Remain focused, intensify your grounding if you need to, and brighten your boundary so you'll have a greater sense of definition around yourself. Welcome your emotions—whatever they are—and use them to move these ideas and behaviors out of the shadows of habit and into your conscious control. If you feel angry, it's safe to express it here. You can throw these ideas onto your parchment (or draw intensely on your real paper), or you can imagine a color, movement, sound, or quality that you associate with anger and place it alongside your images. If you feel fearful, you can speed up your movements and fling these ideas out of you. If you feel sad, you can lay these ideas onto your parchment slowly and mournfully. If you feel depressed, you can darken the images or your parchment (or slow your movements to a crawl), as you welcome your depression to this process.

Don't repress your emotions or pretend you're feeling something else. Don't draw rainbows and dancing kittens if you're enraged. Be emotionally honest. You're safe here. Remember that you're focused, grounded, and safely protected inside your own peripersonal boundary, and you can breathe in and exhale downward to intentionally relax yourself whenever you need to. You don't have to repress, avoid, or demonize your emotions here. You can just get to know them. You can feel the way you feel, name your emotions, and learn how to work with them. You can complete the actions your emotions require and learn how to respond in many different ways as you learn how these responses feel in your body. This is what channeling your emotions feels like—it's dramatic, imaginal, emotive play that helps you increase your Empathic Accuracy and your Emotion Regulation skills at the same time.

If your first parchment (or your real paper) becomes full, move it aside and create a fresh one. Keep working through the situation until you feel some sense of completion. When you feel done for now, and your parchment (or parchments) is full of words, images, feelings, or sounds, please roll it up. This parchment personifies the contract you've forged with this behavior, belief, attitude, or relationship. Roll this contract (or your real paper) tightly so that you can't see what's inside it—in this way, it immediately becomes less powerful. Tie your contract or your paper with a cord, if that feels right. Grasp your rolled-up contract and imagine tossing it outside your boundary and away from you. When it lands, imagine burning it up with whatever emotional energy feels right. You can blast it with anger, strike it with fear, engulf it with sadness, or use your depressive energy to create a funeral pyre. Your emotions will provide the exact intensity you need to destroy that contract and set yourself free. If you used a real piece of paper, you may want to tie it up strongly with many pieces of twine, throw it away, burn it, bury it, or rip it into tiny pieces. Whatever feels right is the perfect thing to do.

When your contract is gone, refocus yourself, check your grounding by breathing in and releasing any tension you might feel, and brighten your peripersonal boundary once again. You'll probably notice changes in your skills—you may feel a difference in your grounding, you may sense a stronger focus or a relaxation of your focus, or you may sense changes in the condition of your boundary. If so, congratulate yourself—your imaginal and proprioceptive systems are communicating with you empathically! Note each of these changes and gently bring yourself back to center; breathe in and reground and refocus yourself gently, and set your vibrant boundary at a healthy arm's length away from you at all points. That's it!

||||||||||||||||||||||||||||||||

Burning Contracts *is* emotional channeling. It helps you raft through the eddies and rapids of your emotions. Instead of haphazardly expressing your emotions at the outer world (or haphazardly repressing them back into your inner world), this process helps you become empathically aware of each of your emotions. Your grounding skills allow you to stay focused and integrated, even when strong emotions flow through you; your defined personal boundaries create a protected and sacred space where you can do your empathic work in safety and privacy; and your ability to imagine your behaviors and stances as *contracts* (rather than unchangeable destinies written in stone) allows you to amend and destroy them at will. This skill can work wonders in situations where you repeat behaviors (like my runaway healing) for what seems to be no good reason. If you can use your imaginal skills and your Einfühlung capacity to feel your way into the behavior, you'll discover absolutely amazing emotional truths that you simply can't get to with mere words (or with practices in which the focus is to extinguish your emotions).

You can burn contracts at any time and in any place. No one needs to know you're doing it. Once you're focused and grounded, you can imagine your peripersonal boundary as a kind of brightly colored, portable sacred space. Within your sacred space, you can do whatever work you need to in complete privacy. You can pull out a parchment at work, while you're driving, or even when you're in the middle of an argument (though it's very hard to remember your skills when you're fighting). This process is fully portable. It's a fully embodied, emotionally welcoming, empathic process that was created for people with busy lives; it can be used whenever and wherever you like.

CONSCIOUS COMPLAINING

Conscious Complaining is an emotional-channeling technique that's goofy and surprisingly healing. Although focus, grounding, and clear boundary definition are things to aspire to, no one can maintain them at all times. In fact, constant focus isn't actually healthy (you have to be able to let go and drift every now and then), and life is a drag if all you do is work. Resting, daydreaming, fooling around, laughing, napping, procrastinating, and playing are extremely important parts of a whole and happy life. It's important to keep things light. However, if you *can't* ground, focus, or define yourself when you want to, that's a horse of a different color.

It's easy to get into troubling moods or stagnant places and lose all of your skills and forget all of your emotional wisdom; it's easy to fall into emotional repression and incompetent expression. When this happens (and it will), your ignored and mismanaged emotions will intensify and repeat themselves. If you continue to ignore your emotions (and you will), they'll become more intense. What started out as mobile, supportive, action-requiring emotions can become monotonous, tormenting, and chronic responses to the world. If this is your current situation, worry not! You can use each of your new skills to address this situation. For instance, you can ground and refocus yourself through relaxation and deep breathing or simply by taking a walk in nature or taking a hot bath. Then, you can define your boundaries to create sacred space, and burn your contracts with your cycling thoughts and emotions. However, there's a much easier and goofier way to restore your grounding and your flow: Conscious Complaining to the rescue!

I first learned of the importance of complaining in Barbara Sher's wonderful book *Wishcraft: How to Get What You Really Want*, which puts forth the idea that wishes and dreams are not silly diversions; rather, they are actually crystal clear pointers that can lead you to your most important work. Sher writes that if you dream constantly of writing, training horses, traveling, going back to school, or becoming a doctor, that dream is actually a specific treasure map that will lead you to the central vocation of your life. Hers is not an ordinary self-help book, because Sher has truly lived the material inside it and knows that moving toward your dreams is often the most terrifying, ridiculous, infuriating, and impossible task imaginable—which is why so few people attempt it and why so many attempts fail. Sher's position is that if you don't look at the problems, the terrors, and the impossibilities in a conscious way, you simply won't survive the often-harrowing process of bringing your dreams into this world.

She suggests taking regular timeouts to complain—both to de-steam and to get a clearer understanding of whatever it is that's holding you back.

Although Sher suggests finding a complaining partner (we'll do that in Chapter 8), I modified the practice because there are very few people in this world who can deal with the amount of complaining I can produce. Most people are so uncomfortable in their own skins that they can't let me be uncomfortable in mine; they want to stop me, fix me, or help me see the world in a peppier light (which is just a form of repression if I'm in a foul mood). So I created a solitary practice for complaining, which has been a real lifesaver. Now, every time I lose all faith or come up against impossible obstacles, I can whine, moan, kvetch, and reinvigorate myself with the grim truth of what I'm experiencing. When I'm done, I'm not depressed—instead, I'm often able to get right back to work, because I know exactly what the problems are and just how hard life can be. This practice doesn't bring me down; it lifts me up, because it clears all the complaints out of my system, helps me be emotionally honest, and restores my grounding, my focus, and my sense of humor.

What Conscious Complaining Will Do for You. This intrapersonal skill addresses the first three aspects of empathy so that you can clear the decks and become more able to empathize skillfully:

> Emotion Contagion—you can verbally identify and work your
> way through any situation of emotional overwhelm, which
> increases your Empathic Accuracy and helps you create some
> distance from situations or emotions that destabilize you
> Emotion Regulation—complaining consciously and intentionally
> is an excellent way to regulate your emotions while you listen
> to, honor, and explore them

In regard to the six dimensions of your emotional style, this safe and private expressive practice addresses your Resilience in both directions by helping you slow down and focus on troubling situations so that you can recover more quickly. This practice also helps improve your Outlook in both directions, because you really need a safe way to focus on your allegedly negative emotions so that you can develop full-scale emotional intelligence. Conscious Complaining also helps increase your Self-awareness by helping you become more honest about how you truly feel, and it helps with your Attention levels in both directions as you learn to focus intently on your internal state, resolve the issue, and then move into a soft focus that allows you to be gently aware of multiple environmental inputs.

||||||||||||||||||||||||||||||||||||||||||||||||||||||||||||||||||||||||||||||||||||

HOW TO COMPLAIN CONSCIOUSLY

Ready? You can be grounded or not, inside your strong boundary or not—it doesn't matter. All that matters is that you're in a foul mood and you have some privacy. Start your complaining with some sort of phrase, like "I'm complaining now!" If you're inside, you can complain to the walls or furniture, to a mirror, or to whatever strikes your fancy. If you're outside, you can complain to plants and trees, animals, nature, the sky, the ground, or your God. If you're a strong complainer, like I am, you might want to create a complaining shrine for yourself (maybe on top of a dresser or an out-of-the-way table), with supportive pictures of grumpy cats, bratty kids, barking dogs, political cartoons, and whatever else calls to your complaining nature.

When you've found your perfect complaining site, let yourself go and give a voice to your dejected, hopeless, sarcastic, nasty, bratty self. Bring dark humor out of the shadows and really whine and swear about the frustrations, stupidities, impossibilities, and absurdities of your situation. Complain for as long as you like (you'll be surprised at how quickly this works). When you run out of things to say, thank whatever you've been whining or yelling at. Thank the furniture, the walls, the ground, the trees, your complaining shrine, or your God for listening, and then end your complaining session by bowing, shaking off, and doing something really fun. That's it!

||||||||||||||||||||||||||||||

People who try this practice are astonished to find that complaining doesn't pull them further down into the doldrums. In fact, most people find that they start laughing during these complaining sessions, because they can finally break through stagnation and repression and tell it like it is—without repercussions. It's an amazingly freeing practice in which you restore your flow again, you tell the truth again, you clear the decks, and you get an important time-out. And because this is a solitary practice, there's no danger of losing face or hurting someone else's feelings—instead, it's like a quick lube for your soul. Afterward, you'll find that you can revisit your struggles with renewed vigor and vision. Conscious Complaining is especially helpful in a life of striving, empathic good works, and personal growth, where complaining is often considered less than saintly (which is a shame, because all by itself, a prohibition on complaining can trigger unresolving, repetitive mood states like worry, situational depression, and apathy).

When you don't pay attention to the difficulties of trying to live a conscious, empathic life in a sea of distractions and emotional illiteracy, the conscious life becomes less and less appealing, and the distractions start calling to you and shimmering seductively. If you only make time for work, and you never make time for play and rest *or* for kvetching, grumbling, whining, and complaining, your emotional flow will evaporate, you'll deteriorate into perfectionism, and you'll have no fun at all. Conscious Complaining gives a voice to your struggles, and in so doing, it restores your flow, your energy, your emotional honesty, your sense of humor, and your hope. It may sound contradictory, but you just can't be happy unless you complain.

COMPLAINING VERSUS POSITIVE AFFIRMATIONS

Positive thinking and affirmations are the opposite of Conscious Complaining. They're also a function of valencing, since many (most?) positive-thinking programs valence the hell out of emotions. The idea behind positive thinking is that you hold on to thoughts and emotions that may get in the way of your health and well-being. Thoughts like "I'm unlovable" or "No one can be truly successful" or "Life is too hard" can really slow down your forward progress. Positive-thinking techniques teach you to unearth and then replace those thoughts with more helpful affirmations, such as "I have love around me all the time" or "Success belongs to me" or "Life is absolutely wonderful." Seems like a good idea, right?

Well, although it can be quite healing to ferret out interior statements that crush your well-being, positive thinking tends to be too much of a quick fix (and it tends to be emotionally repressive). If you look at the practice empathically, you'll understand the problem. Positive affirmations look at issues—for instance, a lack of love or an eating disorder—and apply a kind of reverse psychology. Instead of helping you sit with the issues and honor the emotions that are trying to arise, positive affirmations teach you to override the real situation with enforced statements that erase the true-but-uncomfortable emotions. Affirmations such as "I am surrounded by kind and loving people" or "Food is healing and slenderizing for me" *do* provide a more pleasant inner dialogue, but they don't tell the truth or honor the truth that's trying to come forward with the help of your emotions. These affirmations don't speak to the myriad issues behind your eating problem, nor do they heal or address your broken and weary heart—and your emotions know it. Most positive affirmations elevate verbal–intellectual statements above emotional realities. In essence, you're *telling* yourself how to feel instead of *feeling* the way you feel.

Empathically speaking, I haven't seen or experienced deep or lasting change with positive affirmations. I've seen people deal with the surface of their issues, and I've seen them get some of the things they wish for, but I haven't seen them deepen or mature empathically. Look at it this way: If you place a conflicting or overriding verbal command in the midst of strong emotions, you'll set up warring factions within yourself. Each of your affirmations will deny or repress the truth of the situation, which means that your emotions will have to intensify in order to get you to wake up and take effective, emotionally coherent action. Positive affirmations attempt to deal with deep emotional issues in incomplete and repressive ways.

Conscious Complaining is healing because it speaks to your real issues from within your actual emotive sense of things—it addresses your actual concerns, and it welcomes your real emotions and gives them a voice. When you can complain consciously, you don't sugarcoat or attempt to transform anything; you simply tell it like it is. When you allow yourself to be yourself, and when you allow your emotions to tell the truth *without valencing them,* no one gets hurt. When you can stand up and complain in a conscious way (rather than just griping to people without any purpose), your vision and your focus return, your emotions flow, you release your stored-up tensions, and you get to have the fun of translating everything you feel into choice words and phrases. And then it's done—and you move on.

If we have to valence thoughts and ideas, then let's look at them intelligently and empathically: "positive" thinking is helpful when it's true, just as "negative" thinking is helpful when it's true. If the phrase "I'm wonderful and marvelous!" comes barreling out of you, it's a sign of contentment moving through you in its own way and its own time. Embrace it! It's true! You *are* wonderful and marvelous! Similarly, if the phrase "I can't go on this way!" comes out of you, it's a sign of sadness, fatigue, or situational depression moving through you in its own way and its own time. Embrace it! It's true!

You *can't* go on this way—so don't try! Use your skills, bring your emotions forward, and deal with the truth of whatever you're feeling—whatever that truth may be. Dance with your marvelousness in its time, and complain, cry, whine, and burn contracts with your situational depression in *its* time. Then, move on to your next emotion, your next idea, or your next task. Your Empathic Accuracy and Emotion Regulation skills aren't supposed to create an unmoving and unchangeable sense of slaphappiness in you; their purpose is to help you clearly identify your emotions and respond uniquely to each of them in turn.

Conscious Complaining will help you develop your emotional vocabulary and your emotional awareness in safety and privacy and it will help you restore flow to repressed emotions or emotions that are stuck in a feedback loop. It will also help you refocus yourself and release ideas and behaviors that aren't working anyway, which is naturally grounding. Conscious Complaining is a silly practice, but it has a serious purpose—to connect you to your real emotions in a safe, lighthearted way.

REJUVENATING YOURSELF

Our fifth empathic mindfulness skill is a rejuvenation practice that you can use whenever you need to, wherever you are. This empathic rejuvenation practice is very simple and takes almost no time at all; however, you can turn it into a long and luxurious practice when you have the time.

What Rejuvenating Yourself Will Do for You. This self-rejuvenation skill addresses the following aspects of empathy:

Emotion Contagion—you can fill your body and your personal
   space with the precise emotional and sensual feelings that
   make you feel wonderful

Emotion Regulation—this soothing practice helps you restore
   yourself to equilibrium and can even be used in the middle of
   a conflict or when you lose your focus, your grounding, and
   your emotional skills

Concern for Others—this rejuvenation practice creates a
   compassionate and loving internal environment that helps you
   feel compassion for others, which increases your capacity for
   Perceptive Engagement

In regard to your emotional styles, this simple rejuvenation practice increases your Resilience; it refreshes your Outlook; it makes Self-awareness delicious; it increases your Sensitivity to Context in a safe way by helping you learn how to tune in to relaxation and delight; and it helps you learn to soften your Attention intentionally as you rejuvenate yourself.

||||||||||||||||||||||||||||||||||||||||||||||||||||||||||||||||||||||||||||

HOW TO REJUVENATE YOURSELF

If you're ready, please sit down, breathe in, and ground yourself as you exhale. Just let go. Now, lean forward with good posture and focus yourself; imagine that your peripersonal boundaries are very bright and distinct at the correct arm's-length distance from your body—in front of you, behind you, on either side of you, above you, and below the floor. Imagine your boundary as whole, distinctive, and vibrant.

In the space between your body and the edge of your boundary, imagine your favorite place in the world at your favorite time of day. For instance, use your full-bodied Einfühlung skills to feel yourself surrounded by a mountainside on a late spring evening, or beside a creek in a redwood grove at dawn, or in a cave on a tropical island where you can see and hear the ocean. Choose your favorite place and imagine it surrounding you. Remember that you can also feel or smell or sense this scene if visualizing isn't your skill. Just surround yourself with a feeling of beauty and relaxation and delicious, sensual pleasure.

You may feel your focus soften here, and that's perfectly fine. This is an interior exercise; you don't need to be completely aware of the outside world. Let your focus drift naturally.

As you sense your gorgeous nature scene around you, breathe some of it into your body. Take a deep breath, and imagine breathing the felt sense of this peaceful, beautiful place into your body. Imagine embodying the way you feel when you're in your favorite place. Breathe this feeling into your head and neck, and breathe it down into your chest and your arms and your hands. Breathe it in through your chest and abdomen and into your lower belly, and breathe it down into your legs and feet. Breathe this peaceful and delightful feeling into every part of your body. Fill yourself with this feeling of peace and beauty.

When you feel full, just let your body, your emotions, and your focus soften and relax. You can stay here for as long as you like. To complete this rejuvenation practice, bend over and touch the floor with both of your hands and let your head hang down. Just relax. You're done. Thank the emotion that helped you rejuvenate yourself: these are the gifts of healthy, flowing joy. Joy arises to help you feel a blissful sense of expansiveness and connection to beauty, peace, and wonder.

||||||||||||||||||||||||||||||

You can keep this joyful nature scene around you at all times, or you can bring it forward specifically when you want to rejuvenate yourself. For me, it's fun to imagine my nature scene around me at all times, because I can be where I am—in a traffic jam, on a plane, or in a meeting—and also be swimming in the warm water at Ke'e beach on Kauai or sitting next to a stream in a verdant redwood grove. Empathic and imaginal skills are excellent!

You can perform this rejuvenation practice every morning or evening, once each week, or whenever you like. Sometimes, you may feel like Rejuvenating Yourself hourly—go ahead; this is your practice now, and you can use it however you like.

BRINGING THESE PRACTICES TOGETHER

These empathic mindfulness skills belong to you now, and you can use them in whatever ways work for you. You can wake up in the morning, ground and focus yourself, imagine your boundary, and go on your way—or you can take your time with each skill if you need to. You can use very quick versions of Conscious Complaining throughout the day (my favorite is "Okay, I'm complaining. This sucks! Thank you, I'm done."), or you can create a complaining shrine if you're dealing with a lot of repressed or repetitive emotions. You can burn contracts quickly, or you can work extended contract-burning sessions into your day or week as needed.

You can rejuvenate and replenish yourself before bed with a few soothing breaths, or you can take specific rejuvenation breaks throughout your day. It's up to you; these are your skills now. This is your empathic practice. I created these five simple empathic mindfulness skills because I understand the demands of real life and the way we actually live, and I don't want to saddle you with a complex set of healthy activities that you don't have time for. I want to make your empathic life more workable, more understandable, and more manageable.

In terms of your ability to empathize adeptly, these skills will help with an aspect of empathy that many hyperempathic people find challenging, and that's Emotion Contagion.

127

HOW TO TELL IF AN EMOTION
IS YOURS OR SOMEONE ELSE'S

A question I'm asked constantly is how to determine whether an emotion belongs to you or to someone else. The answer involves me asking you some additional questions, the first of which is: How well are you defining your own boundaries? When you can define your peripersonal space, you'll have a physical and imaginal way to identify where you begin and end. For hyperempaths, this can be a game changer.

As I mentioned earlier, before I learned how to define my own boundaries, I felt every emotion around me, and I compared myself to a malfunctioning radio that picked up only static. Learning to ground and focus myself and set boundaries has helped me learn how to identify my own emotions and reactions so that I can tune into the difference between myself and others. Learning about my peripersonal boundaries has really helped me articulate my own sense of identity and contrast it with the very different identities of others. It has also helped my empathy mature from that place of runaway healing (where I compulsively fixed the problems of others because their problems hurt *me*) and into a more patient, eagle-eyed understanding of the natural life span of difficult situations. When I learned how to identify myself as a distinct individual, I was able to observe the pain, emotions, and anguish of others as something I could understand without having to ingest bodily, share viscerally, or fix immediately. Grounding myself and setting boundaries helped me moderate my overactive Emotion Contagion abilities, which, in turn, helped me develop better Empathic Accuracy and Emotional Regulation skills (because I wasn't filled with the confusing static of everyone else's emotions all day long).

Learning to set boundaries also works for people whose empathic awareness is low, because it helps them realize that their emotional realities end at a certain point and that other people live inside their own worlds with their own distinct emotional realities. So whether you're emotionally hypersensitive *or* relatively insensitive, I want you to focus on your boundary-setting skills. That's the first step in learning how to identify whether an emotion is yours or someone else's.

The next step is to understand that sharing emotions with others is completely normal and absolutely crucial to the quality of your relationships. If your dear friends are laughing, laugh with them. If your mate is crying and you feel the sadness alongside him or her, then cry. If your dog suddenly sits up with alert wariness, track with your dog and use your own fear-based ability to find out what's going on. Emotions are essential, action-requiring aspects of everything you think, learn, notice, and do. It's absolutely normal to share emotions. And when you have your own emotional skills, shared emotions are just as easy to work with as internally generated emotions are. You just feel and identify the emotion, ask the questions and track back to the stimulus, and then perform the action for that emotion (or decide not to act if that stimulus is invalid). Then you move on to the next thing. Sharing emotions is normal—it's the Emotion Contagion aspect of empathy.

In fact, if you think about it, Emotion Contagion is central to your Einfühlung capacity to appreciate art, music, comedy, drama, and literature. A novel that doesn't move you emotionally is a failed novel; music that doesn't touch you emotionally is boring; comedy that doesn't send you into fits of laughter isn't working right; and actors who can't evoke emotions in you (or who clumsily do so) are considered bad actors. We actually pay good actors a great deal of money to emote on screen or on stage so that we can feel alongside them—and we put on lavish spectacles every year to reward actors with Emmys, Tonys, and Oscars specifically for their advanced Emotion Contagion skills. If you think about it, Emotion Contagion is not just normal—it's actually something we value very, very highly.

So with the understanding that healthy boundaries help you identify your own emotions as distinct from the emotions of others; that emotional contagion is normal, healthy, and valued; and that you can work with any emotion (no matter what evoked it) if you can identify it and track back to its stimulus, I'll now reapproach this question: Does it *matter* if an emotion is yours or someone else's? When you have empathic skills, does it matter?

No matter where an emotion comes from, the process from stimulus to action is the same, as we learned in Chapter 4: you *feel* and *identify* the emotion, *ask the question* for the emotion, and track it back to its *emotion-evoking stimulus*. Is the emotion true for you, or is it true for another right now? That's the way you tell whether the emotion belongs to you. If the emotion does belong to you, you complete its action; if it doesn't belong to you, you use your grounding skills to down-regulate the emotion, refocus, and soothe yourself. Then you use your imaginal and proprioceptive skills to set your boundaries more distinctly and develop more precise emotional hygiene skills. With the help of your empathic mindfulness skills, you can gently teach yourself how to identify self and other.

This identification process may take a while, especially if you're on either side of the pole of hyperempathy or low empathy. But with practice, you'll be able to retrain yourself and develop better boundaries. This will, in turn, help you develop stronger Emotion Regulation skills and clearer Empathic Accuracy. Your empathic skills flow from your capacity for self-recognition and self-definition (as Doris Bischof-Köhler discovered with babies who could recognize themselves in a mirror). As you develop stronger self-awareness, you'll become more able to identify where emotions come from and what their stimuli are.

But I have a gentle warning, because your brain is somewhat of a trickster (okay, it's a big trickster). Your brain loves to make up reasons for everything. Since all humans have all human emotions, *any* emotion you pick up can have validity and truth for you at any given moment. This is fine. If you can find a reason that an emotion might be true, then you can simply complete the action for that emotion and go on your way. But there's a trickier situation to be aware of, and it tends to occur in the presence of emotions that people have mistakenly valenced into the so-called negative category. When an emotion is characterized as negative, we tend to ignore, suppress, or repress it, and subsequently, we don't develop practical skills with that emotion. What I've noticed in my own emotional evolution is that when I have trouble with an emotion, I'll be strangely drawn to people who overexpress or repress that emotion. It's almost as if my organism is drawn (like a moth to a flame) to people who are living out their trouble with that emotion. And even though that emotion is currently problematic for me, I'll drop into a kind of unconscious contagion and feel the emotion vicariously alongside the troubled people (usually while I criticize them for being so out of control—hello, my shadow!). When I catch myself doing that, I complete the action for that emotion within myself, and I burn contracts with that emotion and those people (and my old approach to that emotion). Then I move forward.

Understand that burning your contracts with people doesn't mean letting go of the relationship itself. Instead, this practice is about letting go of old, unworkable ways of relating; in most cases, burning these contracts will help you reinvigorate the relationship. But sometimes it takes a while, because you might get riled up by how troubling or wrong or deluded those *other* people are and forget that you have skills and options. I just want you to know that there are reasons behind Emotion Contagion that might surprise you.

So as you observe the emotions that you pick up from others, just ask yourself whether those emotions are ones you can deal with well on your own. If they are, you now have options: you can take the opportunity to work with those emotions consciously; you can ground yourself and down-regulate those emotions and then set clearer boundaries; or you can just enjoy those emotions in the way you enjoy emotions that are evoked by engaging music, art, books, or films. However, if the emotions are problematic for you, and you lose your skills every time they're evoked, you may be picking them up precisely because you need practice with them. So instead of blaming people because their emotions are so intrusive (though this is sometimes the case), just ask whether your own preexisting problem with those emotions might be the crux of the matter. And if certain people are difficult for you to be around because their emotional approach or emotional functioning doesn't sync with yours, just check in with yourself and ask whether you have a good relationship with the emotion(s) in question.

The full answer to the question of how to tell whether an emotion is yours or someone else's is a long one, but it comes down to this: if you know how to work with emotions, then it doesn't matter where they came from. Certainly, you don't want to spend your life around emotionally repressive or emotionally explosive people (that's exhausting for anyone, but it's especially problematic for people who want to become healthy, happy empaths), but Emotion Contagion is a normal and healthy part of being human.

Saying that, however, I now want to focus on an emotion that can be problematic to share—not because the emotion is inherently troublesome, but because of the unusual and future-focused actions this particular emotion requires.

THE EMPATHIC DILEMMA OF ANXIETY

Being an author is pretty awesome, but one of the less awesome things about writing a book is that it sort of freezes you in time. It stands as a testament to what you knew the year you wrote it, even though you keep learning and growing long after it's published. Luckily, I've been able to use my website to update my work in *The Language of Emotions* (which I wrote in 2009) and share the new things I've learned about emotions and empathy. The following information on anxiety first appeared on my website.[41]

I continually study emotions and empathy in social science, neurology, and related fields to stay updated. In January 2011, on the San Francisco–based radio show *Forum* with Michael Krasny, I heard an interview with Dr. Mary Lamia, who is a psychoanalyst and psychologist. She wrote a book called *Understanding Myself: A Kid's Guide to Intense Emotions and Strong Feelings*. It's a great book for kids, and Lamia has some very surprising things to say.

In the latter part of the interview, Lamia spoke about anxiety in a way I hadn't heard before, and I mulled it over a great deal. She sees anxiety as the emotion that helps us take action and get things done. I knew that about fear (the question for fear is, *What action must be taken?*), and in my work, I focus on the action-based and intuitive aspects of fear. However, in my previous book, I sort of pushed anxiety off to the side because, honestly, it bothered me when people ran around being anxious. I just wanted them to calm down and focus themselves already. *Sheesh!* When I wrote my book, I didn't see anxiety as a purposeful emotion (I valenced it!); therefore, I completely overlooked its function. What I began to understand after hearing Lamia is that I wasn't able to maintain my grounding or my boundaries around anxiety and that the normal process of Emotion Contagion suddenly became troublesome when anxiety was in the room. This is a problem I share with many, many people, so let's look at it.

PUTTING IT OFF VERSUS DOING IT AHEAD OF TIME

Lamia contrasts *procrastinators,* who put things off until their anxiety kicks in and makes them do their work, with *do-it-aheaders,* who do their work ahead of time. I'm a do-it-aheader. We actually have a joke in our family about thanking Karla from the past—we'll find some job I finished weeks ago or unearth finished pieces to a project that's crucial, or we'll find important papers in my filing system, and we'll say, "Thanks, Karla from the past, for making things easy!" Clearly, this thankfulness is a great motivator, because in each day, I think of all kinds of cool projects and jobs to do for the future happiness of my friends, my family, and myself. It's a total win-win. It's time travel that works!

Before I heard Lamia, I would have said that I didn't *have* anxiety, but I realized with a thud that, "Ooohhhh, I have plenty of anxiety, but I somehow learned to respond to it at very early points in its appearance, so that it almost never gets to the level of a mood." I realized that I've always paid close attention to soft and subtle levels of anxiety and responded at very early points in its life cycle, which meant that I rarely experienced an identifiable mood-state form of anxiety. Consequently, I developed a valenced and unnuanced empathic blind spot about anxiety.

Because I almost never moved into the mood state of anxiety, and because I usually responded to it in its soft, free-flowing state, I mistakenly identified my subtle level of do-it-ahead anxiety as *foresight, conscientiousness,* or perhaps just *being organized.* I didn't realize that I was working with an emotion that was trying to prepare me for the future. Whoops! We live and learn. So I finally learned to identify the nuances of anxiety, and I've since welcomed anxiety fully into my emotional toolkit. It is now easy to maintain my grounding, my focus, and my boundaries when I'm near an anxious person.

When I lifted my veil of ignorance about anxiety, I realized that my behavior only *appeared* to be anxiety-free, because I wasn't in an anxious mood. However, I was using my anxiety about *not* having completed things as a way to help myself out of future troubles. Does that make sense?

We've all experienced what it's like to look for a specific shirt that turns out to need washing (disappointment, frustration), or how it feels to lose important papers (anxiety, fear, disappointment), or how it feels to be late (embarrassment, shame, anxiety). As a do-it-aheader, I work to avoid those unpleasant outcomes by confronting them before they have a chance to happen. I'm time traveling in a way that's different from a procrastinator (who's trying to avoid an unpleasant future by not confronting it), but we're both attempting to achieve the same goals—we're both trying to avoid an unpleasant future.

During the *Forum* interview, a self-avowed procrastinator called in and explained that he could easily finish things that were pleasant, but that he really had to force himself to do things that felt like work or to finish chores that he didn't feel he was good at. He needed his anxiety to get to a fever pitch before he could power his way through his procrastination and into unpleasant tasks. Even as a do-it-aheader, I *totally* get that. When I have a miserable task to accomplish, my entertainment-and-online-game habit takes over, and I hide from the misery and discomfort and doubt. However, I've learned to pay myself with procrastination; for example, I'll tell myself, "Okay, you can play three games of (insert current favorite game here) or watch a show, but then you need to write that difficult letter or clean out the crisper drawer in the fridge." That may sound silly, but I think it helps me remain emotionally honest.

Honestly, I don't *want* to write that letter or clean out the wretched crisper drawer. It's miserable work. Besides, what if I say the wrong thing in the rotten letter and make things worse? We can all stand outside the situation and know that I'll feel better once these miserable tasks are completed, but it's a long slog through foul terrain before that can happen. So if I have to do those odious things, then I need a reward. And though I didn't know which emotion I was working with, I somehow learned to play with and work with my procrastination and my anxiety, rather than being worked over or overwhelmed by them. Score one for the unintentional empath!

REFRAMING YOUR APPROACH TO ANXIETY

Contagion in the area of anxiety can be troublesome, not simply because anxiety is usually negatively valenced but also because anxiety requires actions that are based on the future. If you pick up anxiety from others, you may become overwhelmed with a dozen future plans that you can't act upon in the present moment, or your adrenaline might kick in and make you feel jangled and unfocused. Both of these fairly normal responses to anxiety can cause you to shut down your empathy. It's important, therefore, to understand procrastination, anxiety, and anxiety-prone people more empathically so that this emotion isn't quite so destabilizing.

What I see in career procrastinators and anxiety-prone people (that is, in mood-state anxiety) is that their uncomfortable relationship to procrastination and anxiety becomes a kind of lifestyle and very much a part of their self-image. Procrastinators and anxiety-ridden people may feel some shame about their behavior, but because they're in a feedback loop with the powerful state of anxiety (which affects hormones, stress reactions, eating behaviors, sleep patterns, and more), they may feel as if they have no control over it. As a result, their mood-state anxiety may become an unwanted but persistent houseguest, which they eventually just learn to live with. Some people even begin to champion their anxiety/procrastination cycles (think of those signs that flaunt a messy desk as a mark of genius).

My suggestion for interrupting this feedback loop (in yourself, certainly, but you can also share this practice with the anxiety-prone people in your life) is to turn toward the anxiety and procrastination and ask the question for anxiety: "What *really* needs to get done?" I think the word *really* is key, because if you simply ask your procrastination what needs to get done, it might answer: "Eat chocolate, go blog hopping, play Angry Birds, watch movies," and then it's four hours later and where are you? Did those things *really* need to get done? But if you ask your mood-state or intense anxiety what needs to get done, it might answer: "Make sure you turned off the stove, now polish the doorknobs, now wash your hands. But where are the nail clippers? What about reorganizing the closet or changing the oil in the car? Oh, did you check the stove?" And again, it's four hours later, and you've been sent on any number of fool's errands. If you can slow yourself down and ask yourself what *really* needs to get done, you can bring your full awareness to the situation.

When any of your emotions (or the emotions of others) are caught in a feedback loop, it's very tempting to turn away (or run away) and ignore them, but you can make significant improvements in your Empathic Accuracy if you can clearly identify emotions and engage with them empathically. When you can understand the reasons that emotions arise, you can help them do their proper work so that they can recede naturally and you can ground and focus yourself again. This process of identifying, listening to, and responding to emotions so that they can move onward is how you develop Emotion Regulation skills. This next skill is a specific healing practice for anxiety, which can be a very problematic emotion if you don't understand how it works or how to regulate it.

CONSCIOUS QUESTIONING FOR YOUR ANXIETY

Anxiety has an important purpose and function—it's your task-completion emotion, and it's your procrastination alert system. Anxiety can be an intensely action-focused emotion, and expressing it when it's intense or when it's in a feedback loop can be pretty problematic. It can run you in five different directions at once. However, repressing anxiety isn't a good choice, because anxiety will keep bubbling up—it has tasks to complete! But here's the rub with intense anxiety: even *channeling* it can be problematic if you're highly activated—it might overwhelm or confuse you, especially if it's in a feedback loop. So we have an empathic mindfulness practice for anxiety that's similar to Conscious Complaining.

In Conscious Questioning, you turn toward your anxiety and identify each issue that your anxiety is responding to so you can organize all of your activation. This practice will help you ground and focus yourself again. You can do this verbally, by asking yourself (out loud) about each thing that *really* needs to get done. But I find that it's helpful to write things down as well. Writing is a way to physically express your anxieties, become aware of them, and organize them intentionally. And here's the interesting part: speaking or writing out your anxieties *is* an action. It counts as an emotion-specific action that helps your anxiety calm down a bit so that you can ground and focus yourself. Many of us try to repress or run away from anxiety, but that doesn't work; turning toward anxiety empathically *does* work. Simply voicing or writing down your anxieties will help your anxieties recede. With this quick, focused practice, you can access the gifts of anxiety, identify any upcoming tasks, organize everything you need to do to complete those tasks, and gently confront your procrastination tendencies. When you use Conscious Questioning, it doesn't matter whether or not the anxiety you feel belongs to you, because no matter where it came from, you can turn toward it, question it consciously, complete its specific actions, and move onward.

Empathic mindfulness skills help you make real changes in your behavior, in your approach to emotions, in your outlook, in your tension levels, and in your empathic skills. No matter where an emotion came from, which emotion it is, or how activated the emotion has become, you can use your empathic skills to engage with each emotion and figure out what it's trying to do. Remember, though, that if you do what you can to empathically address an emotion and it's still too much, please reach out for help from a trusted friend, counselor, or health-care provider. Sometimes, especially with a very intense emotion like anxiety, we can all use a little support to bring an emotion back into balance.

FROM YOUR INNER WORLD TO YOUR OUTER WORLD

Your empathic mindfulness skills are a set of intrapersonal skills that you can use no matter where you are or what's going on around you. In our emotionally confused and empathically noisy world, these skills will help you stay focused, grounded, self-aware, emotionally flexible, empathically aware, intuitively attentive, and rejuvenated. In Part Two of this book, we'll explore ways to safely and comfortably bring your empathy into the world. In the next chapter, we'll create a home environment that can support you and your loved ones in these ways and more.

Bringing Your Empathy into the World

CHAPTER 6

Empaths at Home

Creating a Sanctuary Where Empathy Can Flourish

EMPATHY IS A strongly receptive skill, and empathic people are nearly always sensitive in many different ways—emotionally, aesthetically, multisensorially, socially, and so forth. As you learn to engage perceptively and empathically with others, I want you to also become *comfortably* receptive to your environment and to the emotions, circumstances, needs, and wishes of others. Empathy requires receptivity, so it's important to surround yourself with nourishing and nurturing influences that will help you balance all of this necessary receptivity.

In the previous chapter, you learned about empathic mindfulness skills that you can access at any time and in any place. These resources will help you increase your intrapersonal skills, become more emotionally aware, and perform your empathic work in comfort and safety. They will also help you choose how much receptivity you'll engage in at any given moment. Your empathic mindfulness skills give you options in regard to your empathy.

In this chapter, we'll look at your home from an empathic perspective and discover if there are ways to make your home a more supportive and nurturing environment for an emotionally aware, grounded, focused, well-defined, and healthy empath. It's possible that you've already created an absolutely wonderful empathic sanctuary in your home (if so, congratulations!), but if your home is not currently a sanctuary for you, or if you're not sure what a sanctuary would feel like, it's worth taking a close look at your most intimate surroundings.

With your empathic Einfühlung capacity fully activated, I'd like you to observe your home as if you were an anthropologist, or perhaps as if you were a nosy visitor (being fascinated by and nosy about the social world is a prerequisite for cultural anthropologists and other scientists). It will be helpful to take a notebook with you so that you can jot down your observations—but understand before you start that there are no right or wrong answers to the questions I'll ask you.

As you walk around your home, step outside of yourself and ask, "Who lives here?" What kind of person lives in your home, and what is important to this person? Is this person studious or active, solitary or a part of many social groups, organized or free form? Is this person artistic, scientific, romantic, reserved, or gregarious? Who lives here?

Starting from the most social areas and judging by the way you've set up your front room, what's important to you? Does all of your furniture face toward a central television, or have you created conversation areas where people can sit and talk? Do you have a lot of books, or is a computer or a sound system a central feature? Is your front room a kind of meditative space, or is it a very social space? If you live with a mate, are your styles and needs represented equally in this room, or does one person dominate? If you have children, is this room a kid space—and if so, is there any room for you here? If this is a home you're sharing with your parents, is there any space for you in this front room? If you're in a roommate situation, does this room welcome you? What do you (or the people who live in your home) value? And do those values truly represent the way you want to live?

Do your windows look out onto greenery or nature? If not, do you have plants in your home? Nature and greenery create a soothing atmosphere; simply placing a plant in a room can make it feel homier. Art and music can do that, too. Do you use art and music to bring a sense of beauty into your home? Using your Einfühlung capacity, can you identify any themes or leading emotions in the music you love and in the art you like to have around you? What is your color scheme, and what does it evoke for you? Do your musical and artistic themes—and your chosen emotions and colors—speak to you in a healing and welcoming way? If not, why not?

As you continue to investigate your home, do you find that you like order, or are you looser and more free form? What does the presence or lack of order say to you and about you? As you look at photos displayed in your home, are they of single figures or groups? Or are they all of landscapes or buildings? Does your photography identify you as a solitary person, a group member, or a lover of structure or of nature? If you could identify some leading emotions or themes in your photos, what would they be?

As you move into your kitchen, ask yourself about the social nature of the person who lives in your home. Is your kitchen orderly and spare, or is it overflowing with cooking gadgets and colors and places to relax? Is food preparation easy in this kitchen, or is it somewhat of a chore? Are the cupboards and the refrigerator filled with foods you love, or is there more of a mishmash of things you *should* eat but don't actually like? Does your kitchen nourish and support the real lives of the people who live here and gather here? If not, why not?

As you move through your home, continue to observe and explore. You've been leaving clues for yourself in your home; you've been displaying your true nature, your wants, your needs, and your dreams. With your anthropologist's eyes and your empathic capacities, you can begin to pull these clues together into a unified whole. Who lives in your home, and is he or she comfortable, welcomed, and supported here?

I'd like you to end your tour in your bedroom and, if you have one, in your private bathroom. We've gone from the most social areas of your home to the most private areas, and I'd like you to take a close look at the colors, photos, art, organization, and emotional tone of your private rooms. Look at the things you've chosen to place nearest to your private, unclothed, unguarded, and sleeping self. Is the emotional tone of your bedroom different from the tone in the rest of your home? If you have a private bathroom, what's the emotional and artistic tone here? Does it differ from the rest of your home? If so, what's different? What do these rooms say about you? What's important to you in the most private recesses of your home? *Who lives here?*

CREATING A PERFECT EMPATHIC TERRARIUM

I like to focus on your living situation because if you don't have a warm, supportive, nurturing, and replenishing home environment, it can be pretty hard to develop a healthy and happy relationship with your empathic skills. This is true for everyone, but it's especially true for hyperempaths, who may burn out if their homes aren't sanctuaries for them. In the next chapter, we'll focus on the importance (the crucial, game-changing importance) of healthy love and family relationships for empaths because without that, they have no empathic downtime anywhere. But it's equally important for anyone who wants to develop and nurture their empathic abilities to have a home environment that's filled with comfort, real nourishment, beauty, and relaxation. This kind of environment is especially important for you if you're currently working to develop stronger emotional awareness and a keener empathic capacity. If you want to be able to live happily as an empathic person in a fairly unempathic world, your home truly needs to be your sanctuary.

Your home can act as a kind of threshold between you and the outside world. It can act as a supportive backstage area where you can rest, recharge, replenish, and take a break from the emotional needs of others (and from emotional commotion in general). Your home can be an extension of your boundary-setting practice; it can help you learn how to set and maintain boundaries in the physical world as you learn to define yourself and set boundaries in your interactions and your relationships.

I don't want you to think that I'm promoting the creation of a silent monastery, because your home can certainly be a colorful, music-filled social space and a fun party home. Healthy interaction is good food for your empathic nature, and good friendships can help you develop and hone your empathic skills in a safe and friendly environment. A home that is healing and welcoming for you can be very healing and welcoming for others, as well. However, what we're focusing on in this chapter is how to make your home into a kind of terrarium that can nurture a sensitive, emotionally aware, and healthy empathic organism.

I asked earlier whether your home looks out onto any sort of nature or greenery, because greenery and natural environments seem to have a specific healing function for our bodies. At one point in my earlier career, during a five-year period when I wrote ten books and audio learning sets and toured constantly, I reached a point of such overwhelm that my health started to slip away. A counselor I spoke to prescribed hiking to a secluded spot near water and lying down on the ground under some trees. It seems strange, but that was a specifically healing activity. First of all, I was alone and away from the commotion of other people and their needs. Second, I was in a beautiful place where all the sounds were natural and unconnected to me (no phones, no alarms, no voices). Third, I could lie down and feel the grounding support of the earth underneath my entire body—I could let go of everything. And fourth, as I lay there, I realized that nature didn't need me—I wasn't central to the functioning of this place. Unlike my career or my home or my family life, in this place I was welcome but unneeded. The wind didn't require anything from me. The water flowed downstream whether or not I was there. The trees grew and the animals managed their lives—completely without input from me. In this place, I could be a part of nature without needing to do anything. I could just exist.

As you observe your habitat and your home, I'd like you to be aware of beauty and nature around you. Is greenery and growth visible to you? Do you have sources of fresh, clean air? Can you open your windows freely? Do you have plants in your home? Are there places where you can get away and simply be a part of nature—where you are unneeded but welcome, and nurtured but basically ignored? Are you connected to the natural sounds of the nonhuman world? If not, you can create many aspects of a healing natural environment for yourself.

When I have lived in noisy urban areas, my bathroom became an oasis where I created a sense of being enveloped in quiet, natural sounds and sensual delights. Hot baths or long showers with low lights and soft music (if you like music), wonderful scents (if you're not scent sensitive), and soft, clean towels can bring you a sense of release and relaxation. Think about how many of the gifts of sadness you can access during bathing. You can let go of lots of things that aren't working anyway, like dirt and grime, mental clutter, and muscle tension, and you can intentionally rejuvenate yourself, your skin, your mind, and your musculature. Water can be wonderfully healing and relaxing, and it's readily available. If you're surrounded by noise and bustle, even inside your home, your bathroom can become a mini-spa and sanctuary. Water, nature, and greenery are wonderfully healing, yet if you can't get to nature, you can still create a small healing oasis inside your home.

Relaxation is such an important part of a whole and healthy life, yet I find that it's not something many of us make time for, which is why I created such simple grounding and rejuvenation practices. I noted earlier that most meditation and relaxation practices use sadness without realizing that they're doing so; it's fascinating to me that instruction in how to access the gifts of sadness has become a kind of cottage industry. I mean, it's a good industry, but it's remarkable that people actually need direct instruction in how to access the gifts of their own emotions and that people need to be taught how to relax. As you observe your home, make a note of how many areas are relaxing or are set aside specifically for you to relax. If there are few or none (besides your bed, of course), ask yourself why.

For very empathic people—or for people who are learning to increase their emotional and empathic abilities—interaction and emotional availability are vital learning activities. You have to get out and interact, engage in relationships, use your empathic skills, and be willing to be intimate with others or with your interests out in the world. These are wonderful activities, but they're activating (and sometimes fatiguing); you need to balance all that activation with relaxation, grounding, self-care, and rejuvenation. This is why we're focusing on your home, because it can be your empathic recharging station.

THE HEALING POWER OF ARTISTIC EXPRESSION

As you observe your home and think about how it can support, nurture, protect, and replenish you, look at your artistic practice, if you have one. Have you created a space in your home for your artistic or musical expression? Artistic expression is wonderful and soul-expanding for anyone, but it has a particular healing quality for empaths—it helps you express and channel emotions intentionally. Whether you write, draw, paint, sing, compose, play an instrument, design, do metalwork or paper arts, work with fabric or jewelry, create with wood or ceramics, dance or do martial arts, do graphic arts or photography, do math or science, or work in your garden or your kitchen, artistic and creative expression will enable you to connect with yourself and to tangibly symbolize emotions, thoughts, and ideas.

Artistic expression is specifically healing for empaths because it helps us bring balance to our highly receptive bodies, and it helps us use our empathic Einfühlung skills in self-nurturing ways. We empaths spend a lot of time in receptivity, and if there isn't a healthy way for us to express and channel all of the emotions, sensations, and impressions we receive, we can become overwhelmed and exhausted. We can head toward burnout if we have no expressive practice to balance our natural tendency to be highly receptive to our environment and continually aware of the emotions, needs, difficulties, and wishes of others. Artistic expression can help us express things in a sensual, visual, vocal, intellectual, tactile, or kinetic way, and it can help us develop an internal dialogue and deeper intrapersonal awareness. Artistic expression can also help people with low empathy develop the intrapersonal skills and awareness that lead to stronger Empathic Accuracy and Emotion Regulation skills. Artistic expression is a vital aspect of empathic self-care—and luckily, the art doesn't even have to be any good.

When I was a hyperactive and emotionally volatile little hyperempath, I was fortunate to have artistic parents. My dad was a writer and musician, and my mom was a painter and singer. Art and music, wordplay and singing—these were normal parts of every day in our home. We had a piano, and when I was completely overwhelmed, I'd sit at it to try to learn a song I had heard somewhere. I'd play parts of the melody over and over again, training my fingers and my ears to memorize the song—and once I got it, I'd play the entire song over and over again to get the right cadence and emotional expressivity. I'm talking *hours* on one song. It must have been excruciating for my family, but no one made fun of me or complained, because artists understand that practice—and that being bad at first—is a part of the process.

Although my early music was probably a form of water torture for any listener, the process of creating music was magical for me. I was able to train my hands and my ears to hone in on specific sounds and actions, I was able to exercise my memorization and sequencing skills, and I was able to express emotions in many different ways as I played and replayed my songs. I was also able to spend significant time away from the needs of others and to focus on the exact ways that I wanted to express myself. Art gave me a way to use my intense Einfühlung capacities in safe, intentional, manageable, tangible ways. Art and music helped me learn about myself as an individual, and they helped me develop grounded intrapersonal empathic skills in the way that animals in my neighborhood helped me develop safer and more grounded interpersonal empathic skills. Artistic expression is a specific healing practice for empaths, and it's a wonderful way for people with currently low emotional and intrapersonal awareness to engage with and develop their interior lives and their emotional awareness.

As you observe your home, look for your artistic practice, which can be as elaborate as having a large weaving loom in your front room or as compact as the special journal you use to write haiku. Your art form can be movement based or it can be located in your meditative practice. Your art can be cooking, baking, or home design. It can also be your mathematical or scientific activities, because both of these fields can engage you completely as you work to organize, describe, and express your understanding of natural phenomenon. When I speak of art, I'm looking for something that allows you to express your thoughts, emotions, ideas, dreams, hopes, and visions in an intentional and tangible way. I'm looking for a practice that helps you express your entire self, honestly and ceremonially. We already have expressive practices for your emotions—we have Conscious Complaining, Burning Contracts, and Conscious Questioning—but those practices are specific to situations that trouble you. You also need an expressive practice for things that delight you, for things that puzzle you, and for the wordless concepts you can't quite grasp until you see them expressed in your favorite art form.

Artistic expression can deepen and coalesce you. It can expand and focus you. And it can embolden you so that you can take the joys, excitements, pains, and troubles in your life and immerse them in the beauty and depth of your soul. Art can be a sacred, alchemical healing practice—and, as such, it's a specific practice for empaths.

As you search through your home for your artistic practice, don't be too upset if you don't find anything except some old art supplies at the back of the closet, covered with a layer of dust, hope, and faint shame. Very few of us were raised by artists, and very few of us have ever been able to set aside time for an artistic practice. Even my heavily artistic friends have unfinished projects that collect dust for months or even years. Modern life is busy and hectic, and there's always something dragging us away from self-care, from interiority, and from our art.

Fantasies of perfection are also a big impediment, because many people don't want to do art unless they can do it perfectly. If that's what's stopping you, then please burn your contracts with art as perfection. Unless you're out there trying to make a living as an artist, you don't have to be concerned with perfection; the point is to use art as a supportive expressive practice that is uniquely healing for your empathic self. You need as many forms of healthy expression as you can get, because empathy is a highly receptive process. Expressive practices will help you create balance, and they'll help you avoid (or heal from) burnout.

If you don't currently have any art or craft that engages you, take some classes. Supporting other artists and helping them make a living is a wonderful way to perform empathic activism, and it's a great way to meet people who share your interests. Of course, classes are social activities where you'll need to be empathically receptive for at least part of the time, but gaining artistic tools and skills will help you embark on your own artistic practice. If you can't make time for a class, then try a simple expressive art form and discover what you like and what speaks to you. Even if it's dancing around the living room to your favorite song, writing a short poem, or creating an interesting display on your refrigerator, find a way to express yourself through art and movement, and find a way to make time and space in your home for art. Art heals.

MOVEMENT AS AN ART FORM

Movement is another expressive art form that is specifically healing for empaths. It is also a way to become more aware of your body and your emotions if your empathic awareness is currently low. If you don't have time for a traditional artistic practice, you can work with your existing movement or exercise practice to bring some of the specific healing aspects of art into it. Besides improving your muscle tone and your metabolism and warding off the diseases of inactivity, movement practices can provide you with the opportunity to get away from everything, so you can let your mind and your emotions wander freely while you express yourself physically. Of course, if your movement practice is highly social, like team sports, exercise classes with blaring music, or gym workouts in front of a television, they'll tend to be too activating for our purposes. Instead, see if you can bring some of the flowing, expressive, and intentional movements of dance and martial arts into your existing movement practice. If you can, you'll create a three-for-one: good exercise, artistic expression, and a specific healing practice for empaths. Score!

I want you to notice that I'm not exhorting you to exercise. You know and I know that exercise is absolutely imperative. However, the busy, hectic pace of modern life often means that self-care, relaxation, and movement get pushed to the back of the closet, right next to those dusty art supplies. Sleep also gets thrown into that closet and I'd like to take an empathic look at what many of us do with whatever extra time we have. If we're not relaxing, exercising, doing our art, or sleeping, what *are* we doing?

I notice that many of us use entertainment as a relaxation and self-care activity—TV, movies, or the Internet—and those can certainly be a good way to wind down. However, all of these entertainments are interactive, visually stimulating, and somewhat noisy. They also require that you stay in a receptive mode—even though watching TV and movies can feel relaxing, it's activating for your brain, and the lights, movement, sudden sound shifts, and action on a monitor can keep your fear-based orienting skills activated. As such, screen-based activities can be more distracting than truly relaxing. Distraction, which is a form of emotional repression, is a nice skill to have—it's a nice thing to be able to do every now and then—but if it's a regular practice for you, I'd like you to take an empathic look at it.

If you spend a lot of time in front of a screen, and if that's your central relaxation technique, just check in with yourself. When you're engaged in screen-based entertainment, is it grounding for you? Are you able to let go of the tensions of the day and refill yourself with calm and focus? Is your screen time truly rejuvenating? Does it fill you with delicious, full-bodied beauty in the way your rejuvenating practice does? Do you come away feeling refreshed and refilled? If not, can you think of other relaxation activities that would refresh and replenish you? Would movement work? Would artistic expression work? Would a short nap work? Would your empathic mindfulness skills work?

Entertainment and the Internet are central to many of us, and I'm not suggesting that you banish them. However, if you notice that they take up the time you could spend on movement, relaxation, art, and home tending, then I want you to gently ask yourself why. If you scan yourself empathically when you're in front of a screen and you notice that your screen-based activities keep you activated or even hyperactivated, it might be good to set some boundaries around them. This is especially true with interactive electronic activities such as texting, social media, and checking your e-mail continually. On one hand, this kind of interactivity is awesome for your empathic skills, because it keeps you engaged with many people. On the other hand, this engagement—especially texting and IM-ing—can become a type of addictive distraction that is actually overstimulating and ungrounding for you. As we see every day in online commenting flame wars, people can get so riled up and ungrounded by social media that they completely lose their social skills and their Emotion Regulation skills.

As you work to create a life that will nurture you as a healthy and happy empath, take a close look at your electronic interactions. If they're supporting your emotional awareness in a welcoming and healthy social environment, then hooray! But if your social media interactions are troubling or conflict based, or if they're pulling your focus to a screen pretty much every minute of the day, then it's time to set some time limits on social media so that you can have some privacy, reduce your receptive activities, and restore your equilibrium with healthy, intentional expressive practices like art, movement, or your empathic mindfulness skills.

It's especially important to be aware of your social media and screen-based activities in the hours before bedtime, because the social engagement, the sounds, the visual stimulation, and the flickering lights can tell your brain that it's still daytime and that you should be up, active, and fully engaged. For many people, screen-based interactions and entertainment can actually interfere with healthy sleep. The suggestion from many sleep researchers is that you should shut down your electronics at least an hour before bed (two hours is better, but I'm being a realist here).

So, as we create a healthy home environment for you, let's look at possibly the most important contributor to your health and well-being (and of course, your empathic skills), which is the quality of your sleep.

TO SLEEP, PERCHANCE TO DREAM

When you observed your bedroom, what did you find? Did you find a private, comfortable, quiet, peaceful sanctuary where the primary activity is sleep? Or did you find an entertainment space, a family space, or a room where the clutter gathers? Your answer will describe what sleep researchers call your *sleep hygiene*. How sleep-supportive is your bedroom? How sleep inducing is your bed?

In the past few decades, research into sleep has blossomed, and new findings about the importance of sleep seem to appear every week. Good sleep has been found to increase your cognitive skills, help you integrate knowledge, strengthen your memory, help you heal from injuries, help children grow, help you reset your circadian rhythms and regulate your hormones, and help you regulate your mood. All of these positive benefits of sleep are necessary for your whole and healthy life, but for your empathic skills specifically, the mood and cognition benefits of good sleep are particularly important. Good sleep helps you think clearly, and good sleep helps your emotions stay balanced and well regulated.

In his book *The Promise of Sleep,* pioneering sleep researcher William Dement focuses on the essential benefits of good sleep hygiene so that your sleep architecture (the process of falling into sleep, sleeping, and waking) will be ideal. In his book, Dement asks these questions to help you decipher how sleep smart your lifestyle is:

1. Do you carefully avoid caffeinated drinks in the evening?
2. Do you typically schedule your evening meal at least three hours before you go to bed?
3. Do you have a regular bedtime, which you follow with rare exceptions?
4. Do you have a bedtime ritual, such as a hot bath and perhaps reading a few pages, relaxing, while drowsiness sneaks up on you?
5. Is your bedroom generally a quiet place all night long?
6. Is the temperature of your bedroom just right?
7. Do you think of your bed, particularly the mattress and pillows, as the most comfortable place in the world?
8. Are your bedclothes (blankets, quilts, comforters) exactly right for you?

These questions help reveal how you approach sleep. Is sleep a thing you do because you have to, or do you treat sleep as one of the key contributors to your physical, mental, and emotional health? Is your bedroom primarily sleep-focused, or is it a catchall room? Do you take your sleeping life seriously and practice good sleep hygiene, or is sleep an afterthought for you?

Although Dement doesn't suggest that you have to answer yes to all of his eight questions (we all have different sleep needs), these are questions to ponder seriously. Is your bedroom a sleep-focused room? Is it dark? Dement also asks about the light pollution in your bedroom. His book was published in 1999, but recent studies[42] have suggested a link between light in your bedroom, poor sleep, cognitive depletion, and depression—and that idea has certainly caught on, because you can now buy room-darkening blackout curtains in almost every home store. The relationship between sleep and health is something we're now more aware of, and a tremendous amount of research suggests that sleep is beneficial for your memory, learning, heart health, emotional health, blood pressure, weight control, and endocrine balance.

Everything we're looking at suggests that good sleep is vital for your health, your emotional balance, your cognitive abilities, and your well-being. So my questions are: How sleep-smart is your lifestyle? And how sleep-supportive is your bedroom?

As you observe your bedroom again, look at it in terms of protecting your sleeping body from light, noise, extremes in temperature, and commotion. If there's a lot going on when you're sleeping, your body will still have to be in a receptive mode, and that means you won't have a sensory break or a chance to fully relax at night. That's a problem, but it's a problem you can address with good sleep hygiene. Creating darkness with the use of blackout curtains is pretty easy, but what if some of the light sources emanate from within your bedroom itself? If you have a TV or computer in your bedroom, Dement would tell you to take them out (most sleep researchers suggest that your bedroom should be focused on sleep and sex, and nothing else). But if that's not workable, at the very least, cover your electronics at night so that none of the lights shine on you while you sleep. Also, if you have a glowing clock, turn it to the wall or cover it.

Noise is somewhat harder to deal with, but earplugs can help, as can moving your bed away from windows, doors, or walls that you share with noise sources. However, if one of the noise sources is your snoring mate, know that snoring is often a sign of sleep problems in itself, and it can interfere with sleep for both of you. In his 2012 book *Dreamland: Adventures in the Strange Science of Sleep*, journalist David K. Randall reports that many married couples who sleep separately report feeling better because they no longer have to spend uncomfortable nights struggling with mismatched sleep patterns, snoring, kicking, or blanket-and-pillow requirements that simply don't mesh. Randall reports that there is some loss of intimacy when couples sleep apart—men reported feeling lonelier about nighttime privacy than women did (these were heterosexual couples). Some counselors suggest that partners who sleep apart should set aside time for cuddling, skin-to-skin contact, chatting, and lying down together to reconnect, because even if their shared sleeping times were miserable for both of them, cosleeping can be very important for intimacy and empathy.

Commotion in the bedroom will also be an issue if you have young children (who often love to spend a part of each night in their parents' bed, flailing their limbs around and heating up the entire bedroom) or if you allow your pets to sleep with you. Sleeping with children is an important bonding experience, and every parent has his or her own boundaries around cosleeping. I simply ask you to look at the quality of your sleep. If it's not good, perhaps find a way for your child to sleep in a bed near yours rather than in your bed with you. It's not the same, but it may help both of you get much-needed sleep. It's the same with pets. Some people feel more relaxed with their pets in the bed, even if their sleep is regularly disturbed.

As you consider your sleep needs, know that you can choose to make your bed into a social gathering space, but that will probably reduce the quality of your sleep. If that trade-off is worthwhile for you, then I support you in making it. However, empath to empath, I would ask whether the trade-off is *truly* something you have chosen. If it is—if a bed full of pets or kids or a snoring, kicking mate is necessary for your happiness—then no matter how much sleep you lose, I'm all for it. But if the social nature of your bed is a function of runaway healing and hyperempathy—where you can't say no to the needs of others, and you wouldn't dream of turning off your receptivity, even when you sleep—then I'm going to raise a red flag and ask you to look at this situation very carefully. We'll focus on the often swashbuckling and self-abandoning nature of empathic relationships in the next chapter, but for now, remember that *self-care and concern for others must and should coexist.* Your sleep quality, your privacy, and your comfort have direct effects on all six aspects of your empathic capacities and all six dimensions of your emotional style. Sleep is a magical healing balm, and your bedroom can be a nightly recharging station for your body and your well-being; so please take your sleep hygiene seriously. Thank you!

WHEN HEALTHY EATING GOES WRONG

In the area of self-care, many of us can be pretty unfocused about our relaxation practices, our art practices, our mindfulness practices, our exercise, and our sleep hygiene. This lack of self-care is a fairly common tendency that's not restricted to empaths—pretty much everyone could do a better job with self-care practices. However, in the area of diet and eating behaviors, I've noticed that highly empathic people can sometimes swing in the opposite direction. For many sensitive and hyperempathic people, an overly focused and rigidly ideal dieting behavior called *orthorexia* is almost an occupational hazard.

Your diet and nutrition are vital aspects of your health, your self-care, and your ability to greet each day with energy and focus. Eating a healthy and varied diet is a wonderful way to take care of yourself. However, there's a form of obsessive, super-healthy eating that Dr. Steven Bratman saw among his patients and half-jokingly named *orthorexia nervosa*.[43] Bratman was making a connection between the intense health-food obsessions he saw in his patients and the intense food obsession-and-avoidance behaviors that characterize the eating disorder *anorexia nervosa*.

The idea of orthorexia caught on and is a very helpful concept, especially for sensitive and empathic people who don't currently have many other self-care skills beyond controlling their diets. In the empathy inventory in the first chapter, I included a question about the effects that food and changes in diet have on you, because I notice that highly empathic people are often deeply food sensitive. Foods affect some people very strongly, and it's natural to be careful with and choosy about which foods you eat. But for empaths, food often gets valenced into distinct camps, where some foods are toxic, addictive, and frankly evil, while other foods are exquisite, restorative, and miraculous. As a former orthorexic, I've seen that extreme healthy eating can be a way to create strong boundaries around food that may act as a kind of surrogate protection from problems that don't have anything to do with food at all.

We all use comfort food to soothe ourselves after a rotten day, or when we're lonely, or when we're anxious or angry or bored. Food is delightful, and it can be a surrogate for just about anything—love, happiness, friendship, emotional regulation, relaxation, freedom . . . anything. What I notice in extreme healthy eating is that food can become not just a comfort but also a kind of magical talisman that creates order, structure, and the appearance that you're managing your life and taking top-notch care of yourself. The problem is that orthorexia isn't self-care; it's an obsession. The way you can tell the difference is to look at the rest of your life. If your eating behaviors are standing in for other forms of self-care or if they're taking a tremendous chunk of your time, just stand back and take an empathic look at your kitchen, your medicine cabinet, and your refrigerator.

In your anthropological observation of your kitchen, I asked: Are your cupboards and refrigerator filled with foods you love, or is there more of a mishmash of things you *should* eat but don't actually like? Does your kitchen nourish and support the real lives of the people who live in and gather at the house? If not, why not? When I consult with people, I ask about their eating, their exercise, their sleep, their emotions, their art practice, the quality of their relationships, their work life, and their social justice work. We focus on areas where there is trouble or confusion. In many cases, people report trouble in every area but their eating, which leans into an orthorexic condition that they actually view with pride. It's almost as if they're saying, "The trouble in the rest of my life is clearly an aberration, because look how perfectly I'm eating!"

I don't usually address the eating first, because it's often a lifeline and a surrogate. I address the rest of the situations and help the person develop skills, set boundaries, regulate emotions, find an art practice, and support his or her health with sleep and gentle exercise. When orthorexia is active, I suspect that I'm looking at a life in turmoil. Here in this book, empath to empath, we can talk about this frankly, but I want you to be very careful if you discover orthorexia in yourself or others. If you see extreme healthy eating; magical foods (that change regularly); endless herbs, vitamins, tinctures, potions, remedies, cleansing and purging practices; and unusual healing modalities, please put your anthropologist's hat back on. Look around and identify whether this obsessive dietary behavior is standing in for healthy sleep, self-care, self-love, love from others, healthy relationships, a happy family, meaningful work, safety, empathic skills, healthy exercise, an art practice, Emotional Regulation skills, stability, or hope itself. If orthorexia *is* acting as a surrogate, let the dietary behavior be as you work on those other things.

Sometimes, orthorexia might exist in a person whose life is otherwise healthy. It could be a situation ignited by true food sensitivities that get intensified by peer pressure and the hypnotic quality of compulsive health seeking itself. Once you get into miracle foods, for instance, you could spend years in search of the perfect berry or the perfect herb. Orthorexia is often a socially learned obsessive-compulsive behavior, and it is possible for it to exist in an otherwise healthy life. (I haven't seen that situation yet, but I'm still looking, and I don't want to rule it out.) If you find orthorexia in yourself or others, and you empathically study the conditions that surround it and *don't* find trouble, then fine. Let it be. If you're the orthorexic person, gently focus your Einfühlung capacities on your eating and ask yourself what's going on. If you have an otherwise balanced orthorexic in your life, you can practice grounding and refocusing yourself when your orthorexic friend starts extolling the virtues of special Andean mold tinctures, magic water, and massive quantities of this year's miraculous leafy greens.

I grew up in the 1970s in the alternative healing culture of Northern California, where orthorexia was and still is a required social behavior. A lot of people outside the culture laugh, criticize, or mock the people within it, but as an insider, I can tell you that most of my peers were highly sensitive people, outsiders, and hyperempaths who were never comfortable in the conventional world. In many cases, these unusual people found their first sense of belonging, their first true relief from their symptoms and hypersensitivities, and their first sense of hope in the outsider beliefs and orthorexic extremes of the alternative healing culture. And nowadays, many orthorexic practices have moved into the mainstream, where this year's magical food gets inserted into chips and sodas (acai berry coconut water, anyone?), and people at the grocery store talk casually about fasting and cleansing. The benefits of orthorexia, which give people some sense of control over their bodies and hence their lives, can be valuable for just about anyone.

When I challenged my own orthorexia, I swung to the opposite pole—and I absolutely do not suggest that anyone follow my lead. I burnt all of my health and diet books on a pyre (this is huge; I revere books and don't ever write in them or even bend their pages); I stopped taking all of my vitamins, herbs, and tinctures; and I stopped fretting over the perfection of my meals. And nothing happened. Nothing at all. I didn't feel worse; I didn't feel better—my digestion didn't change, my skin didn't change, my sleep didn't change. Nothing happened. But I did soon become aware of the multiple sources of misery in my life, which I had ingeniously hidden from myself with obsessive decades of extreme health behaviors. Orthorexia is awesome for hiding painful issues from yourself!

So be gentle if you discover orthorexia in yourself or others. It may be a surrogate for any number of currently uncontrollable or seemingly unobtainable (yet vital) aspects of a truly healthy life. It may also be a specific response to hyperempathy, and for people with few empathy-moderating skills, orthorexia may be a lifesaver. When orthorexia is active, gentleness, empathy, and compassion are called for.

DEVELOPING BODILY SOURCES OF STABILITY, COMFORT, AND EMPOWERMENT

I support any practice that helps sensitive and empathic people feel comfortable and empowered, which is why I don't challenge orthorexia in people who consult with me. If it's helping, I say let it help. However, when empathic people are able to ground themselves and focus on their inner lives, on their own emotions, and on their empathic skills, they'll often become able to question any obsessive or compulsive practices they may have. This is great, but because obsessive and compulsive practices exist for a reason, suddenly halting them can be a shock to the system. This is especially true with physical practices that stand in for things like Emotion Regulation, grounding, boundary setting, relaxation, self-love, healthy relationships, meaningful work, or hope. Simply ceasing a practice like this is rarely a good idea, and it can actually make your body feel stripped of its defenses and resources.

Luckily, there's a wonderful and simple practice that I derived from the Somatic Experiencing therapy, created by trauma-healing expert Dr. Peter Levine.[44] This practice can help you find healing resources inside yourself. You can perform this practice anywhere, and you can complete it in less than a minute—or you can extend it into a luxurious practice and take as long as you like. It's called *resourcing*.

|||||||||||||||||||||||||||||||||||||||||||||||||||||||||||||||||||||||||||||||||||||||

HOW TO RESOURCE YOURSELF

At any time of the day or night, no matter where you are or what's going on, there are places in your body that feel strong, stable, capable, and resourceful. Even if you're in pain and even when you're dealing with extreme difficulties, there are strong, calm areas in your body that you can access intentionally. Let's try this now.

Sit quietly. With your eyes open or closed, use your Einfühlung capacity to feel into the words *strong, stable,* and *resourceful.* Locate an area in your body that feels this way right now. This can be a large area, like your abdomen or your thighs, or a small area, like your left foot or the upper part of your right arm. Where does this feeling reside in your body in this moment?

Right now, where do you feel strong, stable, and resourceful? Focus on this area and breathe deeply as you feel into this innate and effortless sense of strength and stability that already exists inside you. Use your intrapersonal skills to empathically interact with this area and with these qualities. They belong to you. They're available to you at any time and in any situation. This is resourcing. It's very simple, and yet it's nearly revolutionary, because very few of us ever learned how to connect to the preexisting strength, calm, and resourcefulness that exist inside our own bodies.

||||||||||||||||||||||||||||||

I learned how to resource myself in only the past few years, and I notice that it's sort of the opposite of how I used to behave around pain and trouble. In the past, the pain and trouble would pull all of my attention, and I'd focus everything on it. There's a way that pain and trouble can sort of dampen or silence the parts of you that feel fine, strong, and resourceful; in the presence of pain and trouble, it's easy to hyperfocus on difficulties and lose your awareness of the fact that you also have sources of comfort inside you that are fully accessible, right now.

With resourcing, you can learn how to pay attention to more than one thing. So, if you have a horrible headache, you use resourcing not to pretend that your headache is gone, but to open up your focus to include the comfort that exists in, for instance, your arm or your knee. Or if you're dealing with intense emotional upheaval, you can focus inside yourself and find an area in your body that feels stable and grounded right now. You aren't repressing the upheaval with this practice; rather, you are opening up your focus to also include the physical sense of stability that exists inside you during upheavals.

When you're in a social situation filled with emotional trouble that you can't read, or if you feel yourself being dragged into hyperempathy or runaway healing behaviors, you can quickly focus inside yourself and locate an area in your body where you feel grounded, resourceful, and stable. The point with resourcing isn't to repress the fact of what you're experiencing. Instead, resourcing helps you connect to another set of facts, which are that more than one thing is going on and that you always have the resources you need to address and deal with whatever confronts you.

I've found in my own life that resourcing is a workable and healthy replacement for compulsive orthorexia. Instead of applying extreme discipline to my eating in order to enforce structure, I simply locate sources of structure within myself. Resourcing is a wonderful self-soothing behavior that can and does coexist with difficulties. It can also help you learn that one condition doesn't erase the other. Resourcing can help you open your focus to *include* trouble and difficulties in the full-bodied narrative of your whole life, rather than hyperfocusing on the troubles and losing your perspective and your skills. Resourcing is a wonderful way to unvalence your inner world.

Resourcing is naturally grounding and focusing, and it helps you set internal boundaries around emotional and social stimuli. With resourcing, you can feel a very strong emotion, *and* you can sense the calm groundedness of, for instance, your calves. Or you can have a headache *and* feel the flexibility, ease, and gracefulness in your right hand. Or, when you're in the presence of someone who's in emotional turmoil, you can experience intense Emotion Contagion, *and* you can connect to internal sources of grounding, peace, and stability. Resourcing gives you ways to clearly identify difficulties *and* clearly identify your extensive internal resources at the exact same time.

Resourcing is also a wonderful practice to use when you're unable to sleep. Instead of struggling to clear your mind or fretting about how you really need to get some sleep, resourcing can help you locate the areas of your body that are tired and ready to sleep. You can feel your bed underneath you and let yourself sink into your mattress. Even if you don't immediately fall into sleep, resourcing is a wonderful way to achieve relaxation during sleepless periods. Resourcing helps you open up your focus, and at the same time, it helps you create a kind of boundary or threshold between your difficulties and your resourcefulness. Resourcing can help you learn to identify multiple internal states and to transition gracefully between them, which will help you create and maintain a healthy terrarium environment for your empathic self, even when you're not at home. Resourcing can help your body become a portable support system for your empathic awareness—an empathic sanctuary that's available wherever you go. The skill of *thresholding* can help you in a similar way.

LEARNING TO CREATE THRESHOLDS

Defining Boundaries, which you learned about in the previous chapter, helps you create a kind of threshold between yourself and others, between your emotions and the emotions of others, and between your ideas, attitudes, and behaviors and those of others. Establishing your boundaries is an imaginal way to create a sense of privacy and sacred space around yourself so that you'll have the internal security, self-awareness, and emotional flexibility you need to empathize skillfully.

In this chapter, we've been expanding that sense of sacred space to include your home and your most intimate surroundings. As we move forward, we'll work to create a sense of boundaries for you in many different environments and situations. For instance, on my website, an actor posed a question about finding ways to access different internal states quickly, and it really got me thinking. This is an excerpt of the question:[45]

> One of my biggest struggles, though, is how to make the transitions between situations in which it is not safe to be my fully emotional and empathic self (e.g., many business environments) and situations in which I am in a safe place (e.g., with a close friend) or in which I need to tap into my emotions fully (e.g., as an actor).

I immediately thought of the *threshold,* which is a clear physical or behavioral boundary between one thing and another. For instance, a physical threshold at a door tells you that you're moving from one space into another, while a behavioral threshold (such as becoming silent before saying a prayer) tells you that you're moving from one behavior to another. Thresholding of one kind or another is an important part of almost any ritual you can name. A threshold tells you that you're entering into a new space (think of ornate church doors), a new attitude (think of removing your shoes when you enter a Buddhist's home), or a new position (think of the aisle in a wedding, where the wedding party walks in a deliberate cadence toward the threshold of the altar). Even when you're not consciously aware of them, thresholds tell some part of you that a change in behavior, demeanor, or position is required.

I view our threshold awareness as an empathic skill, and I'd say that we all have it, to some degree. Therefore, when I need to be in an area where emotional awareness is low to nonexistent, I create thresholds and physical boundaries around myself, as if to say, "Yeah, there's disorder or emotional trouble all around me, but inside my area, there's order, calm, emotional awareness, and freedom." Thresholding is a physical form of setting my boundaries, but it's also a part of my resourcing practice, because it helps me find sources of calm and freedom within myself—especially when those things are not available in the external environment.

So, for instance, if I'm working in a cubicle (for some reason, writers are often put into cubicles in noisy rooms, *sigh),* I might create a threshold by posting funny or beautiful pictures at the entryway, so that anyone coming in will get a sense that they're entering a new area where new behavior is required. I set more thresholds by making sure my cubicle is orderly and appealing. Then I set a behavioral threshold around myself with the respectful and appropriate use of the gifts of anger and shame. (I set clear behavioral boundaries for myself and others without violence.) When I create good thresholds, my area sets boundaries *for* me so that I don't have to work so hard fending off unaware people and their random demands. Through thresholding, my personal workspace seems to tell people that this is not a place for shenanigans or disruptive behavior. Thresholds are awesome.

You can also use thresholding at home if your living space is not yet supportive enough, quiet enough, or spacious enough for your specific needs. Even if you only have a small room in a shared home, you can use your artistic and spatial skills to create beautiful thresholds that announce that yours is a private and unique space and that a new kind of behavior is required within.

FRONT STAGE, BACKSTAGE, AND THRESHOLDING

If you want to see a world where thresholds are central to just about everything, focus your Einfühlung capacities on live theater, which is where professional specialists in empathy and Emotion Contagion (actors!) work. In live theater, there's a distinct separation between backstage (where you can slump over and read a book when you're not in a scene) and front stage (where you have to bring all of your skills, project your voice, engage all parts of your self, and become someone new). When you cross the threshold from backstage to front stage, you're actually supposed to become a new person.

Yet the act of thresholding doesn't stop once you get onstage. There are unseen, but very real, thresholds between upstage and downstage, and between stage left and stage right. There's also a strong threshold between the audience and the front apron of the stage itself. In a traditional theater, there's another threshold, called the *proscenium arch* (usually, the curtains are a part of the proscenium), which delineates the stage proper from the front apron of the stage (where actors might come to break the fourth wall of the stage and intentionally break a threshold to interact with the audience).

Although I don't think it's entirely conscious, the theater world as an entity understands that intensive, multilayered thresholding allows actors to access the amazing behavioral, empathic, emotional, physical, gestural, and subtextual changes they must undergo in their work. I'm going to go out on a limb and suggest that without thresholding, live theater could not have evolved.

As you think about thresholds, remember that they don't have to be large or obvious. For instance, some actors can switch personae simply by changing their clothing or their posture. Many athletes use a portable sort of thresholding, which anthropologists call *fetishes*—for instance, a lucky hat, a lucky pair of shoes, a specific preperformance meal or ritual, and so forth. These things can help a performer cross the threshold and make the behavioral leap from regular life to full-blown performance mode. In a way, these fetishes are make-believe tools, but in another way, they're a potent imaginal signal to the performer inside that person: *Regular life with all its distractions is now fading away, and I must now be intensely focused and at the absolute peak of my abilities.*

Many performers create entire personae that can act as fetishes and thresholds. For instance, the singer Beyoncé, who's a shy and quiet person in her real life, created a performance persona named Sasha Fierce. Sasha, the world-class performer, is a fetish and a threshold for Beyoncé, the person, and she's brilliant. So this imaginal process truly works.

As you travel through the emotional landscape of modern life, play with the idea of thresholds, personae, and fetishes. Skillful and subtle thresholding can help you signal to yourself—and to others—that no matter what's happening on that side of the room or with those people over there, *you* have a private, protected, sacred space in which to feel your emotions, understand the emotions of others, engage in skilled empathy, perform at the top of your game, and access your intrapersonal skills and resources at the same time.

As you become more comfortable and skillful with the six aspects of empathy, you can also use thresholding with your empathic skills so that you can have some privacy in social interactions. If you look back at my scene with Joseph and Iris in Chapter 1, you'll see me thresholding when Iris looks over at me, and you'll see the place where I could have actively entered into their interaction. Right before Iris dropped into a submissive gesture in response to Joseph's shock and anger, I was preparing to stand up and don a more outwardly empathic persona (if things had gone sour). But Joseph and Iris handled everything beautifully, so there was no need for me to move into that persona. Thresholding gives me options.

As you consider the physical forms of thresholding you already use (we all create thresholds in some way), go outside of your home and look empathically and aesthetically at the threshold you've created at your real front door. Does the threshold to your home say everything you want it to say to others? Is it orderly, inviting, and attractive? And most important, does it help people make a clear distinction, as they cross your threshold, between the bustle of the outside world and the empathy-supporting sanctuary of your home? If not, why not?

EVALUATING YOUR EMPATHIC SANCTUARY

Your home can be a getaway and a sanctuary for you—a place where you can live openly as your real self and be surrounded by the uniquely healing influences and practices that refresh, delight, and rejuvenate you. Your home can be the recharging and resourcing station you need if you're going to develop and maintain your emotional awareness and your empathic skills in what can be an emotionally confusing world. Your home can be a specifically nurturing habitat for the specific needs of your unique organism; it can be a threshold between the outside world and your inner sanctuary.

Notice that I qualified each of the sentences in the preceding paragraph with the word *can*. Yes, your home *can* be these things, but if you've never seen yourself as an empathic healing presence in a world that needs you—and if you've never considered that you have the right to be a happy and *healthy* empath—then your home might be kind of a drag right now. It might be yet another thing that's always clamoring for your attention. It might be a place that doesn't honor your unique needs or your unique sensitivities.

If that's true, congratulations. You've discovered trouble in an environment where you actually have control and where you have the right and the power to make changes. When we look at your workplace in Chapter 10, you won't often have that power; so at work, we'll have to make whatever changes we can in an imperfect situation. But in your home? We're golden. In your home, even if you share it with parents, children, or roommates, you can carve out a private space for yourself and start to create a specific terrarium that will meet the needs of your unique empathic self.

If you can't—if your home environment is currently unsupportive and there's not much that you can do—you can still use your empathic mindfulness skills, resourcing skills, and thresholding abilities to create a portable empathic sanctuary inside your own body. You can also reach out for the support of sensitive and empathic relationships—through artistic expression, intellectual pursuits, movement, nature, animals, and other empathic people.

Empathic and social support can be lifelines that will help you transition out of a currently unsupportive environment and into a place where you can live and breathe as your authentic self.

As we move outward from your body, into your home, and into the social world, we'll focus on the quality of your relationships. When they're healthy and supportive, your relationships can facilitate your emotional and empathic development in marvelous ways.

CHAPTER 7

Empathic Friendships, Empathic Love

Relationship as an Empathic Art Form

DEEP INTERACTION IS food for empaths, and no matter where their empathic interests take them, full-bodied interaction is a part of an empath's basic life functioning, and interaction has a central role in the maintenance of an empath's health. Although many hyperempaths (such as our autistic friends) may seem antisocial—in that they primarily interact with animals, nature, art, music, movement practices, science, ideas, computers, or other nonhuman entities—intense Einfühlung interaction is one way that you can tell when you're in the presence of an intensely empathic person.

For those whose intense empathy is focused on human interactions, relationships can be an essential feature of health and well-being or a central contributor to discomfort and empathic exhaustion. As we explore the current condition of your relationships with your friends, your mate, and your family (children are in Chapter 9, and work relationships are in Chapter 10), we'll focus specifically on my six aspects of empathy. We'll also revisit Richard Davidson's six dimensions of emotional style to discover whether you and your loved ones match up well in terms of your current emotional approaches and empathic abilities.

Healthy interactional abilities are essential for healthy relationships and the development of empathy. However, healthy interactions are based on emotional and social awareness and as we've seen, many people have not yet developed strong skills in those areas. As such, many empathic people find themselves doing a lot of heavy emotional lifting in their relationships in order to make those relationships function. This is wonderful in one sense, because it gives empathic people a place to deepen their skills, but it's problematic in another sense because it can lead directly to burnout. If your close relationships ask a lot from you emotionally and empathically—if you're performing continual emotion translation, emotional regulation, and conflict mediation for your loved ones—you may not be able to carve out any empathic downtime for yourself. You may not have the peace and quiet (or the privacy) you need to nurture yourself if you're performing basic emotional and empathic functions for your loved ones. We'll look more deeply at this situation later in this chapter, when we explore the concept of *emotion work*.

Many empaths ignore their needs, their preferences, and their own comfort in their close relationships. They're really good at Perspective Taking, Concern for Others, and Perceptive Engagement, but they're not as good at choosing people who will love, honor, cherish, protect, empathize with, and take good care of them in return. In this chapter, we'll focus on the current empathic condition of your relationships so you can create a social support system for your unique empathic organism.

HOW EMPATHIC ARE YOUR LOVED ONES?

As you develop your own emotional and empathic skills, it's vital for you to have empathic support from your loved ones (or from beloved animals, if people aren't your empathic cup of tea). As we continue to move outward from your intrapersonal awareness to your interpersonal skills, let's observe your friends, family, and mate through the lens of my six aspects of empathy: How well are your loved ones working with their own emotions? And how capable are they of interacting with you empathically?

As you work with your own empathic skills, it's tremendously important to find people who already have empathic skills of their own or who are willing to develop them. As you observe the quality of your close relationships, I'd also like you to think about who is closest to you and why. Who is in your private, innermost empathic circle? Who is in your close friend zone? Who is on the outer boundaries of your personal life? Why are your loved ones where they are? Let's observe your loved ones in regard to my six aspects of empathy.

Emotion Contagion: Can your loved ones read and share your emotions, and can you read and share theirs? If you can't get into sync with a loved one, you may need to back up a bit and start over. (You may want to use the Learning People Intentionally skill in Chapter 8 to home in on each other.) If your loved one isn't comfortable with this skill, you may want to do something together that involves emotion displays—a movie, a concert, or a play—to discover if you share a basic emotional understanding of the world. If you don't, that's a crucial piece of information: this person may not be an empathic companion for you at this time.

Most of us are somewhere in the middle of the Emotion Contagion scale with our loved ones. However, if your loved one shares *all* of your emotions intensely, and vice versa, it can be wonderful or awful, depending on your emotional regulation skills. In situations of mutual contagion, it's really important that both of you get your empathic mindfulness skills under you so that you can begin to individuate, set good boundaries, and develop extensive self-soothing skills. (Please revisit "How to Tell If an Emotion Is Yours or Someone Else's" on page 128.) Hyperempaths can easily burn each other out if they don't have strong emotional hygiene skills, but if they have skills, their relationships can be delightful, deep, and mutually fulfilling.

Empathic Accuracy: Do your loved ones have good emotional vocabularies and emotion recognition abilities? If they do, you're well on your way to a functional relationship. Relationships are built on honest communication, and that comes directly from emotional awareness. If your loved ones understand emotions—yours and theirs—then you have the foundation for healthy communication and empathy right there. The rest is just paperwork.

However, if your loved one is confused by emotions, doesn't want to talk about them, and can't identify them or support them in others (you may not want to hear this, so get ready), he or she probably doesn't belong in an intimate relationship just yet. If your empathically inaccurate and emotionally unaware loved one is a casual friend or distant family member, that's fine. Just be careful that his or her insensitivity doesn't affect you too much, and be sure to use boundary setting and thresholding to reduce your contact time with this person if you need to. With care, you can learn how to gracefully interact with this emotionally unaware person (the communication skills in the next chapter will help).

But if this empathically and emotionally illiterate person is closer to you—or if he or she is your mate—I'm going to raise a red flag. We'll revisit this situation later in this chapter (because choosing emotionally illiterate mates can be an empathic tendency), but emotional awareness and a working emotional vocabulary are prerequisites for intimate relationships. There really isn't a way around this. Certainly your mate can read this book or get counseling and get up to speed emotionally, but until that happens, he or she won't be empathically capable of having a deep and intimate relationship with you. Empathy is first and foremost an emotional skill, and if your loved ones can't (or won't) identify emotions, they won't be able to empathize skillfully.

Emotion Regulation: Are your loved ones able to work with their emotions and regulate their emotional responses? These aren't prevalent skills, so if your loved ones don't have them yet, it's not a big deal. They can work with the skills in this book, or see a counselor, or read Richard Davidson's book and discover their emotional styles so that they can develop vital emotional and cognitive skills. Deficits in emotional regulation skills are not a big deal if your loved ones are willing to work on them. However, it *is* a big deal if your loved ones refuse to regulate their emotions or to learn basic emotional management skills. If these emotionally unregulated people are in your outer circle, you can probably find ways to manage (and restrict) your interactions with them. But if they're in your home or in your bed, then your life as a sensitive and emotionally aware person is going to be pretty rough. You may become a hyperempath simply for survival's sake; you may need to perform extensive Emotion Regulation duties for your loved one. This may involve being hyperaware of his or her emotions, moods, physical condition, body language, and so forth, just so you can stay ahead of the storm. We'll look more closely at difficult relationships like this in a few pages, because they're pretty common for empathic people—and they're clearly an inclination for hyperempaths.

Perspective Taking: Can your loved ones take your perspective or the perspectives of others? Do they have the meta-cognitive and meta-empathic abilities they need to be able to feel their way into and out of the lives and attitudes of others? If so, they'll be able to connect with you and understand you. If not, your relationships might be one-sided.

When we explored Doris Bischof-Köhler's work on the development of Perspective Taking in young children, we saw that self-awareness and self-recognition were actually prerequisites for this skill. If your loved ones cannot take the perspective of others, remember that they may actually need to become more aware of themselves first. Our empathic mindfulness skills will help your loved ones develop better intrapersonal skills, and learning to define their boundaries may be especially supportive in helping them make clearer distinctions between themselves and others. In Chapter 9, I explore the development of empathy in babies, and it might help your loved one to work with the skill of Perspective Taking in the way babies do—through literature, drama, and emotive play. Empathic skills are malleable, and they can be increased at any age if you know which aspects of empathy are underdeveloped.

Concern for Others: Concern for Others is a basic prerequisite for healthy relationships, and its absence is a deal breaker. If your loved one does not have caring concern for you or for others, then this is not a relationship; it's an empathic liability. Remember that this aspect is the trouble spot for antisocial people and people with psychopathic tendencies, which means that people who have problems with Concern for Others can actually endanger your well-being. The only situations in which this deficit is acceptable are in babies, who have not yet developed Concern for Others (remember that babies develop empathy in stages), or in people and animals who are neuro-logically or physically incapable of empathic interactions. In everyone else, Concern for Others is a requirement. If people don't have it, they'll need counseling and social skills training before they can become safe and empath-ically functional partners.

Perceptive Engagement: Can your loved ones read people empathically and act in a way that truly meets the needs of others? Can they read your signals and support you in a way that makes sense to you? If so, these people will nurture you and help you develop and deepen your empathic abilities.

If your loved ones can't quite get this one right (but they want to), then you can help them learn you empathically (see the next chapter), and they can use all of the skills and communication practices in this book to develop their Perceptive Engagement skills. Just make sure that they also develop strong self-care skills so that they don't burn out.

If your loved ones refuse to learn Perceptive Engagement, look back at the five previous aspects of empathy to figure out where their empathic capacities might have broken down. Could they be hyperempathic and burnt out? Do they need help developing Empathic Accuracy? Do they need help with basic Emotion Regulation? Do they need practice with Perspective Taking? All of these situations can be addressed. However, if the problem stems from a basic disregard and lack of Concern for Others, then you simply need to protect yourself; this person is not relationally capable at this time.

YOUR EMOTIONAL STYLE COMPATIBILITY

Richard Davidson's six dimensions of emotional style give you another framework with which to gauge the quality and compatibility levels of your current relationships. Although all of your loved ones will have their own combinations of strengths and challenges in these dimensions, it's important to know where you stand in relation to each one. Does it matter to you if you and your loved ones are very far apart in one or more of these dimensions? Do these differences add to the richness of your relationships, or do they create discord? Your answers will likely be different depending on the closeness of each relationship you examine.

Resilience (from slow to recover to fast to recover): Resilience relates to the speed at which you can move through emotions, situations, and difficulties. Some people can work through difficult emotions and issues in minutes, while others might take weeks or months. Do you have the emotional and empathic room you need to work with a person whose progression through difficulties is different from yours, or do you need someone whose recovery speed is similar? Self-soothing skills, resourcing (from the previous chapter), and Emotion Regulation skills are crucial to resilience and recovery time. Working in these areas may help you and your loved ones increase your skills and your compatibility in this dimension.

Outlook (from negative to positive): We already know about the serious problems that can arise when emotions get valenced into simpleminded categories; similar problems can arise when *people* get valenced. Think about it: When we refer to supposedly positive people, we're generally referring to people who primarily express happiness and joy or who are emotionally calm and relatively unexpressive. When we talk about allegedly negative people, we're often talking about people who simply feel and express a full range of emotions.

Think about people you identify as negative. Usually, it's because they express emotions other than happiness or because they're caught in a feedback loop with emotions like anger, anxiety, or depression. Or perhaps they don't have strong empathic skills, and they trip over your signals and make you feel unimportant or disregarded. When you valence people negatively, you do so, in many cases, because their honest emotional situations and reactions make *you* uncomfortable. This is not an empathic approach.

People can certainly get themselves into a rut and approach every situation with one or two emotions. As I pointed out in Chapter 4, any emotion can be too much. But this problem doesn't reside in the emotions themselves; it resides in the way they're being used and misused. Even happiness can be out of place and too much; it can make you gloss over important problems that other emotions would have alerted you to. So being all the way over to the allegedly positive side of this dimension isn't the go-to position (as Richard Davidson clearly points out in his book).

As you look at the dimension of Outlook, make sure that you're not mistakenly valencing deep and emotional people into the negative category. If you do, you'll disqualify a lot of empaths. Certainly, you want to surround yourself with people who have emotional skills, the capacity to soothe and ground themselves, and the ability to share kindness, laughter, and delight with you. But you may also want to be around people who can understand your deepest emotions and support you when you're feeling them, because they know the territory. Be careful in this emotional style category, and make sure that you're not valencing people.

Social Intuition (from socially intuitive to puzzled): Social Intuition is basically Emotion Contagion combined with Empathic Accuracy and Perspective Taking. It's the crux of emotional and empathic awareness (though without the action component). The question is, How socially intuitive do you need your loved ones to be? Do you prefer to be with people who can read you effortlessly, or is it okay to be with people who need things spelled out? Your answer may change depending on how close your loved ones are to you, and it may change as you begin to develop your own empathic skills. If your loved ones tend to be socially puzzled, you may want to check in and ask yourself if you're doing a lot of *emotion work* for them (see the next section). If you are doing a lot of emotion work, it's important to scale back, because it's healthier in the long run for people to develop their own emotional skills rather than borrowing yours.

If your loved ones have very strong Social Intuition, they may be hyperempaths. If so, make sure that you set good boundaries, and be sure to keep yourself grounded and focused around them. They may need a safe and emotionally hygienic relationship where they can just relax!

Self-awareness (from self-aware to self-opaque): Balanced self-awareness is the foundation for empathic awareness, and this book is focused on helping you develop many different skills in this dimension. However, self-awareness isn't something that most people are encouraged to develop—or if they are, sometimes they can become so self-aware that their inner lives become uncomfortably noisy (the self-soothing skills of grounding and resourcing can really help with this). If your loved ones have been able to develop balance in their inner lives and their intrapersonal skills, consider yourself lucky; you've found a treasure. If they haven't, and you want to invite them into your empathic inner circle, you can share this book or Richard Davidson's book with them, or perhaps find enjoyable Self-awareness activities to share (like art, poetry, tai chi, mindfulness meditations, aikido, yoga, or other inward-focusing practices).

Sensitivity to Context (from tuned in to tuned out): Sensitivity to Context is a key aspect of empathic awareness; it's related to the capacity for Empathic Accuracy, Perspective Taking, and Perceptive Engagement. Joseph and Iris in Chapter 1 (and David and Rosalie in the next chapter) are examples of people who are very tuned into social contexts. Do your loved ones have this capacity to understand different people and situations and to respond empathically? Or are they socially unaware? Do they tend to interact gracefully and engage perceptively, or do they miss obvious changes in social contexts?

If your loved ones are very sensitive to context, are they also sensitive to their own needs, or are they at risk of losing themselves in the needs of others? If they've tuned out, is it because they don't understand social signals, because they're burnt out, or because they can't switch contexts easily? Sensitivity to Context is developed in interactions, and troubles in this dimension can come from many different directions. Empathically speaking, you can help people develop (or calm down) this dimension by engaging with them empathically and respectfully, as well as by supporting them in their development of Empathic Accuracy and Perspective Taking.

Attention (from focused to unfocused): This dimension relates to the capacity to focus and orient yourself to your internal and external surroundings. In our empathic framework, this skill comes from the gifts of fear (and anxiety). Notice that the masking state for fear, *confusion,* helps you take time out from attention; it helps you become unfocused and distracted when you need to be.

How much compatibility do you need in this dimension? Is it okay with you if your loved ones are more or less focused than you are, or does it make you very uncomfortable if you're out of sync with each other? If you're very thrown by differences in focus between you, you may want to check your boundaries, your grounding, and your Emotion Contagion and Emotion Regulation skills. Attention and focus live in the realm of fear, anxiety, and confusion, and if you're not comfortable with these emotions, you might not be able to tolerate differing levels of focus in your loved ones. If this is a regular problem in your relationships, please revisit the Conscious Questioning practice for anxiety on page 135.

INTRODUCING EMOTION WORK

As you examine the empathic and emotional capacities of your loved ones, you may find that you've surrounded yourself with people who need help in one or more areas of emotional functioning, emotional style, or empathic awareness. This is such a common occurrence that there's actually a term for it: *emotion work*.

In her excellent 1983 book, *The Managed Heart: Commercialization of Human Feeling*, sociologist Arlie Hochschild describes what she termed *emotion work*, or the way in which our emotions and emotional states are a part of what we offer (and what is expected from us) in the workplace. In the book, Hochschild gives examples of flight attendants who must not only understand the intricacies of their physical work on airplanes, but must also display an open, welcoming demeanor to passengers. Even when passengers are bad-tempered or overly needy, part of the work of a flight attendant is to continually offer a calm, helpful, accepting face to the public. This is an example of a flight attendant's emotion work.

We'll revisit emotion work in Chapter 10 when we look at the workplace, but I want to speak of it here in terms of the emotion work that some of us do in our relationships. I notice that some empathic people tend to act as external Empathic Accuracy and Emotion Regulation devices for their friends and loved ones. They might be the people others go to for advice, for explanations of the intricacies of the social world, or for help in understanding, managing, and accepting emotions. Some empathic people also help others with Perspective Taking, and they use their own abilities to help people figure out how to empathize with and understand others. If you're the go-to empathy tour guide in your relationships, you're doing a lot of emotion work. Or if you rely heavily on someone to help you figure out the social and emotional world, they're doing emotion work for you.

As you look at the empathic awareness levels in your friends and loved ones, I'd like you to look for trends specifically in the areas of Empathic Accuracy, Emotion Regulation, and Perspective Taking. Do your loved ones tend to be strong in these areas, such that you don't have to help them? Or do they require a lot of emotion work from you in these areas? Or do you rely on them to help you? Do you sense any emotion work discrepancies between you and your loved ones? It's normal to pitch in to help people when they need it—and it's normal to ask for help when you need it—but in the usually hidden world of empathy, emotions, and social interactions, sometimes your emotion-work duties will be deeply unequal.

As you look at the emotional styles of your friends and loved ones, I'd also like you to look for trends in all six dimensions. I asked you about your compatibility in these dimensions because I want you to begin thinking about what a lack of compatibility means for your emotion workload. If there's a large discrepancy between your emotional styles and the styles of your loved ones, how does that discrepancy play out in the area of emotion work? In the area of Resilience, do you or your loved ones do a lot of work to help each other recover (instead of developing internal sources of resilience)? In the area of Outlook, do you or your loved ones work to jolly each other or help each other become more serious? In the area of Social Intuition, do you or your loved ones have to constantly translate the emotional and social world for each other? In the area of Self-awareness, do you or your loved ones work to help each other become more aware of emotions, sensations, and internal realities, or do you work to help each other manage overwhelming interior sensitivities? In the area of Sensitivity to Context, do you or your loved ones work to keep each other tuned in, or do you work to help each other relax and tune out when social contexts are confusing or overwhelming? And in terms of Attention, do you or your loved ones work to keep each other focused and task-oriented, or do you help each other lighten up and learn how to relax?

All of this emotion work is normal and natural, because, empathically speaking, we all work to help each other function (and become more skilled) in the social world. Emotion work is what makes relationships flow smoothly; it's what helps us relate to and support each other; and it's what helps us mature as emotional, social, and empathic beings. However, emotion work *is* work, and if you're not aware of how much emotion work you do (or how much you expect others to do for you), then empathic burnout is a very real possibility—for everyone.

As you empathically observe your relationships, your loved ones, and yourself, take an emotion work inventory and ask yourself: Is this emotion work being acknowledged by anyone? Is it appreciated? Is it even mentioned? Can it become more intentional and conscious? Does it work for everyone? If it doesn't, you can burn your contracts with emotion work tasks that destabilize you, and you can burn your contracts with the emotion work you unconsciously expect from others. Emotion work is an intrinsic aspect of empathic skills and relationship skills, but it tends to be entirely unconscious; it tends to live in the hidden world of nuance, undercurrent, gesture, and unspoken expectations. Burning your contracts with emotion work will help you bring these often-veiled tasks into your conscious awareness, where you can make clear decisions about how you want to approach them now.

We'll explore emotion work more extensively in Chapter 10. In the next chapter, we'll explore a number of empathic communication skills that can bring your emotion work out of the shadows.

IDENTIFYING YOUR INTIMACY ZONES

We're observing emotional styles in your loved ones not to enforce identical approaches to emotions, but to help you understand what conditions and levels of compatibility are important for your unique empathic self. Throughout this book, we've focused on your intrapersonal world so that you can understand yourself more clearly and individuate in healthy ways. In this chapter, we're focusing on your interpersonal world. Who are you in relationship to others? What do you want? What's important to you? What do you need in order to feel loved, safe, respected, and supported? Which kinds of emotion work have you performed, which kinds have you expected from others, and how can you make your emotion work more conscious and intentional?

I'd also like you to put on your anthropologist's hat again and observe the intimacy zones and relationship thresholds you've already built. In terms of your innermost empathic circle, your close friend zone, and the outer boundaries of your intimacy zones, why are people where they are? Who is closest to you, and whom do you hold at arm's length? How do your loved ones' positions relate to their empathic skills and their emotional styles or to the amount of emotion work you do for each other? Why do you bring some of your loved ones close to you, and why do you move others farther away?

As you observe the quality of the love, loyalty, emotional skills, compatibility, and empathic awareness of your loved ones, thank the emotions that help you do this: thank your jealousy and your envy. In their soft, free-flowing states, these two emotions help you focus on what you need from your relationships. They also help you discern the depth of love and care you receive, the loyalty and security you feel, and the quality of your connection to stable sources of love, faithfulness, resources, recognition, and security. If you've created a number of healthy relationships with loving, available, emotionally aware, loyal, and stable people, then your healthy envy and jealousy have been active in your life already—even if you didn't know it until this very second. When these two emotions are free to do their proper work, they'll help you identify and choose safe friends and healthy mates. Thank you, jealousy and envy!

But if these two essential social emotions haven't been able to do their work for some reason, it can be fascinating to discover that you may push skilled empaths away because they don't seem to need you, while you'll pull deeply unskilled and incompatible people (who need full-time empathic heavy lifting and extensive emotion work) into the innermost circle of your life. There's a multimillion-dollar industry devoted to helping you stop doing this, and it's filled with ideas about love addiction, codependence, abuse, and self-abandonment, but let's take a deeper and more empathic look at this self-abandoning tendency, shall we?

SWASHBUCKLERS OF LOVE

We're surrounded by endless fairy tales about love, and we're continually trained to develop deeply unrealistic expectations about what love is supposed to be. Dramas, songs, novels, and art portray love as an ecstatic and life-changing dream, or as a devastating nightmare full of heartbreak and loss. If you sit back and empathically scan the stories we tell each other about love, you'll see grand heroic narratives that don't merely suggest that love can conquer all; they actually *promise* that it can. These stories tell us over and over again that every problem, every condition, and every imaginable failing can be cured with love or by love—and most empaths I know eat these stories for breakfast, lunch, and dinner.

We're all surrounded by these dramatic tales of heroic love. However, for highly empathic people whose central pull is toward relationships and inter-actions, these stories are especially seductive—and especially toxic. They promise that love contains magical healing powers; therefore, many empaths who are under the spell of these heroic love stories tend to seek out peo-ple who are irretrievably incapable of identifying, accepting, or returning love. Instead of taking a healthy jealousy- and envy-supported inventory of the emotional skills, empathic awareness, and interactional abilities of their potential mates, many empaths ingeniously (and usually unconsciously) choose people who have few to none of these capacities.

In their intimate empathic inner circles—in the areas closest to their bod-ies and their hearts—empaths will often choose mates who cannot get into sync with them, don't have emotional skills, and aren't empathically compe-tent. These empaths then throw themselves at these unworkable relationships, as if they're in a game of Red Rover or as if they're on a heroic odyssey through the underworld, filled with impossible tasks and mythical beasts. In the therapy community, people like this are called love addicts, codependents, and victims (and they may well be, if they find people who have no Concern for Others)—but I call them swashbucklers. Swashbucklers of love.

If you think about it, there aren't many places in our lives where heroic and mythic journeys can occur or where brave-hearted warriors and valiant strivers for justice can throw themselves headlong at the deepest troubles of the world. Our homes and families aren't heroic training grounds; they're supposed to be safe places (though they're often chaotic). School is too predictable (unless bullying is allowed, and then it's just grueling) to support a heroic quest. Work is long and often meaningless. Thus, the heroic characters inside us often sit on the sidelines and watch sports or soldiers or dramatic characters or impossibly beautiful, famous, or wealthy people live out mythic and heroic stories for us. There are very few places where everyday people can throw themselves body and soul into intensely meaningful heroes' journeys and fight intrepidly against impossible odds. But there is one heroic training ground that's available to nearly all of us (and it's amazingly seductive to empaths in particular): impossible relationships.

If you choose your mate with heroic and unconsciously swashbuckling ingenuity, you can spend years, decades, and even a lifetime swashbuckling your way through an impossibly heroic journey where more love, patience, dedication, and emotion work than anyone has ever seen will be needed—and you'll provide it, but it still won't be enough. If you manage to get out, people will help you view yourself as a victim and your mate as an abuser; your choices and your sanity will be questioned. But no one will talk about your awesome, heroic, mythic, and swashbuckling love skills. Because these *are* skills—to be able to hold on for dear life no matter how bad things get and to love no matter what happens. These are amazing interpersonal skills. Yes, these amazing skills may turn your life into a living hell if you try to use them with people who have no emotional skills of their own. They may even imperil you if you're with people who have no Concern for Others. But if you're with wonderfully empathic people whose emotional styles are compatible with yours, these skills will lead you into the deepest and most delicious areas of love and communion that you could ever imagine. When you're with people who have the emotional and empathic depth to fully engage with you, to honor you, to match your emotion work task for task, and to protect

THE ART OF EMPATHY

you from your often self-abandoning and heroic empathic nature, then your swashbuckling love will become magnificent.

If you're a swashbuckler of love, bless your heart. Thank you for bringing your wild, boundless, heroic love into this world. You know by now that I'm going to call you out, so I won't even inch my hand toward the red flags you know I'll raise. But let me just say—before I send you back a few pages to observe your impossible relationship(s) in terms of my six aspects of empathy and the six dimensions of emotional style—that I bow to your zany heroism and your majestically out-of-place relationship skills.

Many elements in the dramatic fairy tales you've been told about love are true. Love and healthy relationships are crucial to your survival. You need to love, and you need to be loved. Children need long years of warm, loving, intimate contact or their brains won't develop properly, and the social and emotional well-being of people of all ages is predicated on access to healthy, loving relationships. Love is necessary and vital, and it can change your life for the better—*if* you choose people who can love you back. That's the solution to this dilemma—you have to find people who can hold up their end of the relationship and do their own emotion work. Empathy flourishes in healthy, intimate interactions; therefore, to experience deep and healing empathy in your most intimate relationships, you must be with someone who can love you back.

If you're a swashbuckling runaway love healer, it might take some serious reframing and retraining for you to become able to turn away from emotionally unskilled and empathically unavailable people and focus yourself on people who can love as deeply and as well as you can. You may need to burn contracts continually for a while—with your current relationships, with love as a concept, with your past relationships, with your parents' relationship, with any childhood traumas you may have had, with all of the emotion-work slackers you've known, and with your vision of yourself as a love partner. This is a deep situation, and it's a powerful empathic tendency to offer immense love to people who can't truly receive it, so you'll need to work in a deep, imaginal, empathic, and transformative way to heal this tendency. But as often happens in heroic and mythical journeys, one essential key to this magical transformative process can be found in a very strange and offbeat place.

ARE YOU THE ONE FOR ME?

Yes, my friend, I am suggesting a relationship book (thankfully, you can find it online, so no one will be able to see you buy it). But it's not just any relationship book—this one focuses specifically on your choice of mate, and it's called *Are You the One for Me?* by relationship guru Barbara De Angelis. In this book, De Angelis (who was once a wildly unsafe love swashbuckler herself) writes frankly about the kinds of impediments that will make relationships unworkable, and she teaches you how to identify and avoid them. Four huge impediments in a potential mate—that I never even *considered* before I read her book (twenty years ago)—are (1) a lack of emotional skills, (2) an active addiction, (3) unhealed childhood trauma, and (4) the presence of a toxic ex-mate. I mean, those were practically my mate-selection *imperatives* before I read her book.

De Angelis also puts forth the surprising (to me) idea that it's vital to find a mate who's highly compatible in areas that are crucial to your way of life—for instance, in your approach to finances, child-rearing, politics, spirituality, sexuality, and health care. Basically, she's saying that in your most intimate empathic inner circle, you need to find someone who has relationship skills, is available for the relationship, doesn't require extensive emotion work, understands you completely, supports your decisions, and respects your choices. Otherwise, you may waste your energy fighting over things that aren't going to change, which means you'll probably feel more (rather than less) lonely. For me, this concept of compatibility was life changing, and I had never heard it before, ever. I thought that love was the only thing that mattered, that opposites attract, and that anything could be fixed with increasingly heroic amounts of emotion work and swashbuckling love. But as we all learn sooner or later, incompatibility and emotional incapacity do not lead to healthy relationships.

This book teaches you how to choose relationships wisely, and though De Angelis doesn't frame her work this way at all, she's discovered how to apply the gifts of healthy jealousy and healthy envy *before you commit,* so that your relationship will have the best possible chance for success. She teaches you how to find mates who are secure, emotionally healthy, able to love you, functional, loyal, and as compatible as possible. This compatibility is the key to healthy relationships, but for people who grew up hearing that opposites attract, it can seem frightfully choosy.

So let's move out a bit from your innermost empathic circle and look at friendships that aren't compatible to see what happens there.

In the June 2011 issue of *Scientific American Mind*, science writer Kirsten Weir looked at a number of studies on ambivalent friends, or *frenemies*[46] (friends who let you down, clash with you continually, and just can't get into sync with you). To be clear, frenemies aren't your enemies, and you don't hate them—they're just disappointing and difficult to be around. In numerous studies, frenemies were found to raise blood pressure and increase stress responses and the risk of depression. In addition, frenemies were actually found to be more deleterious to psychological health than actual enemies were.

If you think about this empathically, it makes sense. Frenemies can get close to you, and they can access your personal space and your intimate life, where they can land some pretty solid emotional punches. Enemies, on the other hand, are usually not allowed near you, because when you identify someone as dangerous, you usually keep them the hell away from your inner life. Enemies may throw emotional punches, but you expect them to, and you've created some distance from them; therefore, you can dodge their punches more easily.

The article suggests using behavioral thresholding (the researchers didn't call it that, of course) to contain the amount of damage frenemies can inflict—for instance, don't rely on them to show up on time, don't expect their support, don't be surprised if they make trouble, and so forth. Frenemies are toxic to your emotional and physical health, but if you know that, you can set boundaries around your frenemies and avoid being hit by their emotional shrapnel.

That's a very helpful suggestion, but how can you perform that kind of thresholding in your most intimate relationships? How can you set boundaries and thresholds around a difficult person who lives with you and sleeps in your bed? How can you protect yourself from an incompatible, emotionally incapable, and possibly toxic person who's in your innermost empathic circle?

The answer is, you can't. In your inner circle, you need emotionally awake and empathically attuned people who completely and utterly have your back. Otherwise, you'll be doing emotion work twenty-four hours a day with no breaks. That's a recipe for empathic burnout, and I have a warning: if you're currently in a relationship that's incompatible and based on swashbuckling love, you may want to avoid De Angelis's book, because she's very blunt about your chances for success. If you're on the verge of burnout, but you're still dedicated to your swashbuckling, her book will probably just annoy and offend you. Bless your heart if you need to work in the heroic land of swashbuckling love right now. For many people, relationships can be a place of deep learning—a place to work out childhood traumas, abuse issues, addiction issues, issues with parents and family, and issues of basic self-worth. Some swashbucklers cannot yet identify healthy people or feel any kind of attraction to them, because they're on a quest to find a truly unworkable mate who will require unheard-of amounts of love that, this time, will surely fix everything. As I wrote earlier, this full-bodied heroic swashbuckling can be considered an empathic tendency; we've all done it, and you may need to do it for a while longer. But when you're ready to try something different, and when you're ready to be loved as much as you love others, there's a way out. There are therapists and counselors everywhere; there are abuse and addiction groups everywhere; and your local library is groaning under the weight of books about relationships. There's a lot of help waiting for you when your impossible heroic journey finally comes to an end. Until then, I'll bow to you with reverence, and we'll move on to the next topic.

FINDING EMPATHIC FRIENDS AND COMMUNITY

Intimate relationships are important, but if you're not currently in one, or if yours is fraught with trouble, friendships can be a safe and wonderful way to share and deepen your empathy. Friendships are just as important as intimate relationships, and empathically speaking, they can be less troublesome, because they're not surrounded by quite so much heroic fairy-tale baggage. When I asked you to observe the empathic abilities of your friends and loved ones and to gauge the relative importance of your emotional style compatibility, I didn't do this just to give you a snapshot of your current relationships; I did it to help you identify what's important in your future relationships. When you know what's important to you, you can choose friendships that help you deepen your empathy in safe, healthy, and comfortable ways.

Thankfully, it doesn't seem to matter how many relationships you have; what matters is their quality. The *Scientific American Mind* article about frenemies includes studies that found that the sheer number of friends a person has is not as important as the quality of those friendships; the health-building, empathy-increasing value of friendships depends on the quality of your friendships, and not on their quantity. One excellent friend is all you need. If you can gather more, great; but one will do. Whew!

Personally, I'm working on creating quality time with people in my own community in simple, inexpensive ways. I've also been talking to people about how they fit socializing into their busy lives. Many report that they've created ways to do chores and socialize at the same time (my anxiety finds this idea delightful!). It feels sort of silly to be writing this down, but the loss of social time has affected all of us, and it's important that we address it—not just for our own health, but also for the empathic health of our loved ones and our communities.

Here are some simple ways to increase the face-to-face interactions that will support social, emotional, and empathic health for you and your friends: card and game nights, cooking together, trading chore days at each other's houses, meeting at the local farmer's market, hiking and biking together, taking exercise classes together, washing and vacuuming your cars together, creating arts and crafts parties, singing together, changing the oil in your cars together, trading help on your building projects, cleaning out the gutters at your homes, helping each other organize garages or closets, watching your favorite shows at each other's homes, carpooling to the grocery store, inviting people to create a garden in your yard, and sharing the produce. You get the idea.

In our overly busy modern world, we've become fairly isolated, and we've lost touch with the barn-raising, quilting-bee socializing that kept our hardworking ancestors connected to each other. When I look at our online world—at all the wikis, websites, and blogs that contain all of the knowledge (and wackiness and dysfunction) of humankind—I see that our energetic community-building skills are still very active, but in many cases, they've moved online, where interaction isn't quite as supportive as it might be.

Empathy is developed in interactions, and research is continually suggesting that face-to-face interactions trump online interactions. A great deal of research has been focused on the often unempathic and emotionally explosive behaviors we see online, and of all the possible factors (for instance, anonymity, reaction speed leading to emotional dysregulation, age and maturity levels in the online community, and isolation), it's looking as if one of the most destructive factors is a lack of eye contact.[47] When people can't see each other and read each other's signals empathically, many can't regulate their emotional responses, and they tend to fly off the handle. Eye contact and real-world interactions can be grounding, civilizing, emotionally regulating, and empathy building.

Live, real-world interactions can also teach you how to read all of the rich emotions, gestures, subtexts, nuances, expressions, and pauses that help you truly understand yourself and others. Real-life interactions are food for your empathic soul. Sadly, we tend not to have much time to get together these days, and if we do, it's usually around something that costs money, like dinner, a movie, or a concert. However, since online interactions can actually impede social skills, Emotion Regulation abilities, and empathy in vulnerable people, we must create as many opportunities for real face-to-face interactions as we can. Empathy is a malleable and multifaceted skill that can be increased at any age with healthy interactions—but it can also be decreased at any age if you're not getting the right food for your empathic soul.

In the next chapter, we'll look at some specific communication skills you can use to increase your empathic skills, help make your emotion work more conscious, and revive empathy when your relationships need support.

CHAPTER 8

Empathic Communication

Getting into Sync with Others

EMPATHY IS DEVELOPED in interactions—in infancy, in childhood, during your teen years, and right now. The quality of your interactions has a large impact on your empathic capacities. If you have shallow relationships or inattentive friends and family members, if your relationships are not fulfilling or deep enough, or if you can't find empathic people to interact with, then your empathic abilities may languish. On the other hand, if your relationships are deep and satisfying, if you have family members and friends who can meet you where you are and understand you, if your emotional styles are compatible, if your emotion workloads are equal, and if you have other healthy empaths in your life, then your empathic abilities will most likely flourish. Empathy is developed in interactions, and you can increase and deepen your empathic abilities at any point in your life.

As we move outward in support of your empathic skills, from your inner life to your home and now into your relationships, we'll add specific empathic communication skills that you can use right now to change the quality and tenor of your existing relationships. But first, let's look at one idea of an empathic conversation between a couple who've been together for a while:

> **Rosalie** (frustrated and dejected): It happened *again*. My boss is a jerk, and everything I do is wrong. I'm so tired of this. I'm afraid that I'm gonna get fired, but I'm even more afraid that I'll stay and get sucked into the vortex.
>
> **David** (understanding): I hear you saying that you're sad because your boss is being hard on you, and that you're tired and worried

that you might lose your job. But I also hear you saying that staying put is frightening.

Rosalie (sarcastic): Is there an echo in here?

David is engaging in a kind of pseudoempathy that is currently called mirroring but that was once called reflective listening. My mother told me that she tried reflective listening more than forty years ago on my little sister and me when we were fighting (we were three and four at the time), and that we both got very quiet and rolled our eyes at each other, as if to say, "Our poor mother has developed a brain-wasting disease." Mom said that it stopped our fight very effectively, however, and that we ran outside to play (because she had freaked us out!).

My problem with reflective listening and other allegedly empathy-raising techniques is that they're very obvious *techniques,* and I could see through them even as a toddler. I still can, though I have more patience today than I did then. I realize that people who use mirroring are trying very hard to get into sync with me, and I have empathy for that. But when I talk to you, and especially when I talk to you about trouble, I don't want you to rephrase what I said. I *know* what I said, and I know how I feel. I'm talking to you because I want support or input or help or humor or love or commiseration or a crankfest or a complaining partner. If I'm talking to you when I'm in trouble, it means that I already trust you and believe in you. I already know that you can hear me. You don't need to parrot me to empathize with me. You need to *interact*—honestly, authentically, and as yourself. When I talk to you, I don't want to talk to a mirror; I don't want to see myself. I want to see *you.*

Mirroring and reflective listening can be helpful if you're working with people who aren't very self-aware, because your skillful mirroring may help them become more precise about their own emotions. If you say to someone, "I hear that you're feeling a little bit angry and cheated by that," but the person thought she was being funny, it could really help her begin to become more accurate about her actual emotions, or about the way her emotions are coming across to others. Or if your Empathic Accuracy skills are currently low, learning how to mirror and reflect other people's emotions will help you begin to develop better emotion recognition skills. If you can rephrase what you heard and mirror back the gist of what people say (that is, you don't repeat their words verbatim; instead, you tell them what you think they're feeling, without placing value judgments on their emotions), then you can become more receptive to and precise about the emotional signals people send.

Reflective listening can also be helpful if your relationships suddenly get tangled up and conflicted. It's great to be able to say, "Wait, I heard you say that you felt uncomfortable at my dad's house, so I made other plans!" And then your partner might answer, "Oh, heck, I meant that I didn't want to go there *last Labor Day*, because I don't like watching the game. But now I miss your dad!" And then your communication can move forward because you now understand each other. But using reflective listening for everything? Yeesh, it's exhausting! So let's look at David and Rosalie again, in a situation where David can be a real person with his own opinions, emotions, and truly empathic interactional style:

Rosalie (frustrated and dejected): It happened *again*. My boss is a jerk, and everything I do is wrong. I'm so tired of this. I'm afraid that I'm gonna get fired, but I'm even more afraid that I'll stay and get sucked into the vortex.

David (understanding): Oh, man, I want to listen to you, but I'm really angry with your boss right now.

Rosalie: Thanks. (sighing) I'm angry with myself, for letting this happen.

David: What the … ? You don't make him act like a jerk.

Rosalie: I just keep going over things in my mind: How can I do better? How can I make things work?

David: (softly): Why is it up to you?

Rosalie (angry, explosive): Because! (realizing how ridiculous that sounds, and laughing a bit, and then becoming sad, silent) Because . . . he's just like my dad.

David: Ouch.

Rosalie (quieter): Yeah.

David: (silent, leaving space)

Rosalie (breathing heavily, like a sigh): Yeah.

David (quiet, working with the rhythm of her breathing): What do you need?

Rosalie (final, clear, but very low energy): I need to quit.

David (silent, but very watchful because he doesn't want her to think he's disapproving; he leans in toward her and says softly): Yeah.

Rosalie (crying now): I can't fix it, and I never could.

David (softly): No.

Rosalie (angry): But why do I have to leave and lose my job, and why did I have to lose my childhood—when it's other people's damn problem? Why am I the one who gets hurt but still keeps coming back?

David (smiling gently): Yeah, why?

Rosalie (sighing, more focused, lifting her head): Okay, dusting off the résumé. Do I give notice first or wait? (deciding) I wait. Screw 'em—I can always give notice, but I'm not gonna hurt myself just to make a point. They can pay me until I'm good and ready to leave.

David (laughing softly)

Rosalie (sighing, relieved): Thanks, whew!

What David and Rosalie did was deeply empathic, but David didn't follow any rules or procedures or steps. He kept Rosalie company and let her set the pace. He stood up for her, questioned her, laughed with her, and used silence effectively—but most important, he listened; paid attention to her numerous, shifting emotions; and engaged empathically. This was an *interaction*, not a technique. (We'll revisit this interaction later in this chapter.)

I do have procedures and techniques for specific situations when communication breaks down or when you need to tune in with others. However, it's really important to remember that empathy is a skill you already possess and that you can just relax and hang out with people, listen to them, make mistakes (and apologize if you do), and be empathic simply because you already are.

IF YOU DON'T HAVE ACCESS TO EMPATHIC PEOPLE

Empathy is developed in interactions, but those interactions don't have to be with other humans. If you're isolated, or if you realized in the previous chapter that you're surrounded by people who don't understand you and you're currently stuck in unfulfilling relationships, you can still develop your empathic skills. You can use your Einfühlung capacity to interact with art, literature, nature, science, ideas, drama, dance, meditation, movement, poetry, mindfulness practices, computer activities, hobbies, science, or mathematics. You can still interact even if your relationships with other people aren't currently workable. And, of course, animals are almost always waiting for someone to interact lovingly with them.

If your current relationships with other humans are troubling, you may find that they'll shift or improve if you can simply change the way you approach communication. Remember that most of your empathic work and emotion work occurs in the hidden and rather subtle world of nuance, undercurrent, gesture, and intention. If you can lean into this world empathically and make small shifts in your approach to others, you can often build a better ground for empathy between you.

LEARNING TO IDENTIFY EMOTIONS IN OTHERS

A great deal of the trouble I see in communication springs from incorrect assumptions about what people feel and what they mean—it's a problem of Perspective Taking. However, this problem actually tracks back to poor Empathic Accuracy. Think about it: if you're inaccurate about the emotions and intentions of others (or yourself), your ability to empathize pretty much stops right there, *bam.* You won't be able to understand the person's perspective, because you're not even in the right emotional ballpark. Skillful Perspective Taking springs from your ability to accurately identify what's going on.

Incorrect emotional assumptions can also track to problems in Emotion Regulation, and I notice that people will often lose their empathic abilities in the presence of emotions they themselves don't know how to deal with (anger and anxiety are two that come to mind). All of the empathic skills and practices you've learned so far will help you develop better Emotion Regulation skills. If you identify specific emotions that trip you up, then that's awesome. That's something you can work with intrapersonally so that you can develop better relationships with your own emotions and open up your emotional range to accept those emotions in others.

As you work with troubling emotions in yourself, remember to resource yourself when other people are feeling them (or repressing them). Yes, those emotions may be problematic for you right now, but remember your resourcing practice (page 155) and remind yourself that there are places in your body that are grounded, focused, calm, and resourceful. *Both* things are true—the problem is currently true, *and* you have the internal resources you need to support yourself through difficult times. Both things are true.

Emotion Regulation skills are intrapersonal, and this book gives you many ways to work with and improve them. Your accuracy skills, however, develop in interactions; you learn by interacting, by asking, by listening, and by making mistakes. Some people make your attempts at Empathic Accuracy very simple, because they're open books emotionally—they're easy to read, and what you see is what you get. But in many cases, you actually have to learn people in the way you have to learn a new city or in the way you have to learn how to ride a new horse or drive a new car. I mean, the people you know very well—the people who really feel you and understand you and whose subtlest, secret, wordless glances can send you into fits of laughter—you almost certainly had to learn them, and they almost certainly had to learn you. Although we aren't aware of this learning, the act of learning to read people empathically is intentional (though usually nonverbal) work that occurs in that secret interactional world I referred to in the first chapter—where gestures, body language, subtext, nuance, relational behaviors, and undercurrent are the curriculum. Let's approach this curriculum more deliberately.

LEARNING PEOPLE INTENTIONALLY

Let me be clear before we start: This next empathic technique may have a very short shelf life, and you can't use it with everyone. You'll need to let people know you're using it, and you'll need to let them know why, because this process breaks some privacy boundaries. It's not abusive—I'm not going to teach you to hurt people—but it intimately accesses people's private, peripersonal space, so you have to be sensitive about when and where you use it.

In Chapter 1, I wrote about the ways that body language and facial expressions can give you an entrée into the emotional lives of others, and I gave you some direct examples of how to use body language and facial expressions to open conversations about empathy and emotions. Let's look at those again: "When you curve your body downward and sigh out loud, it seems to me that you're feeling discouraged, or maybe really tired, or both. Is that what's going on?" or "When you use short sentences and don't look at me when you speak to me, it seems that you're feeling impatient and frustrated with me. Is that true?"

In this technique, you use another person's body language to open a conversation and find out whether what you're picking up is true. The trick to this is to keep your empathic mitts off of their behavior until the latter part of the sentence, where you ask about your impressions in the form of a question. So you don't say: "Your gloomy face and your surrendering arm movements tell me that you've given up," because that's not a question, and you've already imposed your own emotions onto the person's body. That violates all kinds of boundaries, and besides, you may be wrong. Remember that body language isn't universal, it's not even fully shared among members of the same family.

That supposedly gloomy face might actually be a tired face, and those arms might be hanging uncomfortably off of sore shoulders—they may have nothing whatsoever to do with surrendering. Body language, gestures, and facial expressions can be an entrée into Empathic Accuracy, but there's really no way for people to retain their boundaries, their emotional realities, or their dignity when you tell them authoritatively what their bodies are doing rather than *learning* what their gestures and expressions mean for them.

In order to respect the boundaries, voice, standpoint, and self-image of others, you let them know that you're working to develop your empathic skills, and ask them whether they're willing to mentor you. If so, let them know about this three-step process, because they may want to try it on you when you're done:

||||||||||||||||||||||||||||||||||||||||||||||||||||||||||||||||||

HOW TO LEARN PEOPLE

1. Take note of two (or three, at the very most) expressions, postures, or gestures, and describe them without any emotional or intentional content whatsoever: So you would say, "When you raise your eyebrows," and not "when you look surprised." Or "When you move quickly," instead of "when you're anxious." Or "When you look down and to the right," instead of "when you're avoiding me." You want to describe the behavior precisely so that the person knows exactly what you're talking about; however, you don't want to impose your own emotions onto his or her body.

2. After you've described these gestures, stances, movements, or expressions without bias, you take responsibility for the emotions you're feeling in response to what you're seeing, and you explain them as clearly as you can. I like to use the word *seems:* "When you look upward and toward the left when I'm talking, it *seems* to me that you want to get away from the conversation. It *seems* like you're feeling frustrated." The word *seems* is boundary respecting in that it qualifies my impressions and makes room for the possibility that I could be mistaken.

3. After you've described the expressions, postures, or gestures without bias and then stated your empathic impressions (as possibilities, *not* as certainties), you follow up with a question

that invites the other person to confirm or correct your impressions. "Is that what's going on?" or "Did I pick that up correctly?" or "Is that how you're feeling?"

||||||||||||||||||||||||||||||

That's it—that's the magic, which isn't really magic at all. This three-step process is meant to help you learn other people. It's an interaction, and it's an interpersonal skill, which means that the other people not only have a say, but also that they get to be the final arbiter of what's going on with their own bodies and emotions. This technique teaches you to use your soft, curiosity-level fear instincts to help you read and report what you see in another. It also uses your soft, self-respecting anger and your soft, other-protecting shame to help you state your impressions without breaking the boundaries of another. When you use this process, the other person can confirm or correct your impressions—and he or she may learn surprising new information about what a certain posture, expression, or gesture might say to another person. In this interactional process, the goal is to develop stronger Empathic Accuracy, but the journey also involves making your emotion work conscious and becoming more deeply connected to the actual lives of other people. Bonus!

This technique may have a short shelf life, because it may only take three to five repetitions before you can tell whether you have a good sense of another person. In some cases, especially with people whose neurology or cultural background is different from yours (for instance, in people with ADHD, depressive conditions, very high intelligence, autism, developmental delays, Tourette's, sensory-processing differences, high or low empathy, or in people from other cultures and linguistic traditions), you may have to use this process for a longer period as you calibrate your empathic skills and learn these new people properly. But in most instances, this technique is more of an icebreaker than anything else. You can also use it in special cases when you and another person lose your empathic bond with each other. But remember, this process is meant as an entrée and not as a main course. The main course is not technique based; it's just being real with people and real with yourself. But you have to develop clear Empathic Accuracy to be able to get to that real place.

This next skill[48] can help you arrive at that real place, because it actually invites people to share one of your empathic mindfulness skills with you.

CONSCIOUS COMPLAINING WITH A PARTNER

You learned Conscious Complaining as a solitary mindfulness skill, but you can also use it as an intentional relationship practice. Conscious Complaining with a partner is an excellent way to de-steam without blowing up, and it can help you create stronger and more honest relationships. I modified this partner-complaining practice from Barbara Sher's *Wishcraft: How to Get What You Really Want.* Sher writes about how important it is for you to complain openly (in a safe and healthy practice), rather than shutting down and losing your emotional honesty and integrity. It's an excellent book.

|||||||||||||||||||||||||||||||||||||||||||||||||||||||||||||||||||||||||||||||||||||||||||||||||||||||||||||||||||||||||

HOW TO CONSCIOUSLY COMPLAIN TOGETHER

In this two-person practice (which you can quickly teach to a loved one), one of you will take the position of the listener, while the other will complain consciously. Then you'll trade places. Let's make you the first complainer: You can start with some conscious recognition that the complaining needs to happen. In our family, we say, "I don't need you to fix me. I just need to complain." Then, you're allowed to bring up whatever's stuck in your craw— "Things are just rotten, this situation is bothering me, and things are too hard."

When you're complaining, make sure that you name out loud any emotion you feel. You may want to have your "Emotional Vocabulary List" (in the Appendix) so you can be very articulate about how annoyed, disappointed, uneasy, enraged, distrustful, or humiliated you feel. Learning to feel and name your emotions will help you become emotionally fluent and will increase your accuracy—but more than that, the act of naming your emotions can help you calm yourself and organize all of the action-requiring programs you have running. So complaining consciously with a partner is also an Emotion Regulation practice.

Your partner's job is to support your complaining with helpful and upbeat *yeahs!* and *uh-huhs!*—no advice, no suggestions, just enthusiastic support. Your partner's job is to create a safe haven for your complaining, which immediately makes it less toxic. Your partner will also get an excellent gift—a chance to practice his or her emotion work out in the open, instead of being an unhappy receptacle for the *unconscious* complaining of other people. Everybody gets a healing in this practice.

An important note: There's a rule in partner complaining—the complainer can't complain about the *listener,* because that wouldn't be fair. If someone is willing to provide support for your complaining, then complaining about him or her would be cruel; it would be like taking a hostage. If there's conflict in your relationship, this is not the right tool to use. This complaining practice is suitable when the problems are *outside* the relationship of the listener and the complainer (I offer two practices for trouble inside the relationship later in this chapter).

When you feel done complaining, you end your turn with gratitude: "Thanks! That's been crushing me," or "I didn't realize I was carrying that much stuff around. Thanks!" Then you get to trade positions: the listener now gets to complain consciously, while you listen and provide support and perform openly acknowledged emotion work. When you're both done, the session is over.

|||||||||||||||||||||||||||

You'll be amazed at how productive (and funny) this complaining technique is. We're all taught to be positive and peppy at all times, which means we have to repress most of our emotions, reduce our Empathic Accuracy, and lose our Emotion Regulation skills. Often, this repression will kick our emotions into repetitive feedback loops, but Conscious Complaining lets us tell the truth and restore our flow. Conscious Complaining is a great all-around stress reliever, but when you can complain with a partner, there's a special set of additional benefits:

1. It teaches you to reach out (instead of isolating yourself) in a safe, boundary-respecting way when you're in turmoil.
2. It teaches you and your complaining partner new ways to function around pain and trouble.
3. It gives both of you the opportunity for your emotion work to be requested, respected, and performed intentionally.

See if you can find more than one complaining partner to share this practice with. If there's someone you regularly call when you're tense and cranky, they'll probably jump at the chance to perform emotion work in a more intentional way. And if there's someone who regularly complains to you, you'll probably love the chance to bring your own emotion work out of the shadows and create better reciprocity in your relationship.

Consciously complaining with your friends is a wonderful way to clear the air and be emotionally honest in the presence of another, and it sets healthy behavioral boundaries around a behavior that's usually unconscious and unrewarding. In this practice, each of you takes responsibility for learning how to name and listen to your own emotions, which will add immeasurably to your emotional skills.

Now, let's look at the emotions themselves and explore how to support people empathically—not by doing emotional heavy lifting for them, but by simply listening to their emotions and helping them connect to their own emotional wisdom.

EMOTIONS AS A PREREQUISITE TO TRULY EMPATHIC COMMUNICATION

Since empathy is, first and foremost, an emotional skill, I focused a lot of attention on emotions in the early part of this book. Here, in the communication chapter, let's bring the emotions back and give you some ideas about how to support people and get into empathic communication with them. You can do this by remembering that emotions are action-requiring neurological programs.

As you recall, anger and shame help you set boundaries, fear helps you orient and focus yourself, sadness helps you let go of things that don't work anyway, and so forth. And, of course, emotions do these things for other people as well. As the neuroscientist Antonio Damasio points out, emotions are evolutionarily ancient and reliably similar, such that fear is going to behave similarly in me, in you, in a person from Germany or Mali, in a wild horse, or in a housecat. Fear will require the same action-completion processes in every case. Emotions connect us to every living being, and I spent the previous chapters unvalencing, undividing, undemonizing, unglorifying, and demystifying emotions because they're the key to truly understanding others—across differences, across borders, across languages, and across species. Emotions are universal, reliable, and profoundly informative.

With that in mind, let's look at each emotion in terms of how you can empathically support people in taking the actions their emotions require. As we explore emotions, I'll sometimes refer to the second conversation between Rosalie and David (page 185), in which he was able to be a real person and not merely a mirror.

ANGER: *The Honorable Sentry*

Anger arises to address challenges to the voice, standpoint, position, interpersonal boundaries, or self-image of another. When anger is present, you can support people by simply asking them what they need. Helping people find their voice is a great way to help them restore their boundaries. David did this with Rosalie, and then he stayed quiet while she found her own solutions and reset her own boundaries. Notice that he acknowledged his own anger at the beginning of the conversation, which helped him intrapersonally, to identify his own state, and interpersonally, to help Rosalie know that anger was okay.

APATHY AND BOREDOM: *The Mask for Anger*

Apathy arises when it's not safe or correct for people to be openly angry, and it can give people a needed time-out. I don't generally address apathy openly, because it's a protective mask. Instead, I might express my own anger in the way David did—in a responsible and nonviolent way—to let the person know that anger is welcome between us. If nothing shifts, I back away and talk casually about other topics, or I end the interaction. The masking emotions (apathy and confusion) are ingeniously protective, and people have to decide to unmask on their own—I don't push.

GUILT AND SHAME: *Restoring Integrity*

Shame arises to help people amend or atone for their problematic behaviors. However, it can be a very tricky emotion if the shame originated in the toxic and shaming messages of controlling parents, teachers, or authority figures. If people express appropriate shame about a thing they actually did and for which they have the power to atone, then you can help them find self-respecting ways to make amends or apologize. But if the shame is inauthentic or toxic, you can gently question it, as David did when Rosalie was taking all of the responsibility for her terrible workplace. You have to be very gentle when you question toxic shame, because people are already in a world of pain. But those same people can often borrow the concern in your question and turn it toward themselves to ask, "Yeah, why do I believe that?" However, if people in your life are really tormented by toxic shame, give them this book and teach them about Burning Contracts. Shame is a vital emotion, but when it's inauthentic or toxic, it can easily be too much.

HATRED: *The Profound Mirror*

Hatred is a very powerful emotion that arises in response to behaviors people cannot accept in themselves and demonize in others. It's a condition of pretty extreme boundary impairment, and it may be that the person just needs to vent in order to reclaim his or her voice and standpoint, calm down, and get grounded again. The problem with listening to this hatred, though, is that it can break your boundaries and include you in a dishonoring practice that may activate your own shame (let's hope). Hatred can be a doozy, so I have some practices for it: certainly, Burning Contracts with the hated person is necessary, and in Chapter 10, you'll learn a skill called Ethical Empathic Gossip, which can be very healing because it sets boundaries around the venting and requires behavioral change once the venting is over. I've also included a list of my favorite books on shadow work in Further Resources; they'll help you work with hatred honorably and uncover the absolute genius inside it.

FEAR: *Intuition and Action*

Fear arises to help people orient to change, novelty, or possible physical hazards. When people around me are afraid, I'll often simply ask, "What are you sensing?" because fear is about instincts and intuition. If people simply pay attention to their fear, they'll usually be able to connect with their instincts and figure out what's going on.

WORRY AND ANXIETY: *Focus and Completion*

Worry and anxiety arise to help people organize, plan for, and complete upcoming tasks, especially if they're currently procrastinating. Anxiety is about the future, so it can be hard to stay grounded and focused when it's active. You can help by suggesting or implementing tangible plans, such as creating a numbered list, a stack of papers, or a pile of whatever item needs attention. These real-world activities will help people figure out what *really* needs to get done. Writing out anxieties is especially healing, because it's an emotion-specific action that can reduce the activation of the anxiety so that people can find their focus and their resources again. Of course, Conscious Questioning (see page 135) helps as well, if people are open to it.

CONFUSION: *The Mask for Fear*

Confusion is a masking state for fear and anxiety that arises when people are overwhelmed by change, novelty, or too much input and too many tasks. Confusion can be a lovely vacation from overwhelm, but if it goes on for too long, people can lose their grounding and their focus. The question for confusion is, "What's your intention?" Sometimes people can lift the mask of confusion if you can help them articulate their real needs and preferences again. David did this throughout his conversation with Rosalie.

JEALOUSY: *Relational Radar*

Jealousy arises when people sense challenges that may destabilize their connection to love, mate retention, or loyalty. These challenges may come from external sources, from an internal lack of self-worth, or both. Jealousy (and envy) contains some of the intuitive focusing gifts of fear and some of the boundary-setting gifts of anger. You can help by asking people what they're sensing (to access their instincts) and what they need (to help them reconnect to their voice and standpoint). Remember, though, that jealousy is one of the most intensely valenced emotions there is, and people may feel shame (or anger, fear, etc.) about the fact that they feel this essential social emotion. Your understanding of clustered emotions, as well as your gentleness and patience, may be required.

ENVY: *Interactional Radar*

Envy arises when people sense challenges that may destabilize their connection to material security, resources, or recognition. These challenges may come from external sources, from an internal lack of self-preservation abilities, or both. Envy (like jealousy) contains some of the intuitive focusing gifts of fear and some of the boundary-setting gifts of anger. You can help by asking people what they're sensing (to access their instincts) and what they need (to help them reconnect to their voice and standpoint). A helpful question to ask an envious person is, "What would be fair?" Envy, like jealousy, is a heavily valenced emotion, and many people react to it as if it's a character flaw rather than an essential part of their social skills. So be on the lookout for clustered emotions. Your willingness to engage and your gentleness can help people uncover the genius in their envy.

PANIC AND TERROR: *Frozen Fire*

Panic and terror arise when a person's physical life is directly and immediately threatened, and the choices are to fight, flee, or freeze. In the moment, there's very little that you need to do beyond helping people pay attention and react in whatever way feels right. However, if the panic and terror track back to an earlier trauma, you can help people get to competent help (see the Trauma Healing listings in Further Resources).

SADNESS: *The Water Bearer*

Sadness arises when it's time for people to let go of something that isn't working anyway. If people let go, they can relax; but if they won't let go, they might become very tense. If people try to hold on tightly to something that doesn't work, you may see anger jump out in front of the sadness. The question "What do you need?" will often help people find their voice again and identify what isn't working. Sadness is a very softening and interior emotion, so it's important that you set good boundaries and don't push or prod at people; gentleness is called for. When Rosalie got to her sadness, David remained very quiet.

GRIEF: *The Deep River of the Soul*

Grief arises when people lose something irretrievably or when someone has died. Grief and sadness are intimately related, but with sadness, people still have a choice about letting go. Grief arises when there's no choice—the loss or death has already occurred, and it's time to mourn and grieve. When people are grieving, you can expect to see multiple emotions arising in clusters or shifting continually. Everyone grieves differently, at different paces, and with different clusters of emotions. If you can simply be present and provide some kind of thresholding or private space for people who are grieving, you can support them in this deep form of emotion work.

SITUATIONAL DEPRESSION: *Ingenious Stagnation*

Situational depression is a specific form of depression that arises when there's an already-dysfunctional situation occurring in people's lives. This situation could be located in any part of a person's interior or exterior life, and it can usually be addressed through changes to lifestyle or behavior. You can help people identify this dysfunction by simply listening as they speak. (I'll introduce a very supportive three-step process later in this chapter that will help you do that.) Be aware, however: If the depression is cyclical or if it doesn't respond to the healing changes people make, please help them seek psychological or medical intervention. Depressions that last too long are not good for people's emotional, empathic, social, or neurological health, so it's vital to take recurring depression seriously and address it responsibly.

HAPPINESS: *Anticipation and Possibility*

Happiness arises to help people look forward to the future with hope and delight. This playful emotion is one of the few that we're allowed to feel comfortable with, so it's not likely that you'll need to do much beyond share happiness when it arises. Yay! You may notice, however, that some people downplay happiness as if it were childish or unserious to feel happy. In these cases, there may be some situational depression that is trying to point to situations that are regularly troubling or that reliably get in the way of feeling happiness. When people valence happiness negatively, they may need to observe their entire emotional realm (and the training they received about happiness in childhood) to find out what's going on.

CONTENTMENT: *Pleasure and Appreciation*

Contentment arises to help people feel pride and satisfaction about a job well done. This emotion can be very tricky, because so many people have an uncomfortable relationship with self-respect and pride. Some people feel that pride and contentment are boastful and shameful, which means they may have a hard time feeling appropriate and deserved contentment about something they did well. Understanding shame will be helpful here, because when shame and contentment work well together, people will be comfortable with their own moral structure and be able to realize when they've done something to be proud of. But when shame and contentment aren't working well together, some people may be unable to feel appropriate contentment, while others may develop strangely inflated contentment levels that don't track to anything real. In Chapter 9, I explore inflated contentment in a section on bullying.

JOY: *Affinity and Communion*

Joy arises to help people feel a blissful sense of expansive oneness with others, with ideas, or with experiences. Joy is a very powerful emotion that usually doesn't require much support from you, and it usually recedes naturally. However, extreme and exhilarated joy should be approached with care, especially if it cycles with depression or sadness. Repetitive exhilaration or flights of giddy mania may be a sign of emotional dysregulation, and it's possible that the person might need psychological support or medical help.

When you know which emotions you're dealing with, it's so much easier to communicate with people and be truly empathic, since empathy is first and foremost an emotional skill that is developed in interactions. However, as you increase your emotional vocabulary, your Empathic Accuracy, and your Emotion Regulation skills, you may come up against a strange situation: Some people don't want to talk about emotions . . . at all.

ANGRY ABOUT ANGER, AFRAID OF FEAR, ASHAMED OF SHAME

Knowing which emotions you're working with is wonderful, but I have a little warning for you: some people feel strong emotions *about* their emotions, and if you say the name of certain emotions out loud, you can trigger strong reactions. For instance, if you mention anger, shame, or fear out loud and suggest that people might be feeling them, you might start a huge argument: "I'm not angry—your *mother's* the angry one!" "Of course I'm not ashamed, shut up, yeesh!" "Fear? Are you calling me a coward?" Whoops.

This is a problem that people have asked me about for years: "If I understand the language of emotions, but no one else wants to hear anything about them, what do I do?" Until recently, my answer was that people should be honest about their own emotions and model emotional awareness as much as possible. But that answer bothered me, because it put a lot of pressure on people who were just learning how to work with emotions themselves. So in 2012, when I taught "Emotional Flow," a live, eight-week online course to people from all over the world, I took advantage of this empathic crowd source to have some fun and to create a new method for addressing emotions honestly, even when other people don't know how to.

WEASEL WORDS[49]

In my work, I refer to stress as a *weasel word,* or a word that people use to hide emotional awareness from themselves. If you observe the experience of stress empathically, you'll see that it's very clearly an emotional reaction. The sense of tension, the rise in cortisol and adrenaline, the tightening of the body, the rise in heart rate—these are all activations that occur in fear and anxiety (and often anger) responses. Luckily, you have skills for each of these emotions, and you can work with your stress responses in the same way you work with any other emotions: You figure out why you've become activated, you listen to each of the emotions you feel, you perform the actions for those emotions, and then you use your empathic mindfulness skills to return yourself to equilibrium. Easy.

However, if you don't know which emotions you're dealing with—or if you use a weasel word like stress to trick yourself out of emotional awareness—things stop being easy. Misidentifying emotions is a way to avoid what you're truly feeling and to dissociate from the situation—"Help! Stress is *happening!* It's an overwhelming force over which I have no control! I'm powerless!" People learn to weasel away from the truth, and they lose their emotional awareness when stressors are present. But stress isn't the only weasel word for emotions; there are dozens—maybe hundreds—and they're used all day, every day. People rely on weasel words like *fine, okay,* or *good,* each of which can mean nearly anything, depending on the context.

Another all-purpose weasel word that we looked at earlier is *emotional.* "Let's not be emotional!" "We can't talk if you're gonna be *emotional.*" "I'm sorry I was *emotional* yesterday." What in the world? Which emotions are we talking about here? If you don't know which emotions you're feeling, your Empathic Accuracy will be kaput, and you won't be able to regulate or work with your emotions, because you won't know which ones they are! Weaseling away from emotions seems to be full-time emotion work for many people, but it's not good-paying work in terms of emotional skills and empathic awareness.

However, we can use weasel words to our advantage. As empaths, we can use weasel words strategically to help people gain a better understanding of their own emotions. If precise emotion words are so threatening to people that they use weasel-ish masking language in ingenious ways, then let's perform a kind of empathic aikido and use those same words in service to emotional awareness.

I and the empathic crowd in the "Emotional Flow" course discovered numerous weasel words that you can use to support emotional awareness in yourself while you set good boundaries around the emotional ignorance of others. We also took advantage of the *soft* category of vocabulary words in the "Emotional Vocabulary List." For instance, if people are clearly angry but they can't even approach the word, you can ask if they feel *peeved, annoyed,* or *displeased.* They may then be able to connect to the fact that their voice, standpoint, or sense of self has been challenged in some way. Or if people are afraid but can't stand the word, you can ask them if they feel *curious, cautious,* or *uneasy.* They may then be able to identify the change, novelty, or possible hazard they're sensing.

We also found some very powerful words that can stand in for pretty much any emotion, and I call them the Wonder Weasels: *stressed, bad,* and *unhappy.* You can use these three Wonder Weasels pretty much anywhere and in relation to any emotion without unduly triggering people. I particularly love the wildly valenced word *unhappy,* because it suggests that happiness is the preferred emotion, while everything else is unhappy.

Two other words are nearly universally useful, and I call them the Lesser Weasels: *upset* and *hurt*. However, you have to be a little more careful with these Lesser Weasels, because both *upset* and *hurt* suggest emotional sensitivity, and a lot of people like to pretend that they're emotionally impervious and invulnerable (like superheroes, except with no emotional or empathic skills). We also have a delicious weasel word from parents of teenagers: *whatever*.

THE FABULOUS EMPATHS' LIST OF WEASEL WORDS!

If people don't seem able to identify or own up to their emotions, you can use soft emotional vocabulary words, or weasel words, to gently bring attention to what is actually occurring.

Weasel Warning: Don't be annoying by naming people's emotions for them or forcing them into the awareness that *you* want. Instead, have fun and know that for some people, even the mention of the real names for emotions can be triggering. If you can gently bring awareness (even weasel-ish awareness) to the actual emotion that's present, and if you can frame your observation as a question (or use the phrase *it seems),* you'll support people in beginning to develop their own Empathic Accuracy. Nice!

In each list, I start with soft emotion words that are less weasel-ish, then I move into weasels, and finally to the Wonder Weasels and the Lesser Weasels if they're appropriate to each emotion.

Anger: Peeved, Annoyed, Frustrated, Displeased, Affronted, Vexed, Tense, Agitated, Disappointed, Whatever, Stressed, Bad, Unhappy, Upset, Hurt

Apathy and Boredom: Detached, Disinterested, Indifferent, Whatever, Unhappy

Shame and Guilt: Awkward, Flustered, Exposed, Demeaned, Stressed, Bad, Unhappy, Upset, Hurt

Sadness: Low, Down, Disappointed, Discouraged, Blue, Bummed, Whatever, Stressed, Bad, Unhappy, Upset, Hurt

Grief: Low, Lost, Down in the dumps, Blue, Whatever, Stressed, Bad, Unhappy, Upset, Hurt

Depression: Disinterested, Detached, Low, Blue, Whatever, Stressed, Bad, Unhappy, Upset, Hurt

Fear: What do you sense?, Cautious, Curious, Uneasy, Jumpy, Unsettled, Off, Stressed, Upset

Anxiety: Concerned, Tense, Agitated, Unsettled, Off, Bothered, Jumpy, Stressed, Bad, Unhappy, Upset

Jealousy: Sensing disloyalty, Insecure, Stressed, Bad, Unhappy, Upset, Hurt

Envy: Sensing unfairness, Insecure, Stressed, Bad, Unhappy, Upset, Hurt

Contentment: Satisfied, Pleased, Proud, Happy, Good

I'm not including happiness and joy in this list, because people are fine saying those words outright. As you go through this list, just notice how many ways we have to skirt emotional awareness and how five weasel-ish words can describe pretty much every emotion, except the three happiness-based emotions. Wow, that's stunning, and it really highlights the problems we have in developing emotional skills and accuracy.

This list belongs to you now; use it with the blessings of an international band of funny empaths! This list may also be useful in the following communication skill.

MOM'S MAGICAL THREE-STEP EMPATHIC COMMUNICATION SKILL

I want to bring my late mother back into this chapter, because she was a brilliant woman and a quick learner; she stopped using reflective listening immediately after my younger sister and I reacted so comically to it. However, as an empath herself, Mom saw the value of reflective listening, and over the years she developed a modified version of the practice that's more interactive and empathic. Now that we'll be learning her practice, I think you should know her name: she was Billie Karyl Lucy Rogers Hubbard; she changed her name to Kara as an adult, though most of her friends called her Sam. If you want to refer to this empathic practice with her name, you now have many options! In my mom's three-step empathic communication process, you learn how to *listen, reflect,* and then *share.*

|||||||||||||||||||||||||||||||||||||||||||||||||||||||||||||||||||||||||||||||||||||||||||

HOW TO LISTEN, REFLECT AND SHARE

1. Listen first: When you're working with someone in turmoil, the first step is to *listen* compassionately, without interruption. You let the person talk his or her way through the issue without turning it into a conversation about what you would do or have done or have thought of doing (and you don't take anything personally—this step is not about *you!*). You don't impede the flow of words, but neither do you just sit there like a rock. Instead, you make supportive sounds like, *yeah,* or *mm-hmm,* while still letting the person have the floor. This step often brings a solution forward on its own, because people almost never get the chance to talk without interruptions or suggestions (usually because the listener can't simply sit with the discomfort and trust the speaker to find his or her own way). Most of us never get to the deeper parts of our stories or issues, because other people are always hijacking the conversation and trying to fix everything or shut down the flow because it's uncomfortable *for them.* However, if we're allowed to really talk things out, we often talk ourselves right into our own solutions.

The empathic practices of Conscious Complaining and Conscious Questioning are solitary ways of accessing the amazing problem-solving abilities that exist inside your internal monologue. My mom's three-step process is a practice you can use with a person who doesn't have his or her own empathic practice yet, but it's also a process you can request from a friend when you have difficulties that don't respond to Conscious Complaining or Conscious Questioning. Sometimes, you really need the support of another person, and this process can help the other person learn how to work with you in empathic, truly helpful, and boundary-respecting ways.

2. Reflect next: If the talking doesn't bring solutions, the second step (when the person tells you that he or she is done) is to *reflect* on what you heard. People have so little chance to be heard that sometimes they skitter around their issues if you just let them talk. So to help them get back on track, the second step is to paraphrase what you heard them say, always checking in with them to see if you heard them correctly. This is the reflecting phase, and it's not about your opinions just yet. If you can correctly reflect another person's words, they may be able to hear what they meant to say, and they may be able to hear their own solution in the words that got away from them.

3. Share last: If your reflections don't help the person see the issue more clearly, then the third step is to *share* your impressions and perceptions. This is the time when you can, you know, *be* an empath! Please realize, however, that you're being empathic when you listen compassionately without stopping the flow and when you reflect accurately. You have to know when to say "mm-hmm" when you listen, and you have to know how to listen well enough to reflect; those *are* empathic skills. But if more input is needed, step three is where you get to call it as you see it—with caveats, of course.

Moving to reflection means that you get to bring your understanding of the emotions into play. When you share your information about what you see, be sure to protect the other person's dignity. If you say, "I think I'm picking up this emotion. You tell me if it's true," then you place that person in a position of power as the final arbiter of what his or her emotional state is. If you try to name emotions for others or tell them authoritatively, "You're feeling afraid," you'll invade their privacy, and you may activate the emotion that protects their standpoint, voice, and self-image (this is a test: name that emotion!). If you can instead ask, "*Could* this be some fear?" you'll honor your emotional intuition by saying the name of the emotion out loud, and you'll also honor the other person's dignity by bringing forth your awareness as a question. Of course, you can also use your weasel words if you notice that the real names of emotions tend to trigger this person.

If you tell people how they're feeling, you'll place yourself above them as the knower of all things, and that's not very empathic. When you engage perceptively, you focus on the other person's needs, rather than on your own need to be an expert. The point isn't to become a magical emotion translator; if you give over with your advice, your insights, and your wisdom, people will learn a great deal, but they won't gain a great deal of *self*-knowledge. Remember that it's an honor to be allowed so close to another person; it's not a right! When someone unmasks before you, you need to behave honorably. Therefore, your sharing should always be done very carefully, with the full cooperation and permission of the other person.

Checking in with other people also helps you hone your empathic skills. If you ask about your impressions, and the person disagrees with you, this may help you understand when you're projecting your own emotions into the situation. If so, you can apologize, ground and refocus yourself, and ask questions to regain your accuracy and clarity.

When you're in the third step of this process, your first two skills—compassionate listening and reflective paraphrasing—are still important. Let's say you pick up on a loose thread in the person's conversation and offer, "I thought I sensed some resentment, like there was something that was still gnawing at you. What do you think?" If you correctly picked up that thread, you may help the person refocus and process verbally again. Then, you'd listen again, without interrupting, and reflect clearly what you heard. Sometimes, all it takes is your picking up that one thread, because uncovering an overlooked emotion often helps people get back on track.

This three-step process makes empathy very manageable and very respectful of the boundaries of both people. Again, the steps are *listen* first, *reflect* next, and *share* last. These three steps take a lot of the mystery out of the empathic process, thank goodness. Thanks, Mom!

WHEN SOCIAL POSITIONS ARE UNEQUAL

This careful, respectful, and question-based process can create a balanced and equal relationship. It can also be an excellent way to create equality if you're working empathically with a subordinate, such as an employee or a person much younger than yourself. If you're in a leadership position (which doesn't lend itself to equal empathic relationships), it's a good idea to equalize a little by being open about your own emotional issues before you start. You can even ask for input and let the other person know that you value his or her ability to interpret emotions and situations. You can't change your age or your job title, but you can be real with people. So go ahead and be a leader or an elder, but use your skills to lead the way to equality in the relationship.

Something to be aware of: When you're in the sharing portion of this process, be careful not to set yourself up as a translator for the other person's emotions. When you can properly identify an emotion and ask the correct questions, it can seem as if you know more about a person's life than they do. This can set up a very unhealthy dependency, in which people may think you're some sort of expert. Make sure that you let people in on the process of asking the right emotional questions. Your skills in listening, reflecting, and sharing are very valuable, but they *are* skills. If you treat your empathic abilities as magical, you'll cripple the people you work with, because they'll begin to think that emotional awareness and Empathic Accuracy come from you. If you can share your skills openly, however, you'll support people in becoming empathically *self*-aware—and then we'll have more healthy and happy empaths in the world. Score!

WHEN PEOPLE DON'T AGREE WITH YOUR EMPATHIC IMPRESSIONS

Sometimes, people will flat out tell you that an emotion you picked up isn't there, that you're imagining it, and that they aren't feeling it at all. You and I know that emotional awareness tends to be low in many people and that emotional honesty can feel threatening for others. Therefore, if you have someone in your life who swears that you're an empathic failure, I want you to think about the many complex factors that can get in the way of skillful empathic interactions:

1. You could be right, but perhaps you phrased things in such a way that the person feels unmasked and unsafe for reasons that may have nothing to do with you.
2. You could be projecting your own current emotional state onto the person, who doesn't feel what you're feeling right now.
3. You could be projecting, yet it's still true that the other person feels it right now.
4. You could feel your own intensity level of the emotion and mistakenly assume that the other person feels it in the way you do (with all of your baggage).
5. You could be having a kind of flashback to emotional behaviors in your family or your childhood—and you could be projecting those into this situation.
6. The person could honestly be unaware that he or she is feeling the emotion.
7. The person could be deeply ashamed of and dissociated from the emotion.
8. The person could view emotions as a sign of weakness or lack of control and misidentify them or ignore them intentionally.
9. The person could be trying to mess with you.
10. The person could be lying.

In the first five situations, your own difficulties with communication or emotional skills are getting in the way of skillful empathizing. All of the skills in this book will help you address those difficulties. Empathy is a malleable skill, and you can increase your empathic skills at any stage of your life. But in the second five situations, the other person's (lack of) skills and emotional awareness are where the problems lie. If this person is in your most intimate empathic zone, you'll need to go back to Chapter 7 to take a closer look at this person's empathic awareness and emotional styles to figure out what's up. In difficult situations like this, clear communication that is emotionally honest and vulnerable can really help—though in some cases, people simply can't tolerate that kind of communication.

The way I deal with people who don't want to be seen and who don't want to be in any kind of empathic communication is to become very clear about my own emotional landscape so that I'm not projecting or leaking, because being seen and being vulnerable can make some people feel truly awful. Therefore, the most empathic response in that situation is to stop trying to be empathic, if you get my drift. When someone sends you clear signals that empathy isn't appreciated, then Perceptive Engagement requires that you back away.

When I'm in the presence of emotionally unaware people who want to dampen my emotional awareness because it feels threatening or exposing to them, I immediately ground, set my boundaries, and threshold by breaking eye contact and moving away slowly, even imperceptibly—in the way you would with a distrustful animal. I also keep up a strong inner dialogue so that I can maintain my voice, standpoint, and emotional awareness, no matter what kind of empathic silencing is going on around me. In our emotional training, we've all learned wildly backward and unhelpful things about emotions, and many people simply can't face their emotions. That's okay.

If these people want to move forward with you, you can share this book and let them know that you're working to develop your empathy. You can use the empathically clumsy situations between you as examples that will help you explore and deepen your relationship. However, if these people state that they're not interested in developing an empathic connection with you, you'll have some very important information about who they are, what's important to them, and how you'll approach them in the future (Wonder Weasels? Check!). Some people will not want to get into sync with you, and that's okay, as long as it's clearly stated and clearly understood.

In your intimate life, however, with people who really *do* want to empathize with you, there will be times when you and your loved ones lose your empathic connection with each other. The practices that follow, which were handed down to me by my mom, can be used when your intimate relationships need some empathic healing.

EMPATHIC MEDITATIONS FOR RELATIONSHIP CONFLICT

When conflicts pull normally close people apart, the resulting separations can be as painful as a physical injury. Although self-soothing and resourcing skills will help, the problem isn't about a lack of resourcing skills; it's about the pain of being out of sync with your loved ones. The following meditations can help mates, family members, and close friends come back together. I appreciate them because they focus on repairing the bonds between people rather than on performing conflict mediation. These empathic meditations help people restore their relationships so that the relationship itself can become a sacred space where people can turn toward the conflict together, as partners and not as combatants. I find that if I can repair the bond with my loved ones, we don't usually need a mediator between us, because when we're able to work as a unit again, we can deal with conflicts ourselves.

My mom called these practices Sufi sitting meditations, but I haven't been able to track them to any particular Sufi teacher or lineage. We can call them Sam's Sufi sitting meditations instead.

|||||||||||||||||||||||||||||||||||||||||||||

FOR A COUPLE

Start by sitting opposite your partner with your knees touching, whether you're in chairs or sitting cross-legged on the floor. Place an item that symbolizes your relationship (a candle, flowers, a plant, a photo, etc.) near the two of you. When you're settled in, place your hands on your knees, left palm facing up and right palm facing down. Your left side is generally thought to be your receptive side, so you turn your left palm up to receive. Your right side is thought to be your expressive side, so you turn your right palm down to express.

Reach your hands toward your partner and gently slide your left palm under his or her downturned right palm as you rest your right palm on top of his or her upturned left palm. In this way, you can create a circle of receptivity and expression, which is what healthy relationships *should* do.

Breathe deeply in this position, but don't speak just yet. Relax into the breaths, and you'll soon start breathing together. When you're breathing together, look into each other's eyes (if eye contact is too activating for you, simply turn your face toward your partner and close your eyes, or make small moments of eye contact that feel comfortable). You can then begin speaking and turn toward the conflict as a couple, instead of turning against each other. If you need structure for your conversation, use my mom's three-step empathic process of *listening* first, *reflecting* next, and *sharing* last.

I have a small caveat: your hands may become *hot*. If so, it's fine to just touch each other lightly so you can cool off.

This practice helps you treat your relationship as a sacred trust instead of a burden, and it's a wonderful way to help both of you become calm and centered together. The communications that can occur in this meditation are usually very deep and meaningful, because your conflict is brought into a sacred space instead of just being allowed to fester. Where you go after breathing together is totally individual, but you go there as a couple rather than as fierce combatants.

When you reach clarity or resolution, close your session in some way that's meaningful to you. Then take the item that symbolizes your relationship and move it to a place of honor in your home. This item can become a visual reminder of the significance of your relationship and the work you do to keep it strong.

||||||||||||||||||||||||||||

FOR A TRIO

A variation of this couple's meditation can be used when people just can't come together on their own. If there's too much conflict, the circle can be opened to admit a neutral third person whose job is to mediate and hold the space for the relationship as an entity. A candle, plant, photo, or other meaningful object that symbolizes the relationship should be placed in the middle of the trio.

In this trio, each person sits with his or her right palm over the left palm of the person to the right, and his or her left palm under the right palm of the person to the left. Each person breathes deeply, focusing on the meaningful item at the center of the group. When the trio starts breathing together, the speaking can begin. The hot hands caveat applies here as well; if you all get too hot, perhaps just touch each other's knees or feet. The physical contact is important, but it doesn't have to be uncomfortable.

With a trio, a triangle is created, so it's important for the neutral third person to focus on the relationship as a whole, rather than taking sides. As the couple speak and hopefully find their own solutions, the third person's work is to remind them of the importance of the relationship first and the issues second. If the couple needs help, the neutral person should use my mom's three-step process of *listening* first, *reflecting* next, and *sharing* last.

When the couple reaches clarity or resolution, the trio should close in a way that has meaning for them and then move the symbolic item to a central location in the home. Using this symbolic item to create a small altar or shrine for the relationship can be a very healing next step that will remind the couple of the importance of their bond.

||||||||||||||||||||||||||||||||

WHEN COMMUNICATION REACHES AN IMPASSE

If the partner meditations above don't work and you arrive at an impasse, please reach out for the help of a professional mediator—a couple's counselor, a therapist, or an actual mediator. Sometimes, you really need a third person who can hear both of you and identify the issues and threads that got away from you.

If you can't afford professional support (or if your partner refuses), there are a lot of books on conflict mediation and communication at your library. However, I haven't found too many of them that treat strong emotions as important carriers of vital information. I can understand this, because conflict can be dangerous, but if you're interested in exploring conflict-mediation techniques, be aware that you'll see all four of the problems that lead to the emotional confusion that we explored in Chapter 3. You'll also see a lot of focus on anger suppression. Even so, some of these books can be very useful.

I found one approach in a book called *Taking the War Out of Our Words,* by Sharon Ellison. Her approach is valuable because it helps you engage in possible conflicts without unintentionally evoking anger in the other person. Ellison's approach is based on tone, body language, and gestures, and she teaches you how to ask questions that aren't unintentionally interrogating or manipulative.

It's fascinating to observe how we've been conditioned to ask questions, with raised eyebrows that denote surprise and need, and an upward change in pitch at the end of the question, which often demands an answer. No matter which words you use, raising your eyebrows and shifting your tone upward at the end of a question feels more like a demand for an answer than it does like an honest request for information. Ellison suggests keeping your forehead fairly immobile and shifting your tone downward at the end of a question. It's absolutely amazing how this changes communication. Ending a sentence with a downward pitch helps you seem surer of yourself. In fact, newscasters are taught very early not to use up tone at the end of sentences, because it makes them seem uncertain. So down tone has some authority to it, yet when you use it to ask a question, it has an amazing effect—it conveys that you're stating something that's true for you rather than demanding a response from the other person.

You don't use down-tone questions for everything, because that would be silly. If you want someone to pass the salt or give you directions to the freeway, you raise your eyebrows and use up tone. But if you're in a conflict and your partner's boundaries are already impaired, simply reducing the amount of need you convey in your questions can help your partner feel like there's space to breathe. Down tone is grounding, and it's boundary respecting, especially if what you're asking is challenging. Try it with an intense question like, "Are you saying that I take advantage of you?" Say it once with eyebrows and up tone, and emphasize a couple of the words harder than the others. This question can be a scathing accusation if you ask it the right (or wrong) way. Even with up tone, which can seem weakening, this question can be a threat or even an ultimatum.

Now calm your eyebrows and ask that question again without undue emphasis on any word, then end on a down tone. Can you feel that there's a space all of a sudden for your partner to answer instead of merely reacting and attacking? Ellison's choice to use down tone at the end of questions is genius, and it can shift a fight *against* each other into a deep conversation about issues that are actually threatening to your health, your happiness, and your relationship.

If you have relationships in your life that reliably devolve into power struggles and fights, Ellison's work can really help you. She also teaches parents how to work with children without unintentionally aggravating them, as well as how to set boundaries without violence, in her audio book *Taking Power Struggle Out of Parenting*.

If you're having serious troubles in one or more relationships, remember to resource yourself regularly. Find areas in your body that feel safe, calm, and resourceful and open up your focus to include the knowledge that you can experience *both* things. You have a relationship that's currently troubled, *and* you have inner sources of calmness, grounding, and focused strength. You have both things. You also have other resources in your life—other empathic relationships with animals, nature, your mindfulness practices, art, music, and friends in your community. Reach out for loved ones and beloved activities when you're having trouble in your relationships. Interaction is food for empaths, and when you have a relationship that's troubled, you need healthy interactions to balance the scales.

In the next chapter, we'll look at the development of empathy in children. As you think about troubled relationships in your life, it may help you to observe how children develop empathic skills. Luckily, because empathy is a malleable skill, you can actually apply the lessons of childhood empathy development to your present-day life. It's never too late to have a healthy empathic childhood.

CHAPTER 9

Empathic Mentoring, Empathic Parenting

Nurturing and Supporting Empathy in Children

SO FAR IN this book, we've delved into your empathic skills, your emotions, your self-care skills, your home environment, and your relationships. We've also focused on you as an adult. However, as we learned in Chapter 2, your empathic skills actually developed very early in your childhood, which is also when a large portion of your emotional training occurred. In this chapter, we'll look at the development of empathy in children—not only to help you work with children (your own or others') empathically, but also to help you understand how your own development of empathy and emotional aware-ness may have been supported or impeded in your childhood. Let's start by observing a game we all played when we were babies but that we may not identify as a specific emotional and empathic teaching tool.

THE EMPATHIC GENIUS OF PEEK-A-BOO

My niece Holly sent me a video of her six-month-old daughter leaping happily in a swinglike contraption (the kind that hangs from a doorway). My grandniece jumped enthusiastically with intense focus, when suddenly Holly said her name, came in close, and said "Peek-a-boo!" My grandniece screamed, loudly! But the scream included a raucous laugh that cycled down in a few seconds to silence and a serious return to her jumping. Holly came toward her again, *Peek-a-boo!*, instinctually knowing, as good parents do, to wait until her baby's fright and shock had cycled down into calmness. The game continued onward in this rhythmic way, and mom and baby had a wonderful time. Without much spoken language, and without intentionally trying to create a teaching moment, Holly and her daughter have created a fully emotive and empathic interaction that's actually helping both of them learn to read each other and develop complex emotional and empathic skills.

Let's look at this interaction in terms of our six aspects of empathy. Holly uses intentional Emotion Contagion to cycle her daughter through intense but manageable (and fun!) shock and fear. By timing her approaches just right, Holly is helping her daughter learn how to calm herself effectively after an emotion is activated suddenly and intensely. The baby is not simply learning how to play and interact; she's also learning advanced Emotion Regulation skills in relation to an intense emotion. My grandniece is also learning how to identify and feel her way into, between, and out of specific emotions by reading them in her mom's face and voice and feeling them in her own body—she's learning advanced Empathic Accuracy skills in this game. At six months old, my grandniece is too young to be able to perform skillful Perspective Taking, and her Concern for Others hasn't fully kicked in, because she's in a developmental stage in which she needs to be very self-focused. She'll develop those skills, and the related capacity for skillful Perceptive Engagement, between her first and second birthday. However, her warm, rich, and interactive bond with her mom (and dad) is setting the groundwork for her eventual development of all six aspects of empathy.

When we looked at my six aspects of empathy in Chapter 2, I included research on the development of empathy in babies. The current consensus is that the capacity for the most developed aspect of empathy—Perceptive Engagement—arises at around eighteen months in normally developing infants. But this is not true for everyone; not all babies are as lucky as my grandniece.

In their 2010 book, *Born for Love,* child psychiatrist Bruce Perry and science writer Maia Szalavitz track the development of empathy in infants and children. Perry is a trauma specialist who works with high-risk children whose empathy was impeded by poor parenting, chaos, trauma, or unsupportive early environments, such as large and understaffed orphanages. Using these unfortunate children as examples of how and why empathy development can go awry, Perry and Szalavitz help us understand what babies need to develop empathy (luckily, it's not hard to provide these things, and games like peek-a-boo are a surprisingly important part of the process). Perry and Szalavitz also provide excellent suggestions for what you can do to support empathy throughout childhood, even in children whose empathy development was disturbed in some way. Certainly, there is an important developmental window that occurs prior to that eighteen-month milestone where babies, like my grandniece, develop skills in Emotion Contagion, Empathic Accuracy, and Emotion Regulation. But these empathic skills can be addressed even into adulthood—just as you're doing right now in this book.

WHAT BABIES NEED TO DEVELOP EMPATHY

Simply put, to develop empathy, a baby needs warm, nurturing attention from one or two reliable, central caregivers who touch, interact with, and respond attentively to his or her unique emotions and needs. Certainly, many other people should interact with and care for the baby so that he or she can learn to trust and read others, but this central bond is crucial. When babies are raised in orphanages, where the staff rotates, they don't often develop strong empathic skills. Even if those babies are fed well, kept warm, and protected from abuse, they aren't able to spend long periods of time connecting with their caregiver—gazing at him or her, learning to smile and smile back, smelling and touching him or her, and learning that whenever they need anything, that trusted caregiver will respond. Babies need to have their emotions mirrored back to them reliably in vocal tone, in touch, and in facial expressions so that they can begin to organize and understand their emotions. They need to interact with specific people whom they can learn very well. As I wrote earlier, empathy is first and foremost an emotional skill that develops in interactions. Babies, especially in their first year, need as much warm, emotive, and intimate human interaction as they can get.

Babies also need to learn how to identify and regulate their emotions, and peek-a-boo is an amazing game for that. But look back and notice how careful my niece Holly's timing was. She let her daughter know that the game was commencing (Holly called her baby's name), and then she let her baby's self-regulation cycles set the pace of the game. If Holly had continued scaring her daughter without waiting for her to calm and self-regulate, this wouldn't have been a game at all; it would have ended in tears, or it would have taught her daughter that Mom is not a source of fun and comfort as much as she is a creator of emotional pain and confusion. Peek-a-boo looks like a simple game, but like all games, it has intricate rules that Holly learned empathically by interacting with her daughter and paying close attention to her unique emotional rhythms.

Babies are interaction-based organisms, and they need to taste, feel, observe, hear, roll in, and experience the world emotionally, physically, and empathically. Babies' bodies and brains are growing at a rapid pace, and they're uploading as much information as they can possibly gather about everything. Babies' fascination with peek-a-boo games is part of this intensely interactional uploading process—it's emotional play and empathic learning focused on the exact skills babies need to develop. Babies and young children need to have their facial expressions mirrored back to them, to have their gurgles and cries answered, to have their emotions mirrored and responded to, and to be lovingly interacted with as much as possible. This is how the six aspects of empathy develop normally—they develop in loving, intimate, and richly emotional interactions that are as simple (and as complex) as a good game of peek-a-boo.

At later stages in their development, when babies develop Concern for Others, Perspective Taking, and Perceptive Engagement skills, you can help them work with and increase their empathic skills through imaginal play, reading and stories, and dramatic reenactments of challenging situations that they've already experienced (or that they might encounter). These dramatic games start very early. In the game of peek-a-boo, my grandniece is already playing with emotions, learning them, feeling them in her body, regulating them, and sharing them with her mom. Peek-a-boo is an emotive, dramatic, and empathic game that encourages and supports empathy development. And as you can see, these games don't have to be formal or difficult. With a preverbal baby, you can simply mime emotions as you name them (overemphasizing your emotional expressions is a sure laugh-getter that never gets old, as we see in all successful comedies), or you can intentionally copy an emotion that the baby is feeling and gently wait to see what happens next as you follow the baby's rhythms. You can also talk about your own emotions: "Ow! I'm mad because I broke that cup, and now I'm sad because it's broken!" You can also talk about the emotions that you and the baby witness in others: "Look, daddy is silly and happy right now!"

We name everything else for babies—colors, body parts, clothing, family members, toys, pets, dishes, everything—but we don't tend to name emotions, not reliably. Providing children with rich emotional vocabularies will help them develop rich empathic awareness, and providing babies with as much warm and intimate interaction as possible will help them develop rich, advanced empathic skills. In Chapter 8, I talked about the trouble of naming people's emotions for them (because it can offend them and make them feel talked down to), but this isn't true for children. Children need to learn the names of their emotions at many different levels of intensity, and they need to learn what their emotions mean and how to work with each one. Children need your help to develop strong emotional vocabularies and strong Emotion Regulation skills.

Storytelling (including reading together) plays an immense role in helping children develop emotional vocabularies, emotional awareness, emotional skills, empathic skills, and, of course, language skills. Storytelling is one of the central ways we communicate emotional information to each other, and it's a wonderful way for children to intentionally put themselves in the place of others and imagine what another feels, thinks, or might do next. Good stories increase all aspects of empathic skills. Of course, good stories teach Perspective Taking, but they also involve Emotion Contagion, which teaches children how to feel and recognize emotions—and this helps them develop Empathic Accuracy. Working through the emotions in good stories helps children develop Emotion Regulation skills, and becoming involved with the characters helps children develop Concern for Others.

Storytelling and reading together also offer other empathy-building features, especially if children can snuggle into their caregivers as the stories are told and then talk about the story after it ends. Talking about stories is a wonderful way to practice Perceptive Engagement in a safe environment. You can ask, "If you were Harold, and you had a magic crayon, what would you draw here in our house? What would you draw for Gramma? What would you draw for the kitty?" Stories and dramatic play can help children try on different aspects of their empathic skills and discover who they are as empathic beings. Storytelling is intrinsic to every aspect of empathy development; stories are delicious food for humans and their empathic skills.

Reading fiction (and watching drama) has been found to increase empathic skills throughout your life span,[50] because dramatic fiction requires that you become an emotionally and empathically invested participant in the stories you read or watch. Good, rich fiction can help you develop all six aspects of your empathy, no matter how old you are. And thankfully, even if your empathy training in childhood was not wonderful, you can still develop your empathy today by intentionally entering the empathic world of fiction.

As you think about fiction as intentional empathy training, consider the quality of fiction you read or watch now. The emotional and empathic training you'll receive from a slapstick comedy is much different from the emotional and empathic training you'll receive from a heroic adventure or a quiet story about relationships. As you look at the quality of the fiction you consume, think about it empathically as well as thematically. What kind of emotional and empathic training are you receiving from your fiction, and what are you learning from it? Does your current fiction diet offer you excellent empathic and emotional nutrition? If not, why not?

WHERE DO SCREEN-BASED STORIES FIT IN?

Frankly, for babies and infants, screen-based stories don't fit in at all. For children under the age of two, television, computer, and tablet viewing, even of baby-directed videos that supposedly help babies develop their intelligence and their vocabularies, is not an empathy-building activity. It's not even good for language development. Empathy develops in interactions and, as it turns out, so does language. If you think about it empathically, it makes sense—televisions, computers, and tablets can't help babies develop empathy because screens don't have any empathic skills. Older children can understand screen-based stories emotively and empathically, but only after they've developed empathic skills in interactions with living beings. Empathic development is built on warm interactions, and a screen cannot interact or respond in the way a baby's developing brain requires; a screen has no way to know whether its viewers are tired, afraid, sad, bored, or asleep. It just drones on.

A television, computer, or tablet can't mirror emotions, understand them, or help babies regulate them. Screens don't wait to see if a baby has heard or understood what's happening before moving to the next idea, the next phrase, or the next scene, and screens don't care who the baby is as an individual. A screen is not empathic, and it can't teach young babies empathy. In fact, screen time can actually impede empathy development, because it's time away from real, warm, interactive intimacy.

Screen entertainment also can't teach babies and young children interactive language skills. Children can learn vocabulary passively in front of a screen, but they can't learn how language is used, how it relates them to others, or how to read the undercurrents, nuances, subtexts, and empathic content of language. Screens aren't interactive, they aren't empathic, they don't provide the necessary interactions that support linguistic development, and they don't care about their viewers in any way. This isn't to say that all screen-based entertainment and teaching are dangerous for older children;

if your older child has strong empathic and emotional skills, then movies, computer games, and shows can be a fun place where he or she can learn about complex dramatized relationships and situations. Screen-based fiction can be a part (I hope a small part) of the dramatic storytelling play that older children adore. But babies don't have those emotive and empathic skills yet, and they absolutely cannot develop empathic skills in front of a screen.

So if screen-based entertainment is a part of your baby's life, be aware. I'm not suggesting that we parents who have parked our babies in front of the tube, computer, or tablet so that we could get a blessed hour of work done are bad people, but I am saying that empathic awareness is called for. Of course, this empathic awareness extends to you as a parent: if your empathic abilities will be increased if you get an hour to yourself while your baby sits transfixed in front of a screen, and you can come back after that hour and be the full-bodied interaction partner your baby needs, then more power to you! An hour of screen time here and there isn't going to harm anyone, and as we all know, television and computers can save a frazzled parent's sanity. But if the TV or computer is on in front of the baby regularly, and if it's his or her central interaction partner for more than an hour a day, then red flag warning—this is a problem. Empathy (and language!) is developed in rich, warm, intimate, emotive interactions with living beings. Screen-based entertainment provides none of these things, and it will actually impede empathy development and language development in young babies. Screen time can be a soothing distraction for overwrought babies, but that's about it.

TEACHING CHILDREN HOW TO SELF-SOOTHE

Screen time can be soothing in its way, but obviously, so can being held, rocked, and loved. However, in order to develop Emotion Regulation skills, babies also need to learn how to soothe themselves. Games can help them learn. My niece Holly's game of peek-a-boo had an important rhythmical flow to it, and that rhythm was guided by her daughter's ability to regulate her emotions and return to a calm, grounded state. Holly helped her daughter cycle up into shock, fear, and raucous laughter, and then she waited until the baby calmed herself down before she scared her again. This cycling is crucial to my grandniece's development of Emotion Regulation skills, because she needs to learn not just how to feel and identify emotions, but also how to ramp up into them, complete their actions, and soothe herself afterward.

Self-soothing is absolutely vital for the development of healthy emotional and empathic skills.

In Chapter 5, I gave you three self-soothing skills—Grounding, Rejuvenation, and Resourcing—to help you return to a calm, focused, resourceful state. These skills help you intentionally down-regulate your emotional activation. I've also given you ways to *activate* your emotions safely, with Conscious Complaining, Burning Contracts, and Conscious Questioning. Notice, however, that all of my emotional activation skills are cyclical. There's a clear beginning, where you set your intentions and get yourself focused; an activation of your emotions; an action component; and a clear ending, where your emotional activation is resolved and you can return to your grounded, focused state. Each of my empathic mindfulness skills helps you learn to work with emotions in the way a healthy developing baby learns emotions.

It's never too late to learn basic developmental emotional skills that help you feel and activate your emotions, complete their actions, and then down-regulate and soothe yourself again. But it's also never too early to learn these skills, since self-soothing skills are essential to a baby's social and emotional development. Peek-a-boo teaches many things, but self-soothing is a crucial part of the game, and it's a crucial part of emotional, empathic, and social development. As you empathically observe the emotional development of your children (or the children you know or work with), take a close look at their self-soothing behaviors—not just in terms of the calming capacities of these behaviors, but also in terms of their fundamental contribution to social, emotional, and empathic development.

Here are some examples of self-soothing behaviors: rocking, self-hugging, reaching for hugs, thumb sucking, pacifier sucking, hair smoothing, hair chewing, making repetitive sounds, scratching, self-talk, toe walking, hand flapping, spinning, humming, devotion to favorite objects (toys, blankets, stuffed animals, etc.), repetitive movements, running, intentional stillness, snuggling, fort building, foot stomping, object stacking or organizing, climbing, sensory seeking, squealing, singing, dancing, or, my old favorite, fidgeting. This list is not exhaustive, but I'm including a lot of different self-soothing examples so you can identify these types of behaviors in the babies and children you know—and, of course, in yourself.

Self-soothing behaviors are crucial for Emotion Regulation and the eventual development of all other aspects of emotional skills, empathic skills, and social skills. If you can look at them developmentally, you'll see that most of these behaviors are rhythmical and that many of them appear in connection to specific activities, emotions, or situations—thumb sucking in an unfamiliar environment, dancing in response to joy or anxiety, humming during intense concentration, spinning after returning from a noisy day at preschool, or floor pounding during angry outbursts. Each child is unique, and each self-soothing behavior is a unique expression of emotional skill and awareness. But *all* children find ways to manage the emotions and situations they encounter with self-soothing behaviors.

Sadly, most of us haven't been trained to look at these behaviors empathically. Instead, we try to extinguish most self-soothing behaviors in children (and we absolutely don't allow them in adults). As a direct result of this repressive bodily control, we don't tend to realize, for instance, that a humming, rocking, self-talking, book-stacking, thumb-sucking child requires a great number of self-soothing behaviors for some reason. Instead, we attempt to shame away and extinguish at least some of these behaviors. *Don't.* Do *not* do this. Self-soothing has a crucial purpose, and taking away a child's coping mechanisms is simply cruel.

If you have a child who self-soothes continually, then you have a sensory-aware, emotionally sensitive, socially receptive individual who's very likely a hyperempath. Your job is to put on your anthropologist's hat and use your full-bodied Einfühlung capacity to empathically assess this child's entire environment—socially, emotionally, nutritionally, aesthetically, and ergonomically—to see if there's any way to make these multiple self-soothing behaviors less necessary for his or her social and emotional survival. Self-soothing behaviors are crucial for Emotion Regulation, and if a child is self-soothing continually, then he or she needs direct physical support, emotional and empathic understanding, and help with thresholding.

A highly sensitive and sensory-aware child might need a quieter environment, less social interaction, and multiple ways to calm his or her body—through movement, water play, regular baths, tactile play (finger painting, clay work), free play with no rules and no enforced purpose, snuggling time, more time with a calm and trusted adult, or more time with animals. Another thing that can help may seem strange, and that is to have less eye contact with the child. Eye contact is very emotionally intense—it's a major factor in Emotion Contagion. Although it helps some children develop emotion recognition skills, eye contact is sort of overkill for some hyperempaths (especially autistic ones). Some of us don't need eye contact to pick up emotions, and eye contact actually creates a kind of emotional over-whelm—it's too much. I wouldn't simply stop meeting the eyes of a child before checking in, but if you can say, "I know that eye contact is very intense, so you don't need to look directly in my eyes. Let's see if there's another way for us to be close," then you can address the unworkable empathic activation in one area while offering workable empathic closeness in another.

If you see children (or adults) who can't meet your gaze, understand this: You may be in the presence of a hyperempath whose Emotion Contagion skills are immense, but whose Emotion Regulation skills may not have caught up yet. One way to tell is to (respectfully) look for rhythmic self-soothing behaviors. In adults, they get pretty tiny, because we're all shamed out of our self-soothing—but if you look, you'll probably see face touch-ing, hair smoothing, finger drumming, subtle rocking or shaking, lip biting, throat clearing, hand gesturing, or some other repetitive movement. If you know these people well enough, you may also find the powerful self-soothing behavior we talked about in Chapter 6—orthorexia. If you've studied books on reading body language, you might mischaracterize self-soothing people as anxious and untrustworthy, or possibly as liars—*sigh*. But self-soothing behaviors are necessary for everyone, and hyperempaths tend to need a rich and varied assortment of them.

When I'm near someone who employs a lot of self-soothing behaviors, or when I realize that I'm in the presence of a very emotionally sensitive person or animal, I move into intentional emotional hygiene behaviors so that I don't make matters worse. I set very good boundaries, ground and resource myself, and soften my focus so that I present a calm and emotionally non-needy presence. I make minimal eye contact, unless the person or animal initiates it, and I subtly get into their rhythm. I have a ton of self-soothing behaviors, so I often rock slightly to empathically signal, "Hi, self-soothing is normal and okay!" And I usually gain a new friend.

Contrast this to the way most of us were taught to behave around hyper-empathic people who are trying to self-regulate in whatever way they can. Even if we don't say anything, we start to feel ungrounded, spiky, distrustful, needy, and pushy. Our very being seems to say, "Hey! Why aren't you *looking* at me? I feel lonely and you're the reason! Why are you so filled with tics? I feel nervous now, and you're the reason! Stop being such a freak; hold still and look me in the eyes, damn it!" I'll tell you a little secret: hyperempaths can hear this wordless behavior loud and clear, and it makes their situation worse.

Sadly, children hear these kinds of messages out loud, because it's completely acceptable to shame a child openly about such behaviors: "Stop fidgeting; do you have worms?" "Look me in the eyes, or I'll know you're lying." "Take that thumb out of your mouth; you're not a baby anymore." "Isn't nine awfully *old* to still sleep with a teddy bear?" These are examples of informal shaming, but there are formal versions as well. In many kinds of socialization therapies, children with autism, ADHD, and other forms of neurological diversity are actually forced to make eye contact and to extinguish their self-soothing behaviors, or to perform them privately, as if they're a source of shame. In the autism therapy industry, these behaviors are called *stims,* which is short for stimulation and which is a pretty creepy way to talk about the self-regulation that these hypersensitive and hyperempathic children are trying to achieve. But adult autistics are reclaiming the word, and the new attitude is: "Love me, love my stims!" I like that. I stim, and I'm proud! Free the stims!

Stims, self-regulating behaviors, and self-soothing behaviors exist for crucial reasons. They have a distinct purpose in the development of Emotion Regulation skills, as well as in the development of emotional and empathic skills. They're necessary, they're purposeful, and they're an intrinsic part of the development of empathy. So respect the stims, my friend. If you see a lot of rhythmic self-regulation behaviors in someone, you're looking at an emotionally sensitive, sensory-aware, and possibly overwhelmed person. If this person is a child in your home, he or she needs a supportive, soothing, empathic terrarium with thresholds, boundaries, and a series of quiet and wonderful places that are set aside specifically for him or her. These places don't need to be big—you can build a secret reading fort with two chairs and a blanket, or you can create a magical ocean getaway in a bathtub full of toys and bubbles. You can create a secret den under a tree in the backyard, or you can help the child create a bed menagerie of stuffed animals so that he or she can sleep, safe and warm, in a forest or a jungle filled with animal protectors.

It's also important to carefully study the physical environment of a sensitive and self-soothing child and to examine everything that comes into contact with his or her body and senses, including clothing, bedding, scents, sounds, lights, and any other sensory inputs. Many of my autistic friends report that when they were little, the sounds of the washing machine next door or the scratchy feeling of tags in their clothing were excruciating, but they didn't have the verbal language to tell anyone about it. Instead, in response to these sensory assaults, they increased their stims and their self-soothing behaviors. Sadly, many of their parents or caretakers focused on these behaviors instead of on what had made them necessary, and the children were punished, isolated, or exhorted to stop stimming. Very few people even thought to check these children's environments. Luckily, stories like this have helped many modern-day parents of autistic children become aware of the purpose of stims and address what's actually going on, rather than just attempting to extinguish these necessary self-soothing behaviors.

If you have a strong self-soother in your home, look at everything from his or her body outward—clothing, sounds, scents, flavors, lights (especially in the bedroom—is it dark enough and quiet enough at night?), social interactions, emotional tone in the home, emotional tone in child care or school, his or her relationships, and the quality of his or her eating and sleep. Find out whether there is anything you can do to help him or her feel more grounded, focused, protected, soothed, and regulated. Our empathic mindfulness skills may also help, so I'm including kid-focused versions of them here.

EMPATHIC MINDFULNESS SKILLS FOR CHILDREN

You can teach children intentional forms of grounding and resourcing when they're old enough to understand how to inhale deeply and exhale and let go of tension or how to find a place inside their bodies that's very comfortable and strong right now. You can also help children learn to do some form of Conscious Complaining so that they can unload all of the emotional impressions they gather during the day. In toddlers, you can even create regular Intentional Tantrum games (we'll explore more about tantrums below) to help them learn to playact, observe, experience, and develop humor about tantrums, which are a very important (though aggravating!) part of children's development of Emotion Regulation skills.

You can also help children create many different forms of rejuvenation play. For instance, you can help them imagine how they feel when they see their favorite place, pet, friend, or grandparent, and to breathe that feeling inside their bodies, from the top of their heads all the way down to their toes—delicious! Or you can create quiet rejuvenation forts and nooks around your home, where children can be surrounded by wonderful things like art, family photos, or collections of their favorite toys and books.

Conscious Questioning for anxiety is also wonderful for children, because so many little ones become filled with worry—especially when they get into school with all of its incessant task-completion requirements. Helping children write down all of their tasks and all of their worries is a self-soothing act, and it's a very specific emotional-channeling skill that may help them (naturally) reduce some of the repetitive self-soothing behaviors that spring up when their worries and anxieties feel overwhelming.

Boundary definition is something else you can teach behaviorally from a very early age. You do this by paying attention to the baby's signals and helping him or her to choose what feels right and good and to avoid what feels uncomfortable and unpleasant. Boundary definition is self-definition; it's about discovering the self as a distinct organism with distinct wants and needs. Favorite animals, toys, and blankies will often become a part of the baby's self-image and standpoint; these items may feel like an intrinsic part of self, so make sure that you pay close attention to these clear signals of your baby's preferences. Also, if there are siblings or if the baby shares space or a central caregiver with others, make sure to spend clear and focused time with the baby so that he or she will feel safely connected to sources of love, recognition, loyalty, and security (we'll explore more about sibling rivalry below).

Boundaries are managed through the skilled use of anger and shame. These emotions can be difficult for little ones to wield. Intentional Tantrums can help children develop anger skills in safe, consequence-free zones. Stories about the misdeeds of others (where you ask children what they would do to make things right) can also help children learn about the remorse, the behavioral corrections, and the amends that need to be made when people do hurtful things (even if they don't mean to hurt anyone). You can make a game around any emotion, and you can help children play with, try on, activate, and then resolve emotional activation as they develop better Empathic Accuracy and stronger Emotion Regulation skills (we'll look at ways to play with emotions below).

As you work with children and their boundaries, keep an eye on how much anger expression you allow. Most of us were raised to squash anger expression in ourselves, and we tend to enforce that behavior with children. This can lead to anger problems for children, so make sure that you make room for anger play and anger talk. In addition, keep a close eye on the way you use shame, because most of us got pretty terrible training with shame, and we tend to apply it from the outside, rather than helping children develop their own healthy forms of shame, remorse, and contrition. Shame is a vital social emotion. Without shame, children can't learn how to tune into the needs, emotions, or pain of others. I'd say that shame is actually the basis for Concern for Others, because you have to care if you hurt someone, and you have to care enough to want them to feel better. Concern for Others springs from the shame, guilt, remorse, and contrition that help you make amends and change any behaviors that injure or offend others. In Chapter 2, I mentioned a patient of Antonio Damasio's who was unable to feel shame and how this deficit led to so much chaos that she was eventually unable to live independently. Certainly, too much shame can make you focus on others to the exclusion of all your own needs, but a healthy amount of appropriate shame will help you engage perceptively with others in a way that really takes their needs into consideration. Healthy, authentic, and appropriate shame is a central feature of healthy empathic engagement.

However, many of us don't have much experience with healthy, authentic shame. Many of us were regularly shamed as children, and we've had to do a lot of work to uncouple those shaming messages from our own authentic sense of shame and self-worth (this is an ongoing process, just so you know). Therefore, it can be hard to know how to support healthy shame development in children. Here's the trick: what you want to do is help children connect to *their own* appropriate shame and remorse (not yours). In the shame chapter in *The Language of Emotions,* I wrote:

> Appropriate shame is something we should all support in ourselves and others. If we discipline a child and it's clear that he or she is truly sorry, the discipline needs to end immediately. What you want to see is appropriate shame arising in response to the original affront—and not to your strict discipline. Continuing onward with the shaming after a child has shown remorse is just abusive, and it often leads to a hardening in the child's soul. . . .
>
> If you're parenting or working with children, it's important to help them connect to their authentic shame in healthy ways. A great way to do this is to let them be involved in setting punishments, if any, for their misdeeds. When I suggest this, many parents scoff and imagine that children will choose extra ice cream as a punishment; they won't take it seriously because they're all little outlaws. But what I found in parenting, teaching, and sports coaching is that most children are very solemn about their acts of contrition—they feel remorse deeply, and the punishments they create for themselves are

often comically medieval. As the parent or authority figure, you can easily lighten their suggested punishments and help children find a way to make amends without (as has been suggested by various little ones I know): Never eating again; paying $2,000 to the police; or giving all of their toys to homeless kids. When children can be involved in deciding upon their acts of contrition, they can connect to their shame in healthy ways (as long as you stop them from inflicting retributive self-flagellation upon their own souls).

Shame is a powerful boundary-setting emotion, but it has to come from within. Otherwise, it will create fundamental problems with setting, maintaining, and respecting boundaries in the self and in others. We'll look at these problems in relationship to bullies later in this chapter.

One empathic mindfulness skill that I'm really not comfortable using with children is contract burning. As children develop their sense of self and their autonomy as individuals, their behaviors are an intrinsic part of their self-identification. Especially in a sibling context or a social group, children often self-identify as the quiet or friendly or musical or angry or smart or athletic child. Their behaviors form an intrinsic part of their boundaries, which is why it can be so painful or almost unbearable for a child to hear that you love them but that their behaviors are unacceptable. Many children really can't understand what the heck you're talking about, because behavior, identity, self, and me are all intertwined. They're not separable for some children until the teen years and, sometimes, not even then. As such, I'd be very careful with anything that attempts to strip a child of behavioral self-identifications. It's far better to play with behaviors and use dramatic, imaginal play and teaching stories to gently help children view their behaviors as choices.

And let's look empathically at a child's connection to behavior in terms of identity and attachment as we observe a child's similar attachment to a favorite stuffed animal or blankie. Nothing about these beloved fetish items is objectively special, and in fact, these items often become hideously disfigured by energetic love and the fact that you cannot wash them without all hell breaking loose. But these fetishes are crucial until the child learns how to manage without them. Behaviors are often the same; they're intrinsic to the child's identity and even to his or her sense of survival—until they're not. As such, I'd say that Burning Contracts is a skill for teens (possibly) and adults (definitely), but not for little ones.

However, there's one area of identity that directly impedes emotional and empathic functioning, and I do suggest challenging it carefully and empathically: gender roles.

EMPATHIC BOYS AND EMPATHIC GIRLS

In Chapter 2, I wrote about the deeply sexist notion that empathy is a female skill and that males are constitutionally less empathic or less emotive than females. This offensive idea often leads people to treat boys and men as if they're not empathic. But little boys can play peek-a-boo like nobody's business! Little boys love stories and cuddling and love and emotional play and silliness and scariness and empathy. Little boys are fully empathic beings. However, gender roles are powerfully enforced and powerfully valenced—as we saw in the experiments I referred to in Chapter 2, where babies were treated completely differently depending on whether they were wearing *delicate* pink outfits or *dynamic* blue ones. Gender valencing is a fact of life, and it even influences whether girls will be encouraged to develop their math and science skills in school. Neuroscientist Lise Eliot, who wrote the wonderful book *Pink Brain, Blue Brain,* notes that there are relatively minor differences between the brains of baby boys and those of baby girls at birth. She goes on to say that the differences that show up later are primarily socially created, in the same way that the brains of people who learned two languages or who learned to play the piano are different from the brains of people who didn't learn those skills.

As I wrote in Chapter 2, Eliot notes that there are some early differences in verbal abilities (girls are sometimes more verbal than boys, but not always), as well as some difference in activity levels (boys are sometimes more active than girls, but not always). However, these differences are not so large as we've been led to believe. In fact, there is more difference *between* girls in these traits and *between* boys in these traits than there is between the sexes. However, parents tend to support these gender-linked behaviors very early. For instance, they may respond positively to baby girls' vocalizations while subtly ignoring their activity levels (and vice versa for boys).

Eliot also notes that the old information about girls being less able to read maps or do math and science has been disconfirmed many times, as has the old idea about men being less emotionally capable than women (or having smaller corpora callosa than women). Yet sadly, these incorrect ideas stay in the culture as people repeat them over and over and expect less emotional awareness from men and much less math and science awareness from girls.

So the biological truth about boys and girls is ignored, while valenced myths and prejudices mold little brains into gender stereotypes.

There are people who can tell us a great deal about the discrimination that this stereotyping encourages: gay, lesbian, bisexual, transgender, and asexual people live in a liminal space between the genders. Because of this, their social and physical well-being is often at risk. Those of us who challenged gender roles as children might have been looked down upon or taunted as tomboys or sissies, but if we *also* displayed conformist gender behaviors (or showed romantic interest in the opposite sex), we probably got away with our challenges to the stereotypes. But people who can't fit into enforced gender roles often experience intolerance, discrimination, and persistent social control attempts—shunning, shaming, bullying, exclusion, isolation, emotional abuse, and often physical violence. Empathically speaking, gender stereotypes are unhealthy for everyone, but they're actually endangering for people who can't force themselves into these binary gender caricatures.

Let's look at the concept of *caricature* empathically, because it tells us something important—that is, gender roles are imaginal. Gender roles are dramatic personae; they're performances that are enforced through incessant social and emotional training that starts the moment we're born (or the moment our parents discover our gender). Gender roles are dramatic roles that we learn in our families, in stories, at school, on television, and everywhere we look—and these roles come complete with costumes, props, and scripted behaviors that fool a lot of people. Those people who thought the same sleeping baby was delicate in pink and dynamic in blue—their Einfühlung capacities were actually fooled by a simple costume change—presto!

Good actors expose gender roles, and they can easily switch genders and convincingly play across and between our make-believe gender divide. This is because they understand all of the social training that's required to play a gender role. Gender roles are thresholds, fetishes, and personae; they are not empathic destiny. Socially created reality can be challenged; you can create thresholds around gender discrimination and individuate from it. It's difficult, because gender valencing is a powerful fetish that many people can't even imagine living without. However, as you work with children, see if you can avoid gender valencing as much as possible in the area of emotions and empathy. If you can intentionally make room for talkative, emotionally aware males and active, scientifically aware females—and everyone in between—you'll create a more empathic civilization, one person at a time. Babies arrive in this world with a full complement of emotional, empathic, intellectual, and linguistic possibilities—so many options are available to them. To the extent that you can, help babies develop all of these human characteristics, and not just the ones that fit into those stifling pink and blue costumes.

Of course, we live in the real world, where gender roles are vigorously and profoundly valenced, and we all know that stepping outside those lines is socially dangerous. My suggestion is that you create a valence-aware empathic sanctuary at home for your little ones and teach them gender roles as a part of dramatic play and as an act of intentional personae creation. If your daughter is a rough-and-tumble individual, let her know that many people will want to change her. Talk about ways to deal with those social control attempts or even ways for her to pretend to be a conformist in unsafe environments. If your son is an artistic or sensitive individual, help him understand the hazards and work around them with the help of dramatic thresholding, playacting, and intentional personae construction. But know that peer pressure exerts powerful social control on children and that your child's friends and schoolmates are learning to valence gender by copying, embodying, and enforcing the endless valencing messages they get from every direction. So your athletic girl may come home from a play date and suddenly become fascinated with princess lore and makeup. Or your artistic boy may turn away from his painting, singing, or dancing and ask to join the football team.

These dramatic shifts may be fine as long as they don't arise alongside increased anxieties, emotional outbursts, sleeping troubles, changes in eating or attention, and other unhealthy shifts in emotional functioning. We all love to put on costumes and pretend to be any number of characters, and if you can help children play with gender identity and individuate (to the extent that they can), you'll help them develop intrapersonal intelligence about who they are and how they feel. This understanding that identity and gender are fluid will also help children develop the interpersonal skills and Perspective Taking abilities they'll need to build a nonvalenced, inclusive, and truly empathic social world that welcomes people of every sexual orientation.

WORKING AND PLAYING WITH EMOTIONS IN CHILDREN

As children are growing, you really can't give them too much information about emotions, because out in the world, they'll receive very poor emotional training. Helping children name their emotions, identify them, play with them, dramatically express them at many different intensities, and talk about them openly will help children develop comfort and expertise with the basic building blocks of their emotive, cognitive, empathic, and social skills. As you explore the actions that each emotion requires, and as you learn many different emotional vocabulary words, you'll be able to approach emotional issues more empathically, share your new knowledge, and help children understand their emotions more clearly.

Depending on their age, you can help children develop their emotional vocabulary to intentionally encompass nuanced emotional awareness and an understanding that emotions often arise in pairs and clusters. As you look at the "Emotional Vocabulary List" (in the Appendix), you can choose a number of kid-friendly words for each emotion at different intensities, or you can just talk about, for instance, a big sadness, a medium amount of fear, or a tiny hint of anger. Children love to grade and sort things, and they may have excellent ideas for how to talk about clustered emotions, such as the large happiness, medium sadness, and pangs of envy they feel when they watch another child open a huge pile of birthday presents. You can also help children unvalence emotions by connecting their emotional vocabulary to the actions each emotion requires. Often, when we name emotions for children, we include direct teaching about whether the emotion is acceptable: "You're angry, young man; go to your room." "There's nothing to be afraid of." "Don't cry, don't cry." "There's that smile—that's what I want to see!"

If you can strip away the good/bad valencing and present each emotion as a tool, you'll really help children become emotionally intelligent. You can do this before children learn to speak by learning to read and respond to their emotions, and by helping them complete the actions for their emotions (instead of praising or punishing children for feeling emotions). As children develop vocabulary, you can incorporate emotions and their actions when you speak about them: "I think you're feeling some fear; what are you sensing?" "It seems like you're feeling envy; what unfair thing just happened?" "You feel proud of yourself because you did good work!" "You feel sad; what isn't working right now? What can you let go of?" "You're feeling angry. What do you need? What would make things right?" These messages, of course, need to be individualized to each child, but even toddlers can learn how to productively complete the actions their emotions require.

EMOTION PLAY!

You can also create games and dramatic reenactments so that children (boys *and* girls!) can have fun exploring emotions in safe ways. With anger, you can have kids think of mean things to say (or repeat mean things they've heard) and then have them explore a number of different ways to respond and reset their boundaries without violence or verbal abuse. With shame, you can have children think up really naughty things that they have done or might do and then playact a number of ways to make amends. With hatred, you can have kids try the emotions on for size and then describe exactly what it is in the hated thing (or person) that makes it seem so dreadfully foreign and unwanted. With apathy, you can laze around on the floor and talk about why you're so bored, fed up, and uninterested, ho hum! This can lead to some very interesting conversations about the child's true interests.

You can also act out Intentional Tantrums. In this fun and silly way, you can help children see what's going on when tantrums occur. For kids from the age of about thirty months to five years, very few things seem funnier than watching adults have pretend tantrums. It's wonderful for children to see the behavior from the outside and to know that adults understand the situation. Tantrums can be very frightening and isolating, so bringing them into the magical world of play can help children feel more capable and calmer about tantrums.

Children tend to create a lot of games around fear already—peek-a-boo, certainly, but also hide and seek, tag, and games where you sneak up on people and scare the wits out of them. With fear and panic, you can create games in which a potentially dangerous thing might happen, and then help the child make quick decisions about what to do. Remember that in panic specifically, there are only three choices: fight, flee, or freeze. Ask, "Which one is best? Let's try all three and see!"

To play with anxiety, you can create a ridiculously large number of tasks that the child has to get done in a very short period of time and then help him or her problem-solve a creative way out of it (getting help from Rumplestiltskin, magic brooms, flying unicorns, and the like *is* allowed, just so you know). To play with jealousy and envy, you can tell the tale of Cinderella and her sisters. Or you can load up one stuffed animal with toys and games while another animal has only one; then have the child talk about what both stuffed animals might be feeling (and how to make things more just and fair). To play with confusion, you can offer the child competing, wonderful options or you can replay a situation in which the child couldn't decide between one thing and another, and then slow down the decision-making process so the child can discover what's significant and meaningful to him or her.

With sadness, you can make a game of finding things that the child has grown out of or no longer needs and then find the perfect person to give them to. This not only helps a child feel the rejuvenation aspect of letting go, but it also helps him or her develop Perspective Taking (Who would like this best?), Concern for Others (Would this make someone feel happy and loved?), and Perceptive Engagement in one fell swoop. (The fact that this game also clears clutter out of your home is a bonus!) With grief, you can play a solemn game and create a ceremony for light versions of loss, such as one of the child's stuffed animals moving to the moon. You can create a small grief shrine, and let the child create a sermon about how much the stuffed animal will be missed, all of the wonderful times they've had together, and the child's wishes for the stuffed animal's life on the moon.

Most children play pretty well already with happiness, but joy and elation can sometimes be a little intense and too activating. I like to help children ramp up into joy and run around—*yay, yeeha!*—and then completely relax, perhaps by laying down and pretending to sleep. Joy can be very tricky to down-regulate, especially since it's valenced so massively as the best possible emotion in the universe. Therefore, it's a good idea to intentionally teach children how to ground and calm themselves when joy is present.

Contentment can also be a tricky emotion, because children are doing such a huge amount of work in the development of their sense of self. Some kids ratchet up into a kind of megalomania of absurd contentment (we'll look at that in the section on bullying later in this chapter), while others are plagued with self-doubts and can't seem to feel much contentment at all. Parenting and teaching styles can interfere with the development of healthy contentment and self-confidence—certainly parents who shame their children can really throw a wrench into this emotional area, but so can parents who overpraise and reward their children for everything. The trick with contentment is to help a child associate it with real actions that are truly commendable and that they themselves feel proud and content about. So a good contentment game might be creating tasks that the child can complete, and then checking in to see if he or she feels satisfied about it. You can find out a great deal about a child's self-concept when you can play with contentment in this way.

TANTRUMS, PHOBIAS, RIVALRIES, AND BULLYING

In most instances, you and your children will be able to figure out what's happening when an emotion arises, and you'll be able to create a number of games to explore the emotion together. However, four specific emotional situations are a little bit tricky, starting with a crucial emotional and empathic developmental phase better known as *tantrums*.

TANTRUMS

Tantrums—loud and annoying though they are—are an intrinsic part of the process of developing Emotion Regulation skills (though it sure doesn't look like it!). If you observe tantrums empathically, however, you'll be able to identify the rhythmical aspect of this important developmental process. Tantrums are a way for children to dramatically cycle between anger (and rage) and sadness (and self-pity) when they confront challenges to their needs, their desires, and their sense of self. Tantrums are not games; rather, they are a form of emotive and dramatic play that occurs as children learn how to work with their emotions. The way you respond to a tantrum will help—or hinder—children in their development of emotional skills and empathic awareness.

In a clever 2011 study,[51] psychologist James Green and fellow researchers at the University of Connecticut gathered audio recordings of numerous real-life tantrums in toddlers. (Tantrums are most prevalent from the ages of one to four, but they can occur at later ages, especially in response to emotional upheavals, loss, or trauma.) Green's team found that there's a very predictable cycle of vocalizations connected to anger (screaming and yelling) and sadness (whining, crying, and whimpering). When challenged, most young children will move between sadness and anger as they ramp up into a tantrum. These distinct emotional cycles are pretty easy to identify (angry yelling sounds very different from sad whining), and Green found something surprising as he listened to how parents dealt with each emotion. In general, nothing helped during the angry phase except calmly setting boundaries for the child. Questioning, arguing, yelling back, pleading, threatening, and joking all made the anger portion of the tantrum much worse; however, making short, boundary-setting declarative statements helped. When parents set boundaries, the child could often reach the sadness phase of the cycle and let go, at which time, he or she could be consoled and soothed.

During a tantrum, I like to name the emotion for the child, without any shame attached. If we're in public, I get the child away from the shaming stares of others (no one needs to hear a tantrum; they're extremely activating if you don't understand what's happening, and the screams could emotionally trigger everyone in the vicinity). So I'll say calmly, without trying to fix anything, "You're very angry about taking a nap right now." "Kelly has the truck right now, and you're angry." "You're very angry because you can't have candy, so we're leaving the store right now until you can calm down." Notice that I also talk about the temporal aspect of the tantrum with the words *right now*. Intense activations of anger and rage can't last—they're exhausting, and it can help a child to know that this feeling isn't going to last forever. It's also important to understand that this behavior isn't intentional and won't be helped by shaming—you'll actually just make it worse if you try to shame a child out of a tantrum. Tantrums are unintentional, and you need to model calm boundary setting to let the child know that even at its very worst, anger is just an emotion, and it's all going to be fine. No shame.

Tantrums *can* become intentional if you handle them badly or if you acquiesce and give the child whatever he or she is screaming about. However, at their core, tantrums are part of an important developmental process. If you can reframe tantrums in your own mind, you can help a child safely ride through these intense emotional storms.

When the rage storm (screaming and yelling) passes and the child moves to the release of sadness (whining, crying, or whimpering), he or she will be able to let go and down-regulate. At this point, the intense activation will cycle down, and the child will be able to focus more clearly on what happened. You can then talk about the tantrum and name the emotions, "Wow, you felt really angry because (something), and then you felt sad. What do you need now?" Sometimes cuddling and reassurance are all a child needs, because a tantrum can be really terrifying and embarrassing for a child. It's important not to punish or isolate children who are having tantrums, because it teaches them that when an intense emotion arises, they're unacceptable and unwanted; they're on their own. That's not a way to help children develop emotional and empathic skills. Children need help to understand and work with their intense emotions. Depending on their language skills, you may be able to talk with them about what happened so that they'll have ideas and options for the next time a tantrum cycle starts to arise.

When a child has a lot of tantrums, it can really help to make Intentional Tantrums a part of his or her imaginative play. Children love to see adults having play tantrums, and they love to stomp around and pretend to have tantrums themselves, because it helps them feel less alone in their emotional lives, less annoying, and less of a burden. Some deeply emotive children just need more time and practice before they can develop Emotion Regulation skills, and dramatic play is a wonderful, safe, empathy-building practice. However, if children are regularly tantrum-prone—and it's not because you bribed them with whatever they wanted and created a monster—you may be looking at a form of self-soothing behavior and not a tantrum, per se.

Sometimes what looks like a tantrum can actually be a sign of emotional or sensory dysregulation. It's important to empathically observe what triggers the tantrums and what's going on in the child's environment. Are the tantrums a response to an anger-evoking situation in which the child's needs or sense of self are being challenged or thwarted? Or are the tantrums occurring in response to sensory overload or fatigue? Underdeveloped Emotion Regulation skills are normal in younger children, and tantrums have a specific purpose in helping them build these skills, but sometimes tantrums are a sign of hypersensitivity and hyperempathy. This is especially true for autistic and hyperactive children, who may be so overwhelmed by sensory overload that they either lose their Emotion Regulation skills, or they ramp into intense emotions as a way to fill their bodies with extreme activation that may temporarily shut out the sensory bombardment they're experiencing. If you have a child who has regular tantrums, don't punish for the tantrums; look for the triggers. If you also see rhythmic self-soothing or self-injuring behaviors during the tantrums, please reach out for the help of a developmental psychologist who can help you create a supportive environment for your hypersensitive and hyperempathic child.

SHYNESS AND PHOBIAS

Each child is born with a unique emotional style, and some children are naturally bold, while others are naturally more reticent. Shyness in and of itself isn't a problem, unless it's connected to a great deal of fear or anxiety. These two emotions are very activating, and they can easily get stuck in a feedback loop if a child does not have effective self-soothing skills. Also, shyness, fear, and anxiety are all seen as signs of weakness, and a shy child may shut down and refuse to ask for help for fear of being further shamed. If you can unvalence the situation for the child, you can help him or her address the fears ("What are you sensing?") or complete the specific tasks that the anxiety is trying to address. Remember to recruit the magic of list-making for anxiety; this anxiety-specific action will address the exact issues that evoked the anxiety in the first place. Playacting and dramatically preplaying anxiety-producing situations are also wonderful activities, because they treat the anxieties as valid, and they give children safe, consequence-free opportunities to develop multiple responses to anxiety-producing situations.

You can also use playacting around phobias, with the caveat that if the fear ramps up too high, you might just overwhelm the child for no good reason. With a phobia, there's a visceral reaction that tells a child to avoid something as if it were toxic. So you have to respect that powerful instinct. However, you can help the child learn to find internal places of calm, strength, and resourcefulness, even when the phobic item is nearby (our empathic skill of resourcing is very healing for phobic people).

Playing rhythmic games with phobias is also very helpful. Let's talk about something specific, like fear of the dark. You can help a child walk a little way into a dark room with you; then you both run away—run!—and hug each other and laugh when you're safely away. Then, when the child has down-regulated, you can approach the room again and go just a tiny bit further, then *run!* This game is ancient and primal—it helps young animals learn to deal with frightening things, and it can help children understand that everyone is afraid of something.

Many online videos show baby animals learning how to approach scary objects. One of the most hilarious is called *Kitten vs. a Scary Thing*,[52] which YouTube user Ignoramusky actually scored with horror film music. Your child will fall down laughing as he or she watches the brave little kitten approach, reapproach, and run away from a very scary thing (A tennis ball? *Auugh!*). But as you watch this brave kitten, notice his rhythmic game: It's a careful approach—a ramping up into intense fear, a quick retreat, and a calming phase. And the kitten repeats the cycle over and over and over again. Eventually, that kitten will be able to look at a tennis ball and feel, "Oh, that thing, ho-hum." But he has to interact with it intensely and learn to play with his emotional reactions before he can get to that calm place.

As you work with a shy or phobic child, look at Richard Davidson's six dimensions of emotional style from Chapter 3 and see if there are any dimensions that can be addressed with support from you or with a change in the child's environment. Specifically, look at the child's overall Resilience, as well as his or her Attention, Sensitivity to Context, and Self-awareness. A shy and phobic child may be a highly sensitive and hyperfocused being who needs many self-soothing, resourcing, and boundary-setting skills. And, of course, kitten videos.

In older children with phobias and anxieties, you can offer support by closely observing their school situation (Could there be so much homework that their anxieties are hyperactivated?), their social world at home (is your home a safe empathic terrarium?), and among their friends, where arguments or run-ins with bullies (see below) could be triggering anxiety, phobias, or social withdrawal.

SIBLING AND PEER RIVALRY

As children develop emotionally, they also develop awareness of their social position in relation to people and things that compete for the attention, resources, love, and recognition of their parents and loved ones. As you know, we're in the sphere of jealousy and envy here, and these emotions arise to make sure that we're securely connected to sources of love and loyalty (in the case of jealousy) and to sources of recognition, security, and resources (in the case of envy). Children can ramp themselves up into jealousy and envy very quickly—partly because their Emotion Regulation skills are still developing, but also because their social position is actually very precarious.

Children don't have a long life full of relationships to look back on when threats to their relationships arise. They have one or two central caregivers, and one family. So their jealousy will be hyperfocused in that sphere. Threats to these central love relationships can be heartrending, and children have to learn how to keep themselves securely attached to the only source of love they know, which means that jealousy will be absolutely necessary. If there are threats to these intimate bonds, you *want* to see jealousy arising in a child; you want to know that the child's emotions are working properly and that he or she has developed healthy attachment.

Most people try to shame jealousy (and envy) out of children, which, if you understand the purpose of these emotions, is a sick, backward thing to do. Forcefully repressing jealousy in a child can turn a normal, healthy emotion into a twisted and dark thing—and that's not a loving or empathic action. If you support love, loyalty, and attachment, you need to support jealousy and help children learn how to work with it. You can do that very simply—by noting the emotion and talking about what the child needs and wants and what would help him or her feel loved. That's it. No shame, no fuss—you just respond to the emotion and help the child complete its action.

Of course, sometimes the child will ask for the moon, but jealousy and envy have an inner core of fairness and justice in them, and you can talk about what would work for everybody so that you can help the child open up the experience of jealousy to encompass the love needs of others.

Envy is another crucial emotion in the lives of children, who don't yet have lists of accomplishments that could help them feel an internal source of recognition or self-worth when threats arise. Children don't own anything, they don't control any resources, and they're completely at the mercy of their caregivers and families for every possible form of security. You bet they need their envy—it's the emotion that helps them begin to have a sense of their value, their worth, and their sense of individuality—of what *I* want, what *I* need, and what's fair. Working with envy is just as easy as working with jealousy if you understand what's occurring in the development of the child's basic sense of self-worth.

Envy itself will help you here. Envy is a surprisingly honorable emotion if you address it respectfully and ask what would be fair for *everyone.* Yes, as with jealousy, sometimes children will demand the moon and the stars when they're learning how to work with envy, but you can help them think about how everyone needs to feel recognized, secure, and resourced. You can help children develop a larger and more nuanced understanding of how their needs relate to everybody else's. I would ask you to protect children from too much self-sacrifice here: definitely help them state and advocate for their specific needs, but also help them ground those needs in relationship to what is available for everyone else. Caring about others is a necessity, but healthy jealousy and envy will support children in balancing their needs with the needs of others.

You'll find that jealousy and envy are some of the most beautiful emotions there are, if you can approach them empathically and engage with them respectfully. They tell us how crucial love, security, recognition, and loyalty are to our very survival. They're powerful emotions because they exist to protect powerful needs.

BULLYING

Bullying is a huge issue in schools, online, and in the workplace. It's a situation in which people feel free to pick on, harass, isolate, shame, and intimidate others. Bullying can start quite early—it's been observed in children as young as three years old (these children were often exposed to a lot of aggressive behavior, including violent movies and TV shows). Luckily, many bullying-prevention programs (NoBully.com is one of the most empathically grounded) have sprung up to address the problem of bullying, which involves poor Emotion Regulation skills, inadequate Concern for Others, and insufficient Perspective Taking abilities. Thankfully, bullying is no longer seen as something to tolerate. So if you have (or work with) children, let them know that bullying isn't okay and that they should report bullying as soon as it happens.

This new movement to openly identify bullying is certainly protective for victims, but it's also protective for the bully. A bully might look strong on the outside, but when someone is lashing out and hurting people intentionally, there's serious trouble going on in their boundary-setting abilities. A lot of problematic emotions are involved in bullying—certainly, you can see the anger dysfunction, but there's also a surprising emotional condition that occurs in bullying. In many cases of bullying, *contentment* has gone completely off the rails.

We can clearly see that abusers and bullies have problems with anger and shame. Their anger gets unleashed constantly, without any moderation from healthy shame, which means they don't have healthy brakes on their anger. Subsequently, they behave in dishonorable and dishonoring ways. But strangely, many bullies score high on tests of self-esteem, which means their contentment is in high gear, even though their behavior is the exact opposite of worthwhile or commendable. In the bullies I've observed, shame becomes unhinged somehow, and it no longer works to help the person manage his or her honor or boundaries. The rules of healthy behavior and Concern for Others get erased, and the person finds a way to feel twisted contentment that doesn't actually track to anything real. The contentment inside a bully seems to be saying, "Yeah, your anger is so righteous! You don't *ever* need to feel ashamed of anything you do, so yay for you and screw everyone else!" It's a hellish, inflated, unhinged form of contentment.

Yet if you look at the way bullies work, you'll notice that they primarily force shame onto others and attempt to break down the self-image and boundaries of their victims. Bullies might crow about the glories of anger, but they don't actually make any room for healthy anger or natural contentment to exist in others. So even though they seem to be very comfortable with anger and wildly full of contentment (and essentially shameless), bullies spend an awful lot of time disabling the contentment, the anger, and the boundaries of their targets with huge helpings of toxic shame. This tells me that their anger posturing, their seeming lack of shame, and their artificially inflated contentment are all a show. No one who is good with anger, shame, or contentment would ever try to disable these emotions in others. Nope. Bullies aren't fooling me.

Many people think that the cure for bullying is to use shame, punishment, and social shunning to bring the bully back into line, but this is precisely the wrong tack to use with a person who already has a severely disabling problem with shame (and a deeply problematic connection to anger and contentment). A chastised bully might publicly apologize and show contrition, but applying more shame to a person with a severe shame dysfunction will backfire. In some cases, it will essentially harden and weaponize the bully. Remember the party scene in Chapter 3 (where our friend shockingly insulted us in front of others)? A person who attacks others already has very poor boundaries. If you attack back, you can easily injure and enrage him or her. That's not smart.

An excellent approach with bullies is to model healthy anger and shame and to allow your own anger to strengthen you so that you can display vulnerability. I know this sounds wildly and dangerously counterintuitive, but it's one of the few ways to help a bully come in off the ledge of severe emotional and behavioral dysfunction. Bullies are nearly always survivors of abuse or neglect (or both), and more abuse just cements them in their behaviors. It also solidifies their worldview, which is that other people can't be trusted and aren't worth caring about. Showing vulnerability to a bully—in a healthy, anger-supported way that isn't self-abandoning on your part—is one of the bravest and most revolutionary things you can do, and bullies *will* notice it. What they do next is individual, but one way to bring bullies back into the realm of functional human relationships is (surprise!) to model functional human relationships for them and to engage with them as if they matter.

Of course, if the bully has power over you or has found a gang (gangs of bullies can goad each other into shocking displays of mindless cruelty), then you'll need support. Just remember that bullying is not a show of strength; it's actually a display of severe boundary impairment, and it's something to be very careful around.

People have a lot of bully-lore about fighting back, but bullies expect a fight, and they're ready for it. They're stuck in a feedback loop with anger, and if you engage clumsily, you'll make things worse. Bullies need to learn how to feel shame properly. As we all know, shame can't come from the outside; it has to be authentic to the individual. Empathy training in a safe space, mediation, and active engagement in reparations (see NoBully.com for ideas) can help bullies reenter the community and become truly commendable human beings again. Certainly, their misdeeds and abuses need to be stopped, but bullying is a sign of emotional dysfunction and an empathy deficit; bullies need to be retrained in how to function socially, emotionally, and empathically.

When I look at bullies, I see a hall of mirrors that reaches back to antiquity to show us just how little understanding we have of emotions—especially of anger. Yes, a bully needs to take responsibility for what he or she has done, but considering the emotional training we all receive, I'm not surprised by bullying and social violence at all. It's just one more example of the very poor Emotion Regulation skills most people have. If you can look at it that way—as a skills issue—it's easier to view a bully as a person in need, rather than as a fiend or a monster.

Something that can really help bullies is to engage them in a form of aggression that includes rules, boundaries, and honor. Aikido and other marital arts, fencing, kickboxing—even some video game communities—can help teach people how to channel aggression in safe, rhythmic, and strongly thresholded ways. The problem isn't that anger exists or that bullies express anger; it's that the bully has no respect for boundaries and no honorable practice for anger. If you can address the actual emotional dysfunction that's occurring, you can help bullies restore their shame to its rightful position, learn how to manage their anger honorably, and learn how to feel healthy contentment once again. I speak to you as a severely bullied child who became a bully extraordinaire—there is healing for victims, and there is hope for bullies.

CREATING A SOLID GROUND FOR EMPATHY IN CHILDREN

We know that there are specific things that help children develop healthy empathy: close ties with emotionally and physically responsive central caregivers, intimate interactions with living beings, dramatic and emotive play that helps children cycle into and out of emotions, the development of multiple self-soothing skills, learning lots and lots of stories, and having many opportunities for healthy social interactions. All of these will help children learn intrapersonal and interpersonal empathic skills. But beyond that, you really have to pay attention to who the child is as an individual.

In interviewing empathic people for this book, I've asked: "What made you feel comfortable when you were a kid? What helped you regulate your arousal? What helped you understand people and emotions? If you could go back and add something supportive to your young life, what would it be?" I got a lot of answers, but only a few were shared among my many interviewees. The only universal needs were having animal friends, having physical freedom, and having numerous outlets for physical activity. Often, these needs for freedom and movement were met at the same time, through a bike, roller skates, stilts, a skateboard, a scooter, or some other form of transportation that enabled the child to travel freely. And some children connected all three of these needs by spending most of their time with a beloved horse.

But the rest of the answers from my interviewees were contradictory. Some empathic children flourished in school, and some (like me) were unrelievedly miserable in the crowded, noisy, stillness-enforcing environment of public school. Some sensitive children loved to be in dance recitals and musical groups, while others absolutely hated being forced to perform in public. Some children loved camping and nature, while others preferred reading books indoors for hours on end. Some delighted in building things (and taking things apart), while others preferred creating intricate drawings or building fictional worlds. Some loved amusement parks and parties, while others were overstimulated and overwhelmed by these exact same things. Some took to water and swimming like otters, while others could take it or leave it. Beyond the need for physical freedom, activity, and animal friends, I didn't find any other shared empathic requirements. Everyone is unique.

However, I did ask specifically about artistic expression and soon realized how strange my own upbringing had been, because I got a lot of blank looks. Most people didn't grow up with music in their homes, with art supplies in more than one room, and with a backyard where extensive fort building and moat digging regularly occurred. This is a problem, because artistic expression and physical expression are specific healing activities for highly receptive hyperempaths. They are also specific emotional-awareness activities for people whose empathic skills are currently low. In Chapter 6, when we observed your home, I asked you to look for your own artistic expression, and I referred to the often sad and neglected art supplies in the back of the closet. If you're not doing your art because you don't have the time, that's different from not doing your art because you've never been shown how to *make* the time. This is something you can learn with the help of children.

IF YOU CAN WALK, YOU CAN DANCE, IF YOU CAN TALK,
YOU CAN SING, AND IF YOU CAN CLAP, YOU CAN DRUM

You may have seen some form of this Zimbabwean saying. I heard it on the first day of an African drumming class, and it really helped relax all of us students; it took the specter of perfectionism out of the experience so that we could all have fun. And we did. Art is fun, it's natural, and it's a part of being human. Art is also an important part of empathy development, because it helps people develop stronger Emotion Contagion, Empathic Accuracy, Emotion Regulation, and Perspective Taking skills in safe, consequence-free zones of discovery. Art can help you try on emotions and attitudes, feel things intensely, and work through deep emotions and difficult situations with the help of whichever medium calls to you. Art is an empathic skill-building tool for people of all ages.

Art is also available everywhere to everyone; it doesn't have to be professionalized or taught by experts. Art can be anything that helps you express yourself emotively in safe and tangible ways. With children, you can create simple art stations at home or outdoors—water tables, sand tables, paint easels, or clay areas—where you and your children can do art together in such a way that both of you get your quiet time while still being together. If you can sit quietly with a child and draw in coloring books or build free-form structures or paint—whatever calls to you—you can model yet another self-soothing behavior for your child. Art, drama, literature, music, and creating things are specific empathy-building activities that you can provide for children and for yourself.

SUPPORTING EMPATHIC DEVELOPMENT
FOR EVERYONE, EVERYWHERE

Your capacity for empathy develops throughout your lifetime. As such, there isn't an age when—*boom*—you either have empathy or you don't. Empathy is a malleable and fluid set of skills that you can share with babies and children, with teens and adults, and with elders. In this chapter, I provided lots of ideas for working with emotions and empathy with kids, but games and stories, art and fun, dramatic play and emotive interactions are not confined to childhood. In fact, they shouldn't be. Empathy belongs to all of us, and these deceptively simple games can support empathic awareness at any age. The development of empathy is a lifetime adventure.

CHAPTER 10

Empathy at Work

Excelling in the Art of Emotion Work

I'M JUST GOING to say this outright: the workplace is problematic empathically. I notice that of all the places where empathy is developed or impeded, the workplace is one of the most obvious culprits in the reduction of emotional awareness and empathy. People focus a lot of energy on schools in terms of providing an empathy-building and antibullying curriculum. But I'd like to focus a great deal more energy on the workplace, since it is by far the most time-intensive aspect of our lives. School obviously occurs during a crucial and formative span in our lives, but unlike work, school ends after twelve years (unless we go on to college, though even then it might only go on for another two to eight years). We might spend twenty years in school, but we'll probably spend forty years or more in the workplace.

Work is where we are: if we work a normal forty-hour week, we spend more time at work than we do with our families or at home. In essence, we *live* at work. As adults, the only thing that we spend more time on than work is sleeping. And yet the world of work has not found ways to create a healthy emotional, empathic, or aesthetic environment for us. If you think about it, the difference between how we approach work and how we approach sleep in terms of the relative importance of each in our lives is kind of bizarre. For instance, in almost any-sized town, you'll find a number of home and bedding stores where you can buy hundreds of different mattresses and choose bedding in nearly any style, from contemporary to sensual to wildly artistic. The bed and bedding industries continually send messages about how vital and important your sleep life is; they've created a competitive sleep luxury market with increasingly expensive beds and sheets with thread counts that reach absurd numbers. The constant message is that your sleep comfort and luxury are crucial to the quality of your life.

Contrast this to your local office supply store—where in most places, small mom-and-pop shops have been replaced by large, impersonal chains. Use your Einfühlung capacity to feel your way into and around a typical office supply store. If you want to organize your office or cubicle, you have only a few choices—usually there are items in black, smoke, or silver mesh, though some designers have created color-coordinated office supplies for what's being called the *home office* (which annoyingly includes canning, sewing, and scrapbook supplies—*sigh*). But in the more serious office supply section, nothing is truly original or even particularly attractive. Look at the mouse pads, which is one place where many people can personalize their workstations. Depending on the store, you'll find some flowers, some pictures of space, some kittens or puppies, or perhaps a print of some painting you've seen before. Even the art is pedestrian, and all of it says, "These are nonthreatening deviations from total conformity." Even though you're using your own money to set up a space where you'll spend the lion's share of your life, your choices are few.

If you're lucky enough to be able to choose your own chair and desk, you might be able to find something fairly comfortable, but it won't be beautiful or artistic, really. The concept of comfort exists in high-end chairs and ergonomic workstations, but the comfort is not about you and your empathic, aesthetic, unique needs as much as it is about making you a better working machine. Of course, in defense of the workplace as an entity, your purpose *is* to be a cog in the machine of the workplace, and you *are* being paid to perform. However, the workplace as an entity has not yet become aware that we are spending the greater portion of our days, our weeks, and our lives away from home, away from our families, and away from an aesthetically pleasing, emotionally supportive, and empathically welcoming environment.

Please put your anthropologist's hat back on and empathically observe your workplace and your office or workstation in the way you observed your home in Chapter 6. Ask yourself whether this place supports you as a unique human being? Is your workplace an extension of your home environment in that it supports your sensory, social, and emotional needs? Or does your workstation create problems for you? Is your workplace a healthy terrarium for you? If not, why not?

As you study your workplace, look at it specifically in terms of the thresholds I mentioned in Chapter 6: Do you have the privacy you need to do your work? Do you have the room you need? Is your sensory environment supportive, or do sounds, scents, lights, or commotion impede your ability to focus? Is your workstation organized and functional? Are there separate areas for you to take breaks or rest or eat? If not, why not?

If you have the power to do so, see if you can make changes to your workstation so that you can feel more physically and aesthetically comfortable. If your workplace is filled with open-minded and caring people, you may want to include everyone in the process, so that all of your colleagues can become more comfortable—that's an ideal situation. But even in a deeply imperfect workplace, you can use thresholding to create privacy and protection for yourself—even in a noisy room where a cloth-covered cubicle divider is your only wall.

I do have a small warning about thresholding at work: some research suggests that the act of walking through doorways or thresholds has a kind of memory-erasing effect. In an experimental study done at the University of Notre Dame,[53] psychology researchers discovered that the act of entering new rooms has a strange cognitive-boundary effect, such that people often forget what they were thinking or doing before they crossed the threshold. The hypothesis is that crossing a threshold or walking through a doorway creates the appearance of a new cognitive event or environment that requires quick orienting behaviors and the clearing of items in short-term memory. This reorienting process may also relate to the problems people have with multitasking. As you probably know, recent research is showing that most people can't multitask at all, even (and often *especially*) if they think they're good at it—their performance actually decreases on every task each time they switch tasks. It could be that multitaskers are continually crossing cognitive event boundaries and losing their train of thought. As I think back to the thresholds I used in my writing cubicles, they did have that event boundary effect, which is why they were so great: people often came in to chatter about something meaningless, but as they crossed into my little cubicle space, their faces would often go blank for an instant, which gave me the chance to refocus them on work. Thresholds are awesome!

But thresholds may have effects on memory, so a word to the wise: if your workplace includes a lot of activity where people have to move from room to room to deliver information or complete their tasks, you might want to *reduce* the thresholds (for instance, by painting the doorways the same color as the walls), so that your coworkers don't lose their flow and their focus every time they cross into a new area. If the thresholds at work can't be modified, and you're one of the people who has to walk through possibly forgetfulness-inducing gauntlets every day, you can support your brain by writing down everything you need to do *before* you move through those event boundaries. Just don't forget to bring your list with you!

The physical condition of your workplace can support you empathically as well as physically, because an organized, well-defined, and comfortable physical environment can help you tolerate the often-disorganized emotional environment at work. Physical and aesthetic comfort can help you feel grounded, focused, and resourced, and this calm, steady state can help you perform some of your most important (yet usually unpaid) work of all: emotion work.

REVISITING EMOTION WORK[54]

In Chapter 7, I introduced the concept of *emotion work*, which comes from sociologist Arlie Hochschild's groundbreaking 1983 book, *The Managed Heart: Commercialization of Human Feeling*. In the book, Hochschild writes about the emotion work of flight attendants who, no matter what perils or discomforts they face, are expected to continually offer a calm, helpful, and accommodating demeanor to passengers. Although these demeanor rules are not written out explicitly in job descriptions, they're an intrinsic part of what we've all learned to expect (and even demand) from flight attendants.

Hochschild's concept of emotion work really helps us look at the often-unwritten emotional rules and empathic behaviors that are expected from us in the workplace—that is, how we must manage our own emotions and the emotions of others in order to get our work done. For instance, if airline passengers are rude, a good flight attendant won't generally snap at them or ignore their requests, as he might if his friends or family treated him rudely. In fact, his normal human reactions would be frowned upon by the airline; therefore, part of his job description (stated or not) is to deal with rudeness and bad behavior in unusual or even counterproductive (to him) ways. This is emotion work, and in many cases, it's actually enforced empathizing. It's a part of our social contract with each other, and though it's not usually spoken of explicitly as a job skill (or written down explicitly in a job description), emotion work is possibly the most important job skill you possess.

As you go through your day, pay attention to the emotion work of the people who serve you and of the people you serve. You probably have very specific (yet unspoken) emotion work rules for the owners and employees of businesses you visit (especially restaurants and stores), even if you've never set eyes on anyone in the business before. One unspoken expectation is that people in service or retail positions *must* be empathic. They *must* appear to care about you and your latte, or your shoes, or your cat food—even if they're making minimum wage and you're wealthy—even if they're well-dressed, and you just got out of the gym with your hair still wet. It doesn't matter—your position as a customer (or even as a potential customer) entitles you to free empathy and respect. Expectations of emotion work and professionalized empathy are everywhere, such that you and I know how every person in a business is supposed to behave toward us, how we're supposed to behave toward them, and how other customers are supposed to behave toward both of us. Everyone has a specific part to play and a specific emotional and empathic performance that is required. Strangely, most of us have never been explicitly taught about any of this emotion work; we're just supposed to have picked it up through cultural osmosis.

At your own job, you have specific emotion work and empathy work expectations for yourself, your coworkers, your employees and contractors, and your managers or bosses. Yet even though we all *know* how everyone is supposed to behave, this knowledge is not made clear, and a great deal of the trouble I see in the workplace revolves around emotion work that either is not being performed (the *problem* employee) or is being performed but not valued (the put-upon or heading-for-burnout employee). In many cases, the rules of emotion work require that we behave inauthentically with each other and toward ourselves. The workplace can become really miserable when there is trouble in the sphere of emotion work.

OUR UNDERGROUND AWARENESS OF EMOTION WORK

As a younger woman, I was hilariously out of place in many jobs, because emotion work was so obvious to me that I didn't realize other people couldn't see it. I tended to get into trouble because I would say out loud, "Hey, why don't you tell your assistant the truth instead of doing his work for him?" or "That person is working *way* past her abilities, and she's bossy and snappy because of it," or "This person is heading for burnout, and if you call yourself a manager, then *manage* the tension in this job and protect your workers!" Empathically speaking, I saw poorly managed emotions, unjust emotion work, and enforced, inauthentic empathy as an integral part of the unprofitability and inefficiency of the workplace. However, until I discovered Hochschild's work, I had no vocabulary for it.

Because I had so many persistent questions about the emotionally detrimental atmosphere of the workplace, I decided to minor in the sociology of work and occupations (this is in addition to my BA in social science and my work as a researcher). I also became certified in career testing and guidance and in human resource administration, because I wanted to know what the experts say about this situation. But after four years of study, I found that the experts say almost nothing.

Career guidance and HR administration programs spend almost *no* time on emotion work and enforced empathy requirements. There are a few psychology courses here and there, but the focus is more about administrative organization first and how to deal with problem employees second. There's very little understanding of the nuances of emotion work and the ways that an unsupportive workplace can create an unproductive emotional atmosphere, which will then create problem employees! There's also very little awareness of *why* people burn out; in fact, a great deal of the burnout response and prevention I was taught focused on making job tasks more interesting or varied, but there was almost no awareness of the burnout potential of unsupported, unjust, or unreasonable emotion work and enforced empathy.

Sadly, unless they've done extracurricular study, the career guidance professionals whose job it is to help us find work and the HR professionals who oversee the workplace usually have no direct education in or understanding of emotion work, which is the central empathic skill that makes the workplace functional (or, more commonly, dysfunctional). There is a saying that "People don't quit their jobs; they quit their managers." The fact is that very few people leave jobs because their daily tasks were too hard; instead, they often leave because the emotional and empathic environment was not managed effectively. It's an ongoing problem that the workplace as an entity does not have a handle on at all. As such, I didn't pursue career guidance or HR after I finished my certifications; however, I did discover precisely why emotion work problems in the workplace aren't being addressed. We have on-site specialists and processes for almost every other problem that exists in the workplace, but the HR professionals whose job it is to humanize the workplace have not been reliably educated or trained to understand emotion work. Therefore, it's up to you and me.

BRINGING EMOTION WORK INTO THE OPEN

Empaths tend to act as emotion work janitors, in the workplace and in their personal relationships. We who are empathically sensitive tend to pick up on—and then address—the emotional troubles around us. However, because emotions and emotion work live in the shadows, we are often unaware that we're engaged in perpetual, unpaid emotion work. We tend to clean up the emotional troubles around us. We mediate between people who can't get along. We jolly the grumpy people in our lives. We translate emotions into easily digestible chunks for our emotionally unaware friends and family. We calm people who are unaccountably anxious. We always seem to sit next to the person who wants a confidante. People tend to bring us their troubles and their conflicts. And no matter what our stated job description is, we have a second full-time job: we're professional emotion workers and professional empaths. But because our work isn't identified *as* work, we tend to burn out.

All of the skills and practices in this book will help empaths and unpaid emotion workers learn what emotions are, how they work, and how to work with them. I developed these empathic skills specifically to make emotion work less taxing: the self-soothing skills address burnout directly; boundary setting and thresholding help empaths develop a sense of privacy, so that their emotion work can become intentional rather than reflexive; and Burning Contracts and Conscious Complaining help empaths address and unload the incredible amount of emotional baggage they carry for others. In addition, these two skills have another vital purpose. Since so many empathic activities occur in the unheralded, unnoticed, yet absolutely crucial area of emotion work, both of these imaginal skills help you bring these seemingly ephemeral empathic behaviors into visual, verbal, and tangible form so you can identify, separate from, and change those behaviors.

Conscious Complaining can help you get to the core of what's bothering you, and Burning Contracts can help you treat your emotion work as a choice rather than as your destiny. When you can visualize or make tangible the persona you've donned as an unpaid emotion worker, you can burn your contracts with that persona and make way for a new, more intentional, and more comfortable approach. You can still do emotion work, and you can still be an empath, but your empathic mindfulness skills will help you do so on your own terms.

IDENTIFYING YOUR OWN EMOTION WORK

What kind of emotion work do you do? Is it stated as part of your job description? (Also, do your friends, mate, and family openly acknowledge your emotion work?) Are you doing any emotion work for a colleague, such as soothing tempers if your colleague blows up, translating for your colleague when others don't understand her behavior or her needs, or taking the lead if another colleague cannot speak up on his own? Are you mediating between family members, translating emotions for friends, or working hard to keep your mate happy, even though your own needs are going untended? What emotion work do you do? Is it being recognized? Is it working for you? And in the larger empathic sense, is it working for other people?

Specifically, how much emotion work are you doing in the area of happiness creation? Is it all right with you when other people feel angry, or do you often try to soothe anger away? Have you become a kind of portable rejuvenation and resourcing station for angry people? If so, could you be training people how *not* to set boundaries for themselves and how *not* to develop their own self-soothing skills?

Do you allow people to feel appropriate shame so that they can learn how to moderate their own behavior, or do you soothe shame away as well? Can you allow people to feel anxiety that may help them get their work done, or do you step in and help them complete the tasks they've been procrastinating about? Are *all* emotions safe in your presence, or are you actually helping people remain emotionally unskilled in the presence of difficult emotions?

As you examine your own emotion work, check in with any valencing you might be imposing upon the emotions of others. In the workplace, enforced empathy often means that you have to keep everyone calm and happy at all times—very few other emotions are welcome. This enforced reduction of emotional awareness has pretty troubling consequences for the workplace as an entity, but it also has troubling consequences for you and your coworkers.

As you observe and improve your physical workspace and your thresholding, think about creating protected areas, times, or practices (such as Conscious Complaining with a Partner) where you and your colleagues can be whole and skillful emotional beings, and not merely emotion work robots.

It's a gift to help people experience their real emotions—to feel the way they feel—and to support them in developing *their own* emotional skills. That's good emotion work, if you can get it!

HIERARCHIES, MERITOCRACIES, AND HIDDEN POWER STRUCTURES AT WORK

Empathically speaking, I love to observe the power differentials in the stated organizational structure of a business—from the owners or the board of directors at the top to the management at the middle to the workers at the bottom. On paper, the power structure is clearly hierarchical; and yet in the real world, you'll often find that the power structure actually exists in a *meritocracy* that the workers themselves create so that they can get their work done. A meritocracy is an organizational structure that places the most talented people in key positions because they *merit* those positions. They didn't get there through family connections, they didn't get promoted past their ability level, and they're actually awesomely good at their work and fully merit the position they have.[55] Most businesses dream of being meritocracies, and most HR departments hope to create meritocracies through effective hiring practices and employee training initiatives. But as we've all seen, many things get in the way of those hopes and dreams.

However, meritocracies are necessary if you want to get anything done. In many dysfunctional workplaces, workers themselves will set up what I call a *shadow meritocracy* of the business. Shadow meritocracies are high-functioning but unacknowledged work groups that arise in response to a failing worker (who's often in a key position or in management), in reaction to an unjust hierarchy, or in reaction to a rigid bureaucratic structure that can't respond quickly to change. I don't use the word *shadow* to suggest that there's something shady going on; I use it because these underground meritocracies can't be seen in the light of day. They're not in the organizational chart, there are no job titles for their members, and you can't even identify them by the relative size of their members' offices or paychecks. You can only see them out of the corner of your eye—in nuances, undercurrents, interactions, whispered communications, and workflow. These meritocracies aren't out in the open because they *can't* be; they have to exist in the shadows because they're covering for, protecting, or working around a problem that cannot be remedied for some reason. Shadow meritocracies are an intrinsic feature of many workplaces, and they're an intrinsic part of emotion work.

We've all seen or worked in businesses where an owner, manager, or key employee just wasn't very functional and where talented assistants, other managers, or the entire staff performed emotion work and physical work to cover for that person's shortcomings. Sometimes the person is beloved, and though the labor needed to cover his or her failings is real, the people who form the shadow meritocracy don't seem to mind it much. They might speak confidentially with one another as a way to relieve tension, but their emotion work binds them together empathically, and they often feel content because they're helping the nonfunctional person, connecting with each other, and making the workplace function efficiently. Shadow meritocracies can be healing and necessary structures in a workplace where troubles or troubled employees can't be addressed openly.

However, if the troubled owner, manager, or employee isn't beloved or is actively obstructionist, always stopping the workflow to go off on tangents, complaining all the time, or bullying others, then the shadow meritocracy can become very shadowy, indeed. This kind of emotion work is grueling, and it can lead to burnout, certainly, but it can also provide a terrible lesson in what kind of work is rewarded. If an untalented, obstructionist, self-pitying, or bullying worker is not challenged by HR, management, or the board, everyone else in the workplace will learn that talent and personal accountability are not the coins of this realm. What workers do with this knowledge is individual, but the knowledge that some people can get away with incompetence and emotional volatility at work can have an explosive effect on the workplace as a whole.

Thousands of books, seminars, and workshops are directed at this kind of workplace problem, but most of them focus on fixing problem employees rather than looking at the entire situation and the emotion work that's occurring. Sometimes these approaches focus on the actual problem employee who created the need for the shadow meritocracy in the first place. But in many cases, that problem employee is in a position of power, and as we've all seen, the rules for people at the top of hierarchies are different from the rules for people at the middle or the bottom. In many cases, the problem employee will be misidentified as the one from the bottom who displays anger about injustices occurring at the top. I cannot even count the programs that target problem employees who are branded as negative (meaning they express any emotion besides happiness and they allegedly drag down the workplace) without studying or even considering the social, emotional, and empathic atmosphere of the workplace.

I saved a particularly awful example of this kind of program in some emails that my husband, Tino, sent me from a rotten job he had. Tino and his fellow managers were asked to identify employees by their leading emotion—Sad Susan, Fearful Frank, Angry Amanda, and so on. They were then told how to manipulate these people into being better workers. Tino knew that this approach would create Angry Karla, and he sent the emails with a kind of "Can you believe this crap?" message—but wow! Talk about zero understanding of emotion work, hierarchies, meritocracies, and basic human emotions. Why are managers with no training in psychology able to interfere with the basic emotional functioning of their workers, yet are not held to any professional, academic, or ethical standards themselves? Yeesh!

Dear workplace, dear managers, dear HR departments: *Wake up!* Emotions are reliable, action-requiring neurological programs that are evoked by reliably specific stimuli. If you follow the emotions, you can gather amazing, game-changing information about what's actually occurring in the workplace, in the hierarchy, and in the shadow meritocracy. For instance, if Susan is always sad, has anyone checked to see whether she's depressed, or has anyone looked to see if there's something inherently depressing in the workplace? Could Susan be a sensitive person who's acting as a kind of canary in the coal mine, pointing to the problems everyone else is ignoring? If Frank is always fearful, what kinds of changes is he dealing with? What is he orienting to, and is he identifying any hazards? Could Frank be an effective early-warning system for existing or upcoming problems? If Amanda is always angry, is she a sensitive person in the middle of a loud room with no protection? You can fix that, and perhaps make everyone else more comfortable at the same time. Or is Amanda performing intense emotion work and needing to set boundaries? You can help her with that. Is her voice or standpoint being threatened? If so, why? Or is she speaking up for people like Frank and Susan, who are so overwhelmed that they've lost their voices? Are Frank, Susan, and Amanda in a shadow meritocracy, doing heavy lifting for a failing manager or a clueless boss? And why are these employee-fixing programs always directed at workers and not at bosses, CEOs, or the entire emotional milieu? Yeesh.

I've read a lot of research about hierarchies, dominance, and employee voice in terms of when employees will (and won't) communicate problems up the hierarchy. Workers often see more than managers and bosses can, because they're actually doing the hands-on labor; yet they tend to keep problems to themselves. This is a huge impediment to workplace effectiveness—it wastes untold amounts of time, energy, and money, and it reduces productivity. In one study,[56] organizational behavior researchers at the New York University Stern School of Business found that *eighty-five percent* of the people they interviewed had chosen not to communicate their concerns to management at one time or another. The researchers found that the reasons for this are primarily social, emotional, and structural; the reasons have nothing to do with the actual work being performed. Many people in the study reported that they didn't communicate because they didn't want to be identified as troublemakers or complainers; they didn't want to rock the boat or lose their relational security. Empathically, I have to ask: Why is there so much tension in the workplace that people can't talk about real workflow problems without endangering their position? Why are people penalized for honesty? Why are their emotions pathologized? And why can't they point to emperors who have no clothes? The answer is this: these honest and productive actions go against the secret, underground rules of emotion work and enforced empathizing. Even if an individual is very honest and forthright in his or her private life, collective dynamics often trump individual skills. The culture drives the behavior.

As you empathically observe your workplace, look at the culture, how problems are handled, and the amount of emotion work that is unacknowledged, yet absolutely enforced. Identify any problem employees, if there are any, and look for shadow meritocracies. If one exists in your workplace, are you a part of it and, if so, what emotional labor are you performing? Does your workplace culture value excellence, which involves honesty that flows up and down the hierarchy, or is excellence just a buzzword in the mission statement? Is there any danger in bearing bad news about products, processes, ideas, supplies, or other workers? If there is danger, then you can expect that a great deal of communication will be redirected. It won't travel upward, but it will still travel, in one of the most important forms of empathic communication there is: gossip.

ETHICAL EMPATHIC GOSSIP[57]

Gossip is usually belittled, despised, and pathologized, yet it's actually one of the most important empathic tools you have. Clearly, this is not the accepted view of gossip, which is usually portrayed as toxic, deceitful, and immature. I understand this view of gossip, because I had a very hard time with gossip when I was a younger person. I saw it as an emotionally dishonest form of communication, and I had very little patience for it. In my family, gossip was the central mode of communication about serious relationship issues, and I watched as people's honest feelings about each other were only spoken in private—to someone else—while the real relationships faltered and sputtered because people refused to talk directly to one another. As a young woman, I continually got myself into awful triangulated problems because I would tell people about what other people were saying about them. I would share the information I learned through gossip because I thought everyone would be better off if all parties knew about the troubles, the issues, the backstory, the emotions, and the truth. Then they could work together to improve their relationships, right? *Hah!* Ack! I got into *so* much trouble that I had to burn my contracts with that behavior, do some research, and work hard to become more intelligent about gossip.

What I discovered in anthropology, sociology, and social psychology is that gossip is a universal practice that is irreplaceably vital to human communication and relationships. Gossip is an essential part of social life, intimacy, and emotional health. Studies have shown that gossip is undertaken by people of all ages and both genders. Gossip is *not*—as I thought erroneously—a sign of cowardice or dishonesty; gossip is the tool you use to form bonds and convey (and become skilled in) the unwritten social and emotional rules of each social situation you encounter. Gossip is a vital social skill, because it gives you a quick and easy way to learn the lay of the land, socially speaking. If someone pulls you aside and warns you that a mutual friend is in a really bad mood because his car just got sideswiped, you've just been saved from making a social faux pas by asking him for that $40 he owes you. Gossip, which we can also call informal communication, can give you social information you can't get any other way.

Gossip can also create an alternative social structure, especially in areas where a great deal of authority is being applied from above. Think of an authoritarian work or schooling environment in your life and how you and your peers created secretive, informal chains of communication to share information about how to behave, how to manage, or how to avoid punishment. Shadow meritocracies function on information-rich gossip, and gossip among peers can reduce the damage that a rigid, hierarchical, and authoritarian system can inflict. Gossip can create an alternative, informal power structure that gives people a certain level of freedom, even in oppressive environments.

Gossip is also a way to signal (or attain) closeness in relationships. For instance, if you enter a new job, and within a few days people begin gossiping with you about coworkers and management, it's probably a sign that they're welcoming you into the informal communication network—and possibly into the shadow meritocracy. Or if your friends and family regularly gossip to you, it's a sign that you're a trusted confidante (whoops, Karla from the past, you *really* screwed up by sharing all those secrets!).

I have a working hypothesis about gossip, which is that the amount of gossip in a workplace relates directly to the effectiveness of the HR department or management. Certainly, if you have a harsh, authoritarian workplace, you'll observe large amounts of gossip as people try to find ways to navigate around oppressive social structures. But you'll also find intricate gossip networks in lackadaisical, poorly managed workplaces, because there's *not enough* structure, and people have to create shadow meritocracies and informal information networks just so they can achieve some order amid the chaos. In both oppressive *and* permissive workplaces, my working hypothesis is that HR and management are either not able to or not allowed to regulate and humanize the social environment; therefore, the workers have to do it themselves—and often, they do it through gossip.

When you see a great deal of gossip and indirect communication occurring in a social group, it can be a signal that you're in the presence of an overly permissive *or* overly repressive social structure. Studying gossip is a fascinating way to empathically observe a social group.

For empaths, because so much of what we see about emotions and the social world is not addressable or mentionable in public, gossip can be a wonderful stress-relieving tool. Gossip can help emotionally sensitive people relieve inner tension, because it allows them to share the emotive and empathic impressions they pick up from others but are not allowed to mention openly. Gossip helps people connect to others, understand human behavior, identify or change their social position, and support (or undermine) rules and set them for others. Gossip is a powerful communication tool that exists in every social group, everywhere.

THEN WHY IS GOSSIP SO DESPISED?

The answer is simple: jealousy and envy. Think about the purpose of gossip, and then think about the things that gossip helps you achieve. Gossip is a powerful communication tool that helps you maintain your social position and your connections to sources of recognition, financial security, loyalty, social support, fairness, and love. Gossip helps you situate yourself skillfully in relation to these vital things; it's a primary tool that helps you complete the actions that your jealousy and envy require. However, since these two vital and irreplaceable emotions are some of the most hated in the entire emotional realm, their communication tool nearly has to exist in a hidden underworld. You can't ignore your social capital and your relational security—it would be foolish in the extreme to disregard your connections to security, fairness, recognition, loyalty, and love—and yet the emotions that help you attain and preserve these connections have been shoved into the deep, deep shadow. And gossip, which is crucial to your social viability, has been shoved into the shadow with them.

Gossip is an irreplaceable tool of informal communication. Gossip gives you an accessible way to connect to others and gather information that you simply cannot get any other way. But when a great deal of gossip is active in a social group, it usually means there is a great deal of trouble that is continually evoking jealousy and envy—there's injustice, disloyalty, and threats to identity and security. Gossip has a purpose. It's necessary for social survival, and when it's very active, it's telling you there are injustices and inequities that need to be attended to. If you can follow the gossip threads and listen to the emotions, you'll discover key issues and crucial structural problems that many businesses hire high-priced efficiency experts to find. I say save your money and follow the gossip. Listen to the emotions, bring the emotion work out of the shadows, and bring your empathic genius to the situation. All the information is there; it's in the gossip network.

Gossip is crucial to social awareness, social inclusion, and social survival, but by its very nature, gossip is indirect, and this can be problematic. If gossip is the only informal communication skill you have, you might learn to talk *about* people, rather than talking *to* them. When you're trapped in a poorly managed social system, this indirect approach can save you from all kinds of trouble. In the workplace, gossip and shadow meritocracies may be your only options. But within your intimate relationships, gossip can lead to unfortunate problems precisely because it *isn't* direct. Gossip can certainly help you navigate safely through social structures and workplaces that are repressive (or permissive), but you can also *create* a repressive social structure if you rely on gossip alone, instead of developing actual relationship skills. You can waste *years* talking about a friend or coworker instead of talking to him or her openly;

therefore, it's often necessary to move gossip aside so that you can communicate directly with people you care about.

Gossip can also be problematic in relationships that you want to nurture, because gossip can lead you to invade the privacy of your gossip targets as you telegraph their behavior to everyone. This is one way that gossip can create a repressive and compromising environment. If you go back to the relationship you gossiped about without addressing the problems more openly, there will always be this *thing* hanging out there—this gossipy information that you hope never gets repeated. Although gossip is necessary, it can be a very messy business if you aren't conscientious and ethical about using it.

Gossip is as natural to us as breathing. Anthropologists see gossip in humans as a primal tool of socialization, almost like the preening and grooming primates use to form bonds. So gossip is primal, and it's necessary. But that's no reason to allow it to be unconscious, derisive, or dehumanizing. If you can understand the tension-relieving, information-gathering, and socialization opportunities that gossip provides, you can turn gossip into a tool that will support your ethics and your relationships. You can turn gossip into an *ethical* empathic practice.

Although this gossip practice is wonderful for your personal life, you can also use it at work if you realize you're in a gossip network or a shadow meritocracy. These networks and shadow structures are often unconscious; you might just fall into them through peer pressures and group dynamics. That's fine, because it's normal to chip in and make things work when there's dysfunction in a social structure—it's a part of the social contract we have with one another. But these social contracts can be brought forward, observed empathically, renegotiated, or burnt. Remember that your social and emotional behaviors aren't concrete; they're not written in stone. They're tendencies that you can change when you become aware of them.

||||||||||||||||||||||||||||||||||||||||||||||||||||||||||||||||||||||||||||||||||||||

ETHICAL EMPATHIC GOSSIP SESSIONS

Gossip is an irreplaceable communication and connection tool that helps you learn the informal rules of a social group. Gossip also helps you become aware of threats to your security and your relationships, and gossip can help you take the actions that your jealousy and envy require. Gossip contains an incredible amount of essential social information, and when you can create an ethical practice for your gossip, you can bring the life-changing gifts of your jealousy and envy out of the shadows. This practice will also help you become more able to empathize with and provide support to the currently unaware gossipers in your life. Here are some guidelines for creating an Ethical Empathic Gossip session with a supportive friend or coworker:

1. Identify a person you gossip about consistently and with whom your relationship has stalled.
2. Open the gossip session by acknowledging your trouble in the situation.
3. Ask your friend for help in dealing with your gossip target and to listen with the goal of providing opinions, ideas, techniques, and skills that will help you re-enter the relationship or situation in a different way.
4. Go for it—just gossip—but be aware of any shadow issues that come forward. Remember that gossip targets nearly always hold some of your shadow!
5. When your friend gives you feedback, pay attention.
6. Close your gossip session with thanks, and then go back to the original relationship or situation with your new skills and insights. Or let it go if it's too damaged to survive. But don't go back in the same old way; that's what led to the need for gossip in the first place.

||||||||||||||||||||||||||||||

When your gossip is conscious and ethical, you'll increase your social skills and your empathy, and you'll become more able to create honest, healthy relationships. What's amazing to me in this practice is that when gossip is made conscious, you can clearly see what a stupendous information-gathering tool it is. When you're able to gossip ethically in this safe, firmly bounded empathic practice, you may be amazed to learn how much intricate social information you've gathered about your gossip targets. This practice will connect you to the deep and emotionally rich undercurrents that flow through your informal gossip networks.

This practice will also remind you that you can ask for and receive help in dealing with difficult emotions, difficult situations, and difficult people. When you've hit a wall, remember to reach out for the assistance of others instead of isolating yourself. None of us knows how to deal with all emotions, all situations, or all relationships, because we simply weren't taught how. For goodness' sake, most of us weren't even taught how to name our own emotions! We're all working without a guidebook here, and we can always use some empathic assistance.

IF YOUR WORK IS EMPATHIC IN NATURE

Not surprisingly, many empathic people choose empathy-requiring jobs in health care, counseling, teaching, and other social support occupations. If your occupation requires high-level empathy and emotion work, then of course, all of the empathic mindfulness skills in this book apply to your occupational health and well-being. You might burn out if you don't have ways to ground, focus, resource, and define yourself in your work, in your workspace, and between clients. High empathy work can be wonderful, and I'm grateful that you're openly using your empathic skills, so let's make sure that your workplace supports you.

Please put on your anthropologist's hat again and use your Einfühlung capacity to observe and feel your way into the physical and aesthetic qualities of your workspace in the way you observed your home. Who works here, and what is important to this person? What is beautiful to you, and why? Which aspects of this workspace support you, and which aspects are problematic? Are you able to create thresholds and privacy for your work? Do you have a comfortable break area? Can you get outside for a walk? Do you have a private place where you can go when you need to resource or rejuvenate yourself during work?

Look at the chair, desk, or station where you do your intentional empathic work: What have you placed nearest to your body? Are you physically comfortable when you work? Is your workplace quiet enough for you? What are you looking out upon? Are there soothing and beautiful vistas or artworks? Are there areas of sensual and visual delight for you to observe as you work? If not, why not?

As a professional empath, please stand back and observe your workspace with the skills you bring to others: If you were consulting with the person who works in this space, what would you change, if anything? Does this physical environment support your body, your emotions, your boundaries, your aesthetic needs, and your unique self? If not, why not?

As a professional empath, the quality of your home life and your relationships will directly affect the quality of your work and your capacity to care for yourself. If your home and your relationships are supportive and healing, they can provide rest, rejuvenation, and real downtime in which you can unwind, let go, and replenish your emotions and your empathic skills. But as I pointed out in Chapter 6, if your home and your relationships are not supportive, then you'll be doing empathic work and emotion work all day and all night as well. There's just no way to keep yourself well if you have nothing in your life that feeds you. If you perform heavy empathic labor at work and then go home to provide basic emotional life support for your emotionally unskilled mate or family members, then something's going to fall apart. I don't want that something to be you.

As a working empath in our emotionally troubled world, you provide a vital and valuable service that can't be replicated. We can't digitize you or replace you with a machine, and we can't outsource your work to other countries. We need you here—happy, healthy, emotionally well fed, and well loved. Your work is vital, and to do it over the long term, you need support from your workplace, from your home, from your loved ones, from your healthcare providers, from your diet, from your sleep, from your artistic expression, from your movement practices, from your empathic practices, and from your empathic friends. But most important, you need support from yourself: you need to identify yourself as a working empath whose unique emotional functioning requires intentional self-care and self-love. I thank you for bringing your empathy and your emotional awareness to our waiting world; please make sure that you're bringing empathy and emotional awareness to yourself as well. Thank you!

CREATING AN EMOTIONALLY WELL-REGULATED WORKPLACE

There are literally thousands of books and programs that target the workplace in terms of how to make people into better workers and thereby increase productivity. Empathically speaking, most of those books and programs fail (or get replaced in a number of months by the next miracle book or program) because they ignore emotion work and focus on the individual instead of the overriding power of workplace culture in driving behavior. With that in mind, I've focused on seven approaches that may help you create an emotionally well-regulated workplace that is respectful of the real needs of real human beings.

1. **Honor emotions in the workplace.** Emotions are reliable, action-requiring neurological programs that arise reliably in response to specific stimuli. They are an intrinsic part of cognition and an intrinsic part of social intelligence. Emotions can lead you directly to crucial issues that affect your

workplace, the workflow, or employee and vendor relationships. Honor emotions and honor the people who feel them. You can do this by copying the list of emotions and their actions from Chapter 4 and having people regularly check in (with themselves or others) about how they're feeling about work, upcoming deadlines, or changes in workflow. A tremendous amount of information is contained in emotions. Use it well.

2. Identify any unsupported emotion work and acknowledge it openly. Put on your empath's hat and observe the emotion work requirements at your workplace. What emotions are required in interactions with customers, suppliers, and coworkers? Is empathy toward customers required but unacknowledged? What emotion rules are active and for whom? Are the emotion rules different at different levels of the hierarchy? For instance, can one person or group display anger, depression, or anxiety, while everyone else must display only happiness and complacency? To the extent that you can, acknowledge this openly. If you can't do it openly, use Ethical Empathic Gossip to help people clearly identify the emotion work they're being expected to perform.

3. Support healthy thresholding and help people become physically comfortable. Remember the stark differences between a bedding store and an office supply store and challenge that paradigm. People *live* at work, and they need to be physically and emotionally comfortable.

4. Create many ways for problems to be communicated upward without danger. Employees will be honest in a supportive work culture where bearers of bad news are welcomed. However, if problem-identifying employees are shunned, shamed, or jollied out of their positions, gossip networks will have to intensify, and a shadow meritocracy may become necessary. If you notice a great deal of gossip in your workplace, yet unusual silence occurs when management or HR show up, there is probably a culture of emotion valencing, repression, or even punishment at work. If your workplace is currently incapable of dealing with problems in a focused and emotionally honest way, your workforce may not trust any changes you might make to this process. Suggestion boxes may be necessary at first, but even those may not be trusted. In a culture of silencing or punishment, you may need to bring in a mediator to help work through the multilayered dysfunctions that reliably arise in a problem-averse workplace.

5. Hire overqualified people and trust them. An old, dusty canard in HR lore is that overqualified employees are a problem because they might get bored and leave. Empathically and logistically speaking, that's nonsense, especially in our new workforce where pretty much everyone job-hops every three years, on average. If you're lucky enough to have highly skilled and experienced workers applying for jobs, you've struck gold. Experienced workers require fewer training days, fewer corrective management interactions, and less time to learn their jobs. They can think on their feet, and they understand the workplace as an entity. In other words, they know what they're doing. If you hire overqualified people, then you're well on your way to creating the true meritocracy that most businesses dream of. All you have to do is acknowledge your concerns about possible boredom levels. If highly qualified and experienced people are not concerned about that, believe them, hire them, and stand back and watch your workplace actually *work*.

6. **Honor shadow meritocracies and support them.** Shadow meritocracies, which form in response to real problems in the workplace, are often the secret, underground machine that keeps everything working. To address these meritocracies, you should fix the problems that they formed to solve—don't shun, shame, or cajole the people who formed them. In fact, throw them *two* parties: one to thank them before you fix the problem (and while they're still making everything work for you), and one to thank them after you fix the problem and they can disband gracefully.

7. **Honor gossip networks, but help them become ethical.** Gossip is a vital and absolutely necessary form of communication, and it strengthens social bonds. However, as we all know, it can strengthen bonds in a toxic way and encourage people to express jealousy and envy harmfully. If there's a powerful underground gossip network at your workplace, it's signaling deep trouble in your social structure, which may be too rigid and overly authoritarian or too loose and unstructured to be truly efficient. If you can formally introduce Ethical Empathic Gossip into the gossip networks, it can help people become consciously aware of all the information that exists in gossip, and it can do so in a way that protects the dignity of everyone involved. If you can't formally introduce this practice, see if you can use it in small work groups or within your own department. Gossip is a necessary tool, and you can learn to use it ethically as an intentional part of your workflow.

WHEN YOUR WORKPLACE IS NOT EMOTIONALLY WELL-REGULATED

If you work in an emotionally unregulated workplace, do what you can to make yourself comfortable. If you can, work with thresholding and Ethical

Empathic Gossip to make your environment and your relationships as supportive as possible, and use your empathic mindfulness skills to keep yourself focused, grounded, and resourced. An emotionally unregulated workplace can really drain the life out of you, so you'll need to create as many thresholds around it as you can. Your social life away from work can provide some of that thresholding, and of course, your home can be a healing getaway and a sanctuary that will give you something to look forward to every day.

If you can't make enough changes to detoxify your workplace, and you can't currently move to a new job, I ask you to treat yourself as a working empath in a situation like this—and to take care of yourself as fully and with as much dedication as I suggested for professional empaths a few pages back. Emotion work is real work, and if your workplace can't support your real work, then you'll need to support yourself in as many ways as you can.

You can support yourself with all of the empathic practices in this book, with art and movement, with time in nature or with animals, and by spending time with people who truly understand you. In the next chapter, we'll look at ways to connect with empathic people and empathic social justice movements so that you can help create a more truly empathic civilization for everyone.

CHAPTER 11

Empathy for the World

The Empathic Art of Social Justice

IN THIS BOOK, we've been working from the inside out. I intentionally focused first on your emotions; then on your empathic skills; then on your home and on your relationships with your friends, family, and children; and then on your workplace. Now, we'll focus on the most outward manifestation of your empathy, which appears in your social justice work.

Social justice work is all about empathy; it's a full-bodied empathic activity that calls upon all of your empathic skills. Attaining the sixth and most developed aspect of empathy—Perceptive Engagement—means that you can take focused and appropriate actions based on your Concern for Others and your capacity for sensitive Perspective Taking. Social justice work, which is intentionally and deliberately empathic, can help you expand your empathic skills in a community of people who want to do the same thing. Social justice work is a full-scale, professional empathy-building activity that will connect you to other empaths. This work can challenge you in the areas of self-care and Emotion Regulation (as we'll explore later in this chapter), but if you want to deepen your empathic skills and enter an empathic community, social justice work is your friend.

When I speak of social justice, I don't mean to conjure up images of large organizations collecting money and advocating for national and international political change. Those organizations are certainly a part of what I'm referring to, but social justice work is empathic, which means it occurs wherever interactions occur. Visiting an elder in your neighborhood and driving him or her on errands, creating a fun afterschool space for local kids, providing a safe shelter for neighborhood stray cats, creating a tool-sharing cooperative on your block, learning Spanish or sign language so you can communicate with your new neighbors—all of these are empathic social justice initiatives. Social justice work doesn't have to be large and lofty activism; it can be anything you do to make the world warmer, more connected, more just and equitable, and more workable for others. You can do that in activist organizations, sure, but you can also do it in intimate and informal settings, such as your home and your neighborhood.

As you think about bringing your healthy, grounded, and resourced empathy to the larger world, I'd like you to put on your anthropologist's hat again to observe the causes that speak to you. You're a unique empathic organism with a unique sense of meaning and purpose. As such, which forms of need and inequity feel meaningful to you? What draws your attention? I'd like you to be as specific as possible, because if you're very empathic, you may be pulled in many directions at once, and your anxiety may kick in to help you plan for the complete healing of every problem facing every species on every continent. Bless your heart, but remember the question for anxiety—"What *really* needs to get done?" Focus your attention closer to you, become very specific, and identify things that you can actually do, so that you can take tangible, real-world actions that will help your anxiety recede naturally.

If your attention is drawn to the environment or to animal welfare, you can support large organizations, but you can also work in your own neighborhood to address local issues. You can help with creek cleanup, work to make bike lanes safer, work with animals at the local shelter, or take neighborhood dogs on walks if they're lonely and bored. If you're concerned about human rights violations at home and abroad, you can support international organizations, but you can also volunteer at local homeless shelters and food banks or with the local battered women's shelter. If you're drawn to literacy or the arts, you can support your local library and become a reading tutor or support your local arts council and teach classes (or support others artists who do). My point is not to provide you with an exhaustive list of places where you can lend a hand; rather, it's to focus you on simple, real-world interactions that will help you develop and expand your empathic skills in your community and in support of causes that already have deep meaning for you.

PROTECTING YOURSELF FROM EMPATHIC BURNOUT

If you follow your own sense of meaning and do your social justice work in a way that works for you, your experience may be pretty graceful and fulfilling—that is, you won't burn out. However, in many larger social justice initiatives, two often-competing needs are active: (1) The social justice work needs to be undertaken in the smartest way possible; and (2) Money needs to be gathered. As we've all seen, this need for money can mean that our inboxes, social networks, and mailboxes are filled with pleas for help. Empathically speaking, these pleas are created very intentionally to activate specific emotions and empathic states in you.

Numerous studies have found that when people are emotionally activated about causes, they tend to be willing to part with their money. If you approach people with information on these same causes *without* trying to activate their emotions, they don't tend to be as generous. If you think about this empathically, it makes sense—emotions require actions, and giving money feels like you're taking action. As you observe your involvement in social justice work, look for the emotions being activated. There's some crossover, but in general, disease-curing activists try to evoke your sadness, fear, anxiety, and pity empathy; environmental activists try to evoke your sadness, fear, anxiety, anger, and indignation empathy; animal rights and human rights activists try to evoke your sadness, anger, indignation empathy, and pity empathy; and so forth. Many social justice and activist groups pour a lot of time and money into marketing pleas that are engineered to activate specific clusters of emotions about that group's special focus.

This doesn't have to be a problem. Intentional emotional activation isn't evil; it's how activism works, it's how advertising works, it's how teaching works, and it's how parenting works. If you need people to do something they might not want to do or if you need them to learn something new, you have to figure out ways to compel or maneuver them—and the fastest way is through their emotions and their empathy. There are certainly more and less ethical ways to do this, but in and of itself, trying to evoke emotions in others is not a problem; it's normal everyday behavior, and we all do it.

Here's something to consider: when activist groups target and activate your emotions, it means that almost all of your empathic skills are engaged (all of them except perhaps Emotion Regulation, I'd say). That's really great in one way, because you may love to feel the emotions that are being evoked. You may love to feel deep empathy and pity as you look upon the images of sad dogs or babies in third world countries, and giving money might feel incredibly healing to you. That's great! You might also love to be angered and energized by activist groups that help you identify injustice and malfeasance.

You may love to feel righteous indignation and share that emotional state with your activist friends as you work to bring awareness and justice to the world. That's great, too! Your activism and social justice work can be as emotionally compelling as any form of drama, art, or literature, and it can absolutely increase your emotional and empathic capacities.

However, because the dramatic and empathic practice of emotion activation is an intrinsic part of the business model of successful activist organizations, there's something to watch out for empathically: As we all know, this emotional activation can become absurd and manipulative ("Who will think of the *children?*"), and it can and does lead to compassion fatigue and empathic burnout. So I ask you, empath to empath, to become hip to this intentional emotional manipulation rather than become a victim of it. Activist groups and social justice organizations feed off of your emotions; it's how they survive. You can use your empathic skills to identify the targeted emotions and decide whether you want to be influenced into feeling them. If you do, great! If you don't, but you really like the work the organization does, make sure to perform emotional thresholding for yourself and stay away from their marketing materials—you should be fine.

Tony Waters, one of my sociology professors, wrote a beautiful book with a fairly inaccessible title, *Bureaucratizing the Good Samaritan.*[58] In it he writes about how humanitarian relief organizations have to focus their advertising efforts in ways that have very little to do with the realities of their work. Many of these large relief organizations have to mobilize quickly and create massive tent cities with food, temporary housing, medical care, transportation, sanitation, clean water, electricity, and security for perhaps thousands of people fleeing wars or natural disasters. The work is massive—it's city-building in a hurry, and it involves intricate planning and cooperation among dozens of governmental and nongovernmental agencies—ships, trains, airplanes, huge trucks full of supplies. Yet to procure donations, according to Waters, these organizations often have to show photos of two or three hungry children or mothers holding babies with tears rolling down their cheeks. They have to humanize the situation and help people feel sadness, love, anger about injustice, pity empathy, and a kind of panicky immediacy about sending money. Often, famous singers and actors are recruited to stand among the refugees and ground the emotional situation for people back home. But sometimes these situations are so emotionally inaccessible that the donations don't arrive, and the massive relief efforts can't function effectively.

The behavioral economist Dan Ariely writes about this very situation in his book *The Upside of Irrationality*,[59] in which he contrasts the striking differences in people's responses to two tragic situations. In the first situation, which happened in 1987 in Texas, a toddler who came to be known as Baby Jessica fell into the bottom of a dry well and got stuck for two-and-a-half days. The media went on an absolute bender, with the new cable TV station CNN providing continuous and breathless twenty-four-hour coverage of the rescue efforts. Baby Jessica was rescued after two days of media frenzy, and though she needed medical attention, she survived and returned to a fairly normal life, media glare notwithstanding. People who had followed the story sent more than $700,000 in donations to Jessica's family. Ariely contrasts this situation to the 1994 genocide in Rwanda, Africa, where more than 800,000 people were murdered in ethnic-cleansing violence that didn't garner even a fraction of the media coverage that Baby Jessica's two-day ordeal did.

Waters was there in 1994, right outside Rwanda, helping to set up refugee camps in neighboring Tanzania, where Rwandans were fleeing for their very lives. But the situation wasn't so simple and emotionally accessible as a little white baby falling into a well. There was extreme violence among people of color, decades of simmering tribal inequities with brutality from both sides, squabbling among African countries, political assassinations, and multiple international relief organizations tripping over one another while UN policy makers argued about the precise definition of the word *genocide*. The media stayed away in droves, and hundreds of thousands of people died because we who might have helped or donated couldn't access the situation emotionally or empathically. These massive rescue and aid organizations don't operate on emotions alone—they actually operate on detailed strategy and extensive infrastructure. Yet if the right emotional frames aren't in place, they can't operate well at all.

In March 2012, in a professionally produced thirty-minute video, an American group attempted to address this very problem by simplifying the search for an African warlord so that people could access the situation emotionally. In the viral *Kony2012* video, an adorable little white boy is shown reacting in horror as his father sits him down and tells him about the exploits of the violent Ugandan militia leader Joseph Kony. I watched the first three minutes of this film just as it started to go viral (by May 14, 2013, the YouTube version had been seen by more than 97.5 million people), but I skipped through the rest, because the emotional manipulation was so ham-handed that all of my red flags went up. I was really offended that the little boy was used as an empathy generator, but I was pretty much alone in that feeling—for about a day. Soon, actual relief workers in Uganda and neighboring countries started asking pointed questions about who was behind this film, why military action (and vigilantism) was being urged, and why the film didn't state that Kony hadn't been in Uganda since 2006 and was thought to have fewer than a hundred followers left.

Numerous professional relief workers were astonished that so much focus was placed on a Ugandan who wasn't actually in Uganda, when neighboring South Sudan was in a full-blown refugee crisis and nearby Somalia was in a full-scale famine. No one suggested that Kony *wasn't* a violent man—Kony needs to be brought to justice—but everyone was left wondering what this over-simplified and emotionally manipulative video was truly intended to do. The filmmaking was very emotionally compelling (for many people), but in terms of its impact on the actual troubles of real people in Africa, it was a failure.

Yet it may be a worthwhile film in other ways, because it has so openly exposed the emotionally manipulative structure of a successful social-justice appeal, and it has made many people much more aware of how activists and social justice groups intentionally manipulate emotions and empathy. Right now, that awareness lives in suspicion, in jokes, and in a kind of reactive rejection of these sorts of appeals. I'll be interested to see how this plays out and how other, more grounded social justice organizations will respond to the *Kony2012* debacle. I hope it will help more people realize that they don't need to be manipulated in order to help and that they should check with responsible organizations before they leap into hyperactivated, emotionally manipulated responses. Empathically speaking, it's important to clearly identify the emotional stimuli that are being used in these appeals and to question their intended purpose. You have the right to know. Social justice work is necessary and valuable, but emotion manipulation is a coin of that realm, and as we've all learned in our own lives, there's such a thing as too much emotion.

THE DARK SIDE OF EMPATHY

I'm currently observing a number of activist groups—or to be more precise, I'm observing a number of my highly empathic activist friends on my Facebook feed. Every day, ten or more of my friends will post about their most pressing social justice concerns, and they all attempt to evoke specific emotions (usually without realizing it) in their Facebook friends and followers.

"How can they *say* that?" "Can you believe the gall of this guy?" "Oh no! My local chapter just found out that . . . ," "I don't usually post these appeals, but . . .," "Oh how droll; I've just been called 'oppressive.'" "You guys, we've got to act right now!" And so on. If you're on Facebook, you may have your own collection of friends like these.

Empathically speaking, I'm fascinated by all of these activist emotion displays and emotion-evoking attempts and by the emotional responses that occur in the comments sections. My Facebook feed is active with activists! Of course, I also have friends who post art, music, and funny pictures of animals, so there's a balance (unless it's election time—then all bets are off!). However, I also have people on my feed who belong to groups that are strongly opposed to one another—skeptics versus New Agers, religious people versus atheists, autism activists from opposing camps, and so forth. The people from these warring camps can't see each other, but I can see them in my feed, griping about each other and creating emotionally manipulative stories that call out, second-guess, chastise, expose, or demonize people from the opposing group. I call these groups, collectively, *conflict cultures,* because they form and coalesce around their antagonism to differences in approach, beliefs, and identity.

We've all seen this behavior, but if you strip away the words, the issues, and the specific activist stances, there's mesmerizing empathic activity going on. No matter which group you look at or what their particular crusade is, group members are being urged to increase their empathy for each other at the exact same time that they're being urged to decrease (or even extinguish) their empathy for their opponents. In this three-party[60] version of empathy, you have self, other, and the intentionally *othered* other who (you will be told repeatedly) does not deserve your empathy. In conflict cultures, you'll find intense appeals for undying empathy for the in-group being encouraged at the same moment that reduced empathy or even antipathy for the out-group is being enforced. *We* become important and more internally cohesive because *they* are wrong. It's so simple—it's valencing for entire groups! It's also deeply seductive.

Don't get me wrong (don't *other* me!)—there are plenty of people (like Joseph Kony) who deserve to be clearly identified as dangerous and brought to justice, so I'm not suggesting that we track down Kony and hug him a lot. But let's be equally clear about what these dramatic us-versus-them narratives are asking us to do: We're being urged to choose *for* one group and to view ourselves as intrinsically righteous. And we're being urged to choose *against* another group and (depending on which conflict culture we're in) to view them as intrinsically wrong, deluded, dangerous, or even evil. We're being urged, cajoled, compelled, and even commanded to reduce or extinguish our empathy for an entire class of people so that social justice can flourish. What? I'm sorry, but empaths say, *What?*

Sadly (but not surprisingly), this empathy-extinguishing behavior has pretty terrible side effects. As I've observed numerous conflict cultures, I've been both fascinated and sickened to watch in-group members turn on each other, especially when one of their own challenges the othering process or asks for balance. One day, when one of the activist groups on my feed was savaging its own members, I posted a note on my Facebook author's page[61] about it. I wrote about biologist Edward O. Wilson's challenging book *The Social Conquest of Earth,* which explores the unusual conditions that gave rise to our highly empathic species. Wilson points out that these contentious intergroup behaviors are a part of what has made us wildly successful in one sense, yet wildly dysfunctional in another. This is an excerpt:

> Experiments conducted over many years by social psychologists have revealed how swiftly and decisively people divide into groups and then discriminate in favor of the one to which they belong. Even when the experimenters created the groups arbitrarily, prejudice quickly established itself. Whether groups played for pennies or were divided by their preference for some abstract painter over another, the participants always ranked the out-group below the in-group. They judged their "opponents" to be less likable, less fair, less trustworthy, less competent. The prejudices asserted themselves even when the subjects were told that the in-groups and out-groups had been chosen arbitrarily.
>
> The tendency to form groups, and then to favor in-group members, has the earmarks of instinct. That may not be intuitive: some could argue that in-group bias is conditioned, not instinctual, that we affiliate with family members and play with neighboring children because we're taught to. But the ease with which we fall into those affiliations points to the likelihood that we are already inclined that way—what psychologists call "prepared learning," or the inborn propensity to learn something swiftly and decisively. And indeed, cognitive psychologists have found that newborn infants are most

sensitive to the first sounds they hear, to their mother's face, and to the sounds of their native language. Later they look preferentially at persons who previously spoke their native language within their hearing. Similarly, preschool children tend to select native-language speakers as friends.

The elementary drive to form and take deep pleasure from in-group membership easily translates at a higher level into tribalism. People are prone to ethnocentrism. It is an uncomfortable fact that even when given a guilt-free choice, individuals prefer the company of others of the same race, nation, clan, and religion. They trust them more, relax with them better in business and social events, and prefer them more often than not as marriage partners. They are quicker to anger at evidence that an out-group is behaving unfairly or receiving undeserved rewards. And they grow hostile to any out-group encroaching upon the territory or resources of their in-group.

When in experiments black and white Americans were flashed pictures of the other race, their amygdalas, the brain's center of fear and anger, were activated so quickly and subtly that the centers of the brain were unaware of the response. The subject, in effect, could not help himself. When, on the other hand, appropriate contexts were added—say, the approaching African-American was a doctor and the white his patient—two other sites of the brain integrated with the higher learning centers, the cingulate cortex and the dorsolateral preferential cortex, lit up, silencing input through the amygdala. Thus different parts of the brain have evolved by group selection to create groupishness, as well as to mediate this hardwired propensity.

When the amygdala rules the action, however, there is little or no guilt in the pleasure experienced from watching violent sporting events and war films in which the story unwinds to a satisfying destruction of the enemy. The horrors make the fascination. War is the strong life; it is life *in extremis*.

This excerpt really struck me. Groupishness seems to be our fallback position, and it's a tendency that won't go away. In studies of the hormone oxytocin,[62] which is being heavily promoted as the *love hormone* by some people, you find this very behavior: when people are under the influence of oxytocin, their groupishness and concern for their in-group intensifies, but often, their aggression against out-group members intensifies right alongside it. If you think about it, oxytocin may be more of a *mama bear* type of love hormone: there's deep groupish love in the oxytocin realm, but there's also deep danger.

Yet as we've all seen, we *can* calm and ground ourselves and activate our empathy across lines of difference. We *can* activate our Empathic Accuracy, identify the Emotion Contagion that's occurring, and use our Emotion Regulation skills to reduce our innate tendency toward toxic groupishness. We can intentionally activate our empathic skills and engage our intrapersonal and interpersonal intelligences. We can perform Perspective Taking across lines of difference—it can be done. We can live more intelligently with one another. Our capacity for empathy for the other, and especially for the *othered* other, is the magical ingredient for intergroup (and interpersonal) harmony.

But there's still this deep, powerful, instinctual part of us that loves its us-versus-them dramas, its monsters, its enemies, and its evil madmen. This instinctual lust for dramatic good-versus-evil narratives is just as powerful as the deep yearnings that the swashbucklers of love I wrote about in Chapter 7 have for their impossibly tragic and heroic relationships. And these powerful, instinctual, and unconscious processes are not something you can just argue people out of (believe me, I've tried, and I have the bruises to show for it). These aggressive and destructive forms of love and empathy are an intrinsic part of what it is to be human.

So here's my thought: Let's intentionally and heroically work to develop empathy for ourselves and our loved ones, for people who are like us and people who aren't, for people who deserve empathy and people who don't. Then, to support the dramatic, groupish, swashbuckling, aggressive, war-loving, bullying, and enemy-addicted parts of our brains in nontoxic ways, we can have a daily round of tug of war, steal the flag, or pin the tail on the outcast. Yes!

I'm joking, but I'm not. As you look back at Chapter 9, on how empathy develops in children, you'll recall the powerful emotional and empathic learning processes that occur during storytelling. In stories, we learn how to feel, how to empathize, how to approach huge emotions like terror and grief, how to interact in love and during conflict, and how to become social and moral beings. Yet this learning doesn't end in childhood, because no matter how old you get, stories continue to provide you with basic emotional and empathic training. Stories (especially emotionally manipulative activist appeals and dramatic us-versus-them narratives) help you understand who you are, who the other is, who the in-group is, who the out-group is, who the monsters are, and exactly how you're supposed to feel about all of it. You live in a social world that's made of stories, and no matter how old you are, these stories teach you how to be a member of your gender, your family, your in-groups, your workplace, your community, your nation, and humanity itself.

CONFRONTING THESE STORIES
AND CHANGING THE WORLD

So, who controls these stories? Luckily, you do. We all do, because we're not merely the characters in these stories, mindlessly reciting our dialogue. We're the *storytellers*.

We can dream new stories, and we can learn how to tell these new stories to each other. We can create stories that will help us address and detoxify our aggressive and conflict-seeking groupishness, in the same ways that we create stories to help children deal with monsters, intense emotions, and grievous losses. We can learn to understand the problematic aspects of empathy, oxytocin, and groupishness, and we can remind each other that (just as it is for children), the more strongly we feel love and attachment, the more activated our jealousies, envies, and angers may become. It's a normal process that we can detoxify by understanding the purpose of our emotions in the stories of our lives. We are imaginal, emotive, and empathic beings, and we are the storytellers.

In your social justice work, it's important to bring your storytelling exper-tise to the process and to listen to activists' pleas and pitches empathically. Which of your emotions are being evoked, and why? Who (or what) are the monsters, and why? What mythological themes are at play? What is the heroic quest, and what is your role in the quest? Do you agree with the role that's been written for you, or do you have a better storyline? Most important, what happens if you bring your better ideas, your new approach, or another set of emotions to the story? Will you be accepted, or will you be exiled? Is there room for a real, live human in this story, or have you been cast in a nonspeaking role as an extra?

I'm not suggesting that you need to be the director of every story you're in (how exhausting!). Some people create magnificent social justice narra-tives, and it's an honor to play a part in them. But I am suggesting that you become emotionally and empathically hip to what's occurring, especially when you're being urged to close your mind and your heart against entire groups of people. That's toxic groupishness, and it's a part of a very old story that always ends badly. You can do better; we can all do better—because we're much better storytellers than that.

We can create stories that magically expand to include the alleged out-group. We can bring new and different emotions to the forefront. We can engage with our toxic groupishness through drama, mythology, literature, and ritualized forms of aggression, like tug of war, steal the flag, aikido, fencing, or kickboxing. And most important, we can learn how to form groups that don't define themselves by whom they exclude. We can tell new stories and begin, slowly but surely, to challenge the dark side of empathy and create a better and healthier empathic world for everyone.

Envisioning an Empathic Civilization, Together

A FRIEND ASKED me the other day what an empathic civilization would look like. I thought for a minute and said, "It looks like this. It looks like the human race." We are an empathic species, and this is our civilization. This, right now, is where we are in our communal development of empathy. Almost every one of us achieved skill in all six aspects of empathy before we were two years old; we are empaths, we created this civilization, and this is what an empathic civilization looks like right now.

If you know what to look for, you can find empathy everywhere. Empathy is our nonverbal language and our interactive skill set, and it's a source of endless fascination. We pay people large sums of money to emote skillfully so that we can empathize with them; we interact empathically with art, animals, nature, and ideas; and we join groups intentionally so that we can feel specific emotions, including delightfully deep empathy for our in-group and deliciously deep enmity for the out-group. Empathy is our first language, our universal bonding skill, our captivating plaything, and our devastating weapon—we are a wholly empathic species.

This book is a part of my swashbuckling empathic quest to bring emotions and empathy out of the deep shadows and into the light of day—because, you see, emotions and empathy are alive and active in our every moment; they're visible everywhere if you know where to look. Emotions and empathy are fundamental tools of human cognition, human interactions, and human culture; they make us who we are. We *are* an empathic species, but if we're going to make a world worth living in, we have to become intentional empaths: emotionally awakened, well-regulated, healthy, happy, and perceptive empaths. This is my quest. This is my zany heroic journey.

Thank you for taking this empathic journey with me. I've sat far too still for many months, alone in front of my computer, yet I've been on a fully interactive journey that could only happen because you were with me. People who call writing a solitary occupation—I don't think they're highly empathic, because writing is a conversation and an extended imaginal relationship that exists in its own unique world. These words on this page, they sit here doing nothing until you bring your Einfühlung capacities, your intelligence, your intensity, and your empathy into our relationship. If you've enjoyed this book, I'm glad, but it's your empathic abilities that made these words speak to you. Thank you for your deep empathic attention, thank you for your emotive presence, and thank you for sharing the art of empathy with me.

Now go out and create some beautiful new stories about empathy. You are the storyteller, you are an empath, and this is *your* civilization.

Acknowledgments

THERE'S THIS CONVENTION in book acknowledgments in which the families and loved ones of authors get thanked last. What a silly convention. I subvert that dominant paradigm. First and always, I thank my husband, best friend, and empathic partner, Tino Plank. My career as a writer could not have moved forward without your support. I thank my son, Eli McLaren; my family, my nieces and nephews, my grandnieces and grandnephews; and my closest friends. I also thank my late mother for doing everything she could to raise a tornado wrapped in an enigma wrapped in emotions—this was full-contact parenting.

I thank all of the empaths and hyperempaths who have worked with me, challenged me to come up with better skills, and helped me realize that I wasn't alone in the world or in my empathic way of framing human interactions. I thank my many neurodiverse and autistic friends, as well as the parents of autistic children, for inviting me into an intensely empathic community and helping me understand empathy at a much deeper level. And I thank the men and boys who show me every day that empathy never was, and never will be, a gendered trait.

I thank my darling Tami Simon and the folks at Sounds True, whose outsider status allows me to be an al fresco academic doing original theory. Haven Iverson, in particular, is a sensitive, pointed, and empathic editor who offers me her ears, her mind, and her heart. Writing for her and with her is an honor. Being an empath is easier because the people at Sounds True have treated my work and my unique approach as legitimate and worth hearing. As I stand on the margins of a highly contentious cluster of academic disciplines whose approach to emotions and empathy is—in my empathic opinion—still struggling with fundamental misunderstandings, I appreciate the fact that my voice and my life's work are being treated as valid by this merry band. Thank you!

I also thank the many people I see who avoid empathy and gleefully create enemies—because although creating a distrusted or hated other is a wonderful way to generate internal cohesion in a group, it's a process that always backfires. Groups and people who engage in othering help me understand just how crucial fully inclusive and non-othering empathy is to a functional community, to functional activism, and to the empathic evolution of humankind.

I thank all of the authors and researchers whose work I reference and learn from every day. When I have intense questions or feel as if I just don't *get* this world, I enter your words and feel into your work, your ideas, your brilliance, your struggles, your arguments, your confusions, and the depth of your humanity. You make a difference, and I thank you.

And of course, I thank *you* for supporting my work in the world. As I wrote this book, I continually thought of you, and I used my Einfühlung capacities to imagine you reading alongside me, arguing with me, pointing out inconsistencies, and whispering all of your hopes, concerns, and emotions into my ears. Thank you for keeping me company as I wrote this book. I appreciate you!

Emotional Vocabulary List

From karlamclaren.com

ANGER

SOFT ANGER

Annoyed ~ Frustrated ~ Cross ~ Apathetic ~ Peeved ~ Irritated ~ Cranky ~ Crabby ~ Bored ~ Impatient ~ Critical ~ Cold ~ Displeased ~ Rankled ~ Detached ~ Indifferent

MOOD-STATE ANGER

Angry ~ Mad ~ Offended ~ Antagonized ~ Bristling ~ Sarcastic ~ Aggravated ~ Arrogant ~ Indignant ~ Inflamed ~ Affronted ~ Resentful ~ Incensed ~ Exasperated ~ Riled up

INTENSE ANGER

Hostile ~ Aggressive ~ Livid ~ Outraged ~ Furious ~ Belligerent ~ Disgusted ~ Appalled ~ Bitter ~ Ranting ~ Raving ~ Contemptuous ~ Hateful ~ Vengeful ~ Vindictive ~ Irate ~ Violent ~ Menacing ~ Seething ~ Vicious ~ Spiteful

SADNESS

SOFT SADNESS

Regretful ~ Disappointed ~ Disconnected ~ Distracted ~ Low ~ Listless ~ Wistful

MOOD-STATE SADNESS

Sad ~ World-weary ~ Down ~ Melancholy ~ Mournful ~ Weepy ~ Grieving ~ Gloomy ~ Dejected ~ Downtrodden ~ Heavyhearted ~ Forlorn ~ Sorrowful ~ Dispirited ~ Discouraged ~ Drained

INTENSE SADNESS

Despairing ~ Bleak ~ Despondent ~ Depressed ~ Anguished ~ Inconsolable ~ Grief-stricken ~ Hopeless ~ Heartbroken ~ Morose ~ Bereaved

HAPPINESS

SOFT HAPPINESS

Smiling ~ Upbeat ~ Peaceful ~ Calm ~ Amused ~ Open ~ Friendly ~ Encouraged ~ Hopeful ~ Inspired ~ Jovial

MOOD-STATE HAPPINESS

Happy ~ Glad ~ Content ~ Optimistic ~ Cheerful ~ Joyful ~ Satisfied ~ Lively ~ Delighted ~ Rejuvenated ~ Pleased ~ Gratified ~ Excited ~ Gleeful ~ Merry ~ Playful

INTENSE HAPPINESS

Elated ~ Exhilarated ~ Manic ~ Giddy ~ Euphoric ~ Awe-filled ~ Blissful ~ Enthralled ~ Rapturous ~ Jubilant ~ Ecstatic ~ Overjoyed ~ Radiant

FEAR

SOFT FEAR

Alert ~ Hesitant ~ Pensive ~ Watchful ~ Cautious ~ Curious ~ Leery ~ Uneasy ~ Doubtful ~ Confused ~ Apprehensive ~ Shy ~ Concerned ~ Disquieted ~ Timid ~ Edgy ~ Fidgety ~ Disconcerted ~ Insecure ~ Indecisive ~ Disoriented

MOOD-STATE FEAR

Fearful ~ Afraid ~ Suspicious ~ Startled ~ Unnerved ~ Anxious ~ Nervous ~ Worried ~ Alarmed ~ Shaky ~ Perturbed ~ Aversive ~ Wary ~ Distrustful ~ Rattled ~ Unsettled ~ Jumpy

INTENSE FEAR

Terrorized ~ Shocked ~ Panicked ~ Dread-filled ~ Horrified ~ Phobic ~ Petrified ~ Paralyzed

JEALOUSY AND ENVY

SOFT JEALOUSY AND ENVY

Suspicious ~ Insecure ~ Distrustful ~ Protective

MOOD-STATE JEALOUSY AND ENVY

Jealous ~ Envious ~ Covetous ~ Threatened ~ Demanding ~ Desirous

INTENSE JEALOUSY AND ENVY

Greedy ~ Grasping ~ Persistently jealous ~ Possessive ~ Resentful ~ Threatened ~ Avaricious ~ Gluttonous ~ Green with envy

SHAME AND GUILT

SOFT SHAME

Hesitant ~ Flushed ~ Self-conscious ~ Speechless ~ Discomfited ~ Awkward ~ Humble ~ Reticent ~ Abashed ~ Flustered ~ Withdrawn

MOOD-STATE SHAME

Ashamed ~ Guilty ~ Embarrassed ~ Intimidated ~ Penitent ~ Regretful ~ Remorseful ~ Chagrined ~ Culpable ~ Reproachful ~ Sheepish ~ Rueful ~ Contrite ~ Humbled

INTENSE SHAME

Humiliated ~ Guilt-ridden ~ Guilt-stricken ~ Disgraced ~ Stigmatized ~ Mortified ~ Demeaned ~ Self-condemning ~ Self-flagellating ~ Degraded ~ Shamefaced ~ Belittled ~ Ostracized

SUICIDAL URGES

SOFT SUICIDAL URGES

Depressed ~ Dispirited ~ Constantly irritated, angry, or enraged (see the anger list) ~ Helpless ~ Impulsive ~ Withdrawn ~ Apathetic ~ Lethargic ~ Disinterested ~ Pessimistic ~ Purposeless ~ Discouraged ~ Feeling worthless ~ Isolated ~ World-weary ~ Humorless ~ Listless ~ Melancholy ~ Flat ~ Indifferent

MOOD-STATE SUICIDAL URGES

Desperate ~ Hopeless ~ Despairing ~ Morbid ~ Sullen ~ Desolate ~ Miserable ~ Overwhelmed ~ Pleasureless ~ Joyless ~ Fatalistic ~ Empty ~ Passionless ~ Bereft ~ Crushed ~ Drained

INTENSE SUICIDAL URGES

Agonized ~ Tormented ~ Self-destructive ~ Tortured ~ Anguished ~ Bleak ~ Numbed ~ Doomed ~ Death-seeking ~ Reckless ~ Devastated ~ Nihilistic

Note: If you're feeling any level of suicidal urges, don't think that you have to wait until you're in the throes of torment to reach out for help. If you can learn to catch your suicidal urges when they're in the soft stage, you can often stop yourself from falling into the pit of anguish. In the territory of the suicidal urge, your capacity for emotional awareness and articulation can literally save your life. For more information on this empathic approach to emotions, see the suicide chapter in my book *The Language of Emotions: What Your Feelings Are Trying to Tell You.*

If you or anyone you know is feeling suicidal, please know that free, safe, confidential help is available. In the United States, you can call the National Suicide Prevention Lifeline at 1-800-273-TALK (8255). For other countries, the International Association for Suicide Prevention has a list of crisis and suicide prevention centers throughout the world—www.iasp.info/resources/index.php.

How to Be Helpful to Someone Who Is Threatening Suicide (from the National Suicide Prevention Lifeline website SuicidePreventionLifeline.org/GetHelp/Someone. The content was developed by the American Association of Suicidology, suicidology.org)

- Be direct. Talk openly and matter-of-factly about suicide.
- Be willing to listen. Allow expressions of feelings. Accept the feelings.
- Be non-judgmental. Don't debate whether suicide is right or wrong, or whether feelings are good or bad. Don't lecture on the value of life.
- Get involved. Become available. Show interest and support.
- Don't dare him or her to do it.
- Don't act shocked. This will put distance between you.
- Don't be sworn to secrecy. Seek support.
- Offer hope that alternatives are available but do not offer glib reassurance.
- Take action. Remove means, such as guns or stockpiled pills.
- Get help from people or agencies specializing in crisis intervention and suicide prevention.

Thank you for your emotional fluency and your willingness to reach out when others are in need.

Your Emotional Styles

THE FOLLOWING THERAPEUTIC suggestions address the six dimensions of emotional style that Dr. Richard Davidson has identified in his research. Full descriptions of these practices and the neurological structures associated with each emotional style, which in some cases include changes in living and working environments, can be found in *The Emotional Life of Your Brain,* by Richard Davidson and Sharon Begley.

Resilience (from slow to recover to fast to recover): Being slow to recover might keep you engaged with a difficult emotion for a possibly uncomfortable amount of time, whereas being fast to recover might speed you through an emotion so quickly that you won't actually gain much emotional depth or the capacity to empathize with others. Davidson suggests traditional Buddhist mindfulness meditations (especially the empathy-focused form called *tonglen* meditation) if you're a little too fast to recover, and cognitive behavioral therapy if your recovery is slow enough to provoke uncomfortably extended periods of emotional activation.

Outlook (from negative to positive): Davidson doesn't glorify a positive outlook, because it tends to interfere with people's ability to plan for the future, learn from their mistakes, and delay gratification. However, he does note that staying in a continually low mood isn't an optimum situation either. To bring balance to an overly positive outlook, Richardson suggests learning to plan for the future and think things through more carefully as you learn to delay gratification. (I suggest that you request some assistance from your healthy anxiety and your healthy shame as well.) To bring balance to an overly negative outlook, Davidson suggests intentionally identifying positive things about yourself and others, expressing gratitude regularly, and complimenting others so you can create healthier social connections based on warm and caring interactions.

Social Intuition (from socially intuitive to puzzled): People who are socially puzzled also tend to be low in empathic awareness. In order to address people at the puzzled end of this dimension, Davidson suggests a number of different sensitivity-raising and social-interaction exercises to help people become more aware of faces, bodies, nuances, gestures, and social signals. To help people on the opposite end of this dimension relieve their intense social awareness, Davidson suggests reducing social interaction and eye contact, managing overstimulation, and working in the Resilience dimension to move toward the *fast to recover* pole.

Self-awareness (from self-aware to self-opaque): If you're too self-aware, you might be so attentive to every change in your body, in your thoughts, and in your emotions that you lose track of the external world, or you might become uncomfortably emotionally activated about every change you sense. On the other hand, if you're too self-opaque, you might continually miss important cues about your health, your emotions, your thoughts, and your preferences. Davidson suggests Buddhist mindfulness meditations for both situations, as they may help you become more aware of your inner world in the case of self-opaqueness and more able to calm your reactivity in the case of overactive Self-awareness.

Sensitivity to Context (from tuned in to tuned out): Being insensitive to context can make people socially inappropriate—they can miss a lot of nuance and become unable to modify their emotional responses in differing situations. There is not a lot of research on this dimension, and Davidson suggests deep breathing and a form of exposure therapy to help people distinguish between different contexts and different levels of emotional activation. For people who are so sensitive to context that they lose track of themselves in social interactions, he suggests that they work in the Self-awareness dimension in order to become more familiar with their own authentic emotions, thoughts, and preferences.

Attention (from focused to unfocused): Davidson suggests two forms of meditation to address people's capacity for Attention. If people tend to be unfocused, he suggests mindfulness meditations that train them to focus on specific objects for increasing periods of time. However, if people are overly focused and unable to see the big picture or attend to more than one thing at a time, he suggests a meditation practice called *open monitoring*, which helps people open up their focus and become aware of their very awareness itself.

Notes

1. What is the difference between the words *empathic* and *empathetic?* Right now, they're undergoing a definitional shift, and it is becoming normal in scientific research to use the word *empathic* instead of *empathetic.* However, the two words are interchangeable, as the words *sympathy* and *empathy* tend to be. I prefer the word *empathic* because it relates more specifically to empaths, whereas the word *empathetic* tends to refer to the process of using empathy.

2. I explore our centuries-long distrust and fear of emotions in my book *The Language of Emotions: What Your Feelings Are Trying to Tell You.* I track this dysfunction throughout human cultures; in philosophy; in religions and spiritual traditions; in the scientific and industrial revolutions; and into compulsory schooling, modern medicine, psychotherapy, and psychiatry. Our deep troubles with emotions are everywhere you look, but luckily, many multidisciplinary theorists are doing wonderful work to bring emotions out of the shadows once again. This book is a part of my continuing contribution to that work.

3. Altruism is one concept that is making the study of empathy very contentious, because it is currently being looked at through a contested avenue of Darwinist thought that assumes self-interest at every level, from the selfish genes of Richard Dawkins' (and others) ideology to the self-centered, winner-take-all frame that some political thinkers assert as the natural truth of human behavior. In these ideologies, empathy and altruism are often viewed with deep suspicion, and this suspicion has actually impeded empathy research for many decades. Accordingly, some of the most interesting research on empathy has been done not on humans, but on the great apes, by primatologist Frans de Waal. If you read empathy research done on humans, you'll empathically sense a thread of defensiveness about the altruistic nature of empathy, because when they research empathy, many scientists have to confront the faction of Darwinists who think that empathy and altruism can only exist in relation to what the central actor is getting out of it. For a startling take on the subject, which proposes an empathy-requiring theory of group selection and evolution instead of individual selection, read

Edward O. Wilson's *The Social Conquest of Earth* (Liveright Publishing, 2012). The story of evolution, empathy, and altruism is still being written.

4. For instance, in the work of German researcher Doris Bischof-Köhler and American researcher Allison Gopnik, among others

5. McLaren, Karla. "Are Men Less Able to Feel Emotions?" March 24, 2010. http://karlamclaren.com/are-men-less-able-to-feel-emotions/.

6. You'll run smack into this valencing if you observe children's toys and clothing: girls get pink, lacy, movement-inhibiting clothes that openly suggest that their work in life is to become pretty and alluring. Beyond the age of two, it's hard to find building toys, math toys, or intellect-developing toys aimed at girls; it's all princesses, ponies, makeup, jewelry, and playing house. If girls want to run and play hard or learn to fight with a sword, they're going to have to shop in the boys' section, and their wishes will probably be challenged as unfeminine. Boys, on the other hand, get blue, rugged, activity-enhancing clothes that tell them their work is to be active and tough. From early infancy onward, boys are encouraged to use their bodies, build things, and learn to fight with as many different weapons as possible. If boys want to create art, or care for animals and babies, or learn to cook, they're going to have to shop in the girls' section, and their wishes might be challenged as unacceptably feminine, or flat-out refused.

7. British psychopathologist Simon Baron-Cohen claims that autistics are unempathic due to a malfunction in their mirror neurons. However, in 2007, Swiss neuroscientists Henry and Kamilla Markram and colleague proposed the "intense world theory" of autism, in which the central focus was on autistic *hypersensitivity,* rather than on a lack of awareness or insensitivity. Then, in 2010, Israeli neuroscientist Ilan Dinstein and colleagues studied mirror neuron responses in autistic adults and found them to be normal. Dinstein proposed that autism might not have anything to do with mirror neurons, but might instead involve "noisy brain networks" that scramble incoming sensory data, making the deciphering of social input more difficult (but not due to any lack of empathic capacity). Added to this is the writing of autistic youth and adults themselves, which clearly chronicles their intense emotional and social sensitivities. For some excellent first-person accounts of autism and empathy, see AutismandEmpathy.com, a site created by autistic advocate Rachel Cohen-Rottenberg.

These more inclusive inquiries are helping us understand that hypersensitivity and sensory integration issues make social cues harder to read and organize for many autistic people, which is why it can appear that some autistic people lack empathy. They don't; in fact, hyperawareness of others (and of multiple sensory aspects of their surroundings) can cause such overwhelm that many autistic people will shut down in order to self-regulate. This can appear unempathic, but it's usually a function of hypersensitivity and, often, hyperempathy.

8. When I use the word *autistic* as a descriptor, rather than saying "person with autism," I am following the lead of the autistic advocates who are framing their struggle as one

of civil rights and fundamental identity (rather than disease). However, if you and I were talking together, and you preferred another way of describing your own autism, then I would certainly defer to your wishes. For a good community discussion of this choice of terminology, see www.journeyswithautism.com/2012/04/25/the-problem-with-person-first-language/ and www.thinkingautismguide.com/2011/11/person-first-language-why-it-matters.html.

9. "Ableism is a form of discrimination or prejudice against individuals with physical, mental, or developmental disabilities that is characterized by the belief that these individuals need to be fixed or cannot function as full members of society (Castañeda & Peters, 2000). As a result of these assumptions, individuals with disabilities are commonly viewed as being abnormal rather than as members of a distinct minority community (Olkin & Pledger, 2003; Reid & Knight, 2006). Because disability status has been viewed as a defect rather than a dimension of difference, disability has not been widely recognized as a multicultural concern by the general public as well as by counselor educators and practitioners." Smith, Laura, Pamela F. Foley, and Michael P. Chaney, "Addressing Classism, Ableism, and Heterosexism in Counselor Education," *Journal of Counseling & Development* 86 (2010): 303–309. From http://disabledfeminists.com/2010/11/19/what-is-ableism-five-things-about-ableism-you-should-know/, accessed August 10, 2012.

10. Criminal behavior is socially defined, and identified criminals are even more socially defined by their lack of access to money, influence, and social capital, not to mention their racial characteristics, which determine in large part whether they will be arrested and charged or enter into the criminal justice system at all. I have strong empathic reservations about the whole category of psychopathy, since definitions change based on the source, while researchers and clinicians disagree about antisocial personality disorder, narcissism, and borderline traits. To my eye, the entire subject is rife with problematic interpretations of antisocial behaviors that might also be applicable to, for instance, outsiders, disabled people, minorities, artists, monks, geniuses, and visionaries.

11. For a grounded and humane discussion of psychopathic personalities and treatment options, Dr. Nancy McWilliams's *Psychoanalytic Diagnosis: Understanding Personality Structure in the Clinical Process* (Guilford Press, 2011) is a wonderful resource. In it, McWilliams notes that two powerful underlying motivations for people with psychopathic tendencies are (1) not to appear weak and (2) not to feel any envy (see my empathic description of envy on page 75). In terms of impediments to the development of empathy in children, there's an early condition that can arise when babies aren't attended to skillfully or empathically. In some children, poor or unskilled early nurturing (and, of course, abuse) can interfere with secure attachment and create a condition called Reactive Attachment Disorder (RAD). RAD children don't develop a sense of trust or reliance on their caretakers and often learn to manipulate them just to get their basic needs met. For a RAD child, love, closeness, and empathy may feel alien, untrustworthy, or even dangerous.

One hypothesis is that RAD children who don't receive early intervention might grow up to be distrustful and manipulative and might develop an almost pathological unwillingness to appear weak, needy, or envious. One hypothesis is that psychopathic people might have been children who learned how to survive without love, caring attention, or empathy.

12. American psychologist Robert Titchener coined the word *empathy* in 1909 (source: http://plato.stanford.edu/entries/empathy/).

13. Vischer, Robert, et al. (reprint and translation from the original German). "On the Optical Sense of Form: A Contribution to Aesthetics." *Empathy, Form, and Space: Problems in German Aesthetics, 1873–1893* (Texts and Documents Series), pp. 89–123. Santa Monica, CA: Getty Center for the History of Art, 1993.

14. See my two-part essay "Empaths on the Autism Spectrum." October 2011. http://karlamclaren.com/empaths-on-the-autism-spectrum-part-1/.

15. "Empathic accuracy is the measure of one's skill in empathic inference [your ability to read the emotions, thoughts, and intentions of others]." From Ickes, W. (ed) (1997). *Empathic Accuracy.* New York, NY: Guildford Press, 1992 (p. 2).

16. The term *display rules* is from P. Ekman and W. V. Friesen. "The Repertoire of Nonverbal Behavior: Categories, Origins, Usage, and Coding." *Semiotica* 1 (1969): 49–98.

17. Seubert, J. and C. Reganbogen. "I Know How You Feel: Good Social Skills Depend on Picking Up Other People's Moods—A Feat the Brain Performs by Combining Numerous Sensory Cues." *Scientific American Mind,* March/April 2012.

18. It also may have much to do with language acquisition, as research on deaf and blind children in Australia in 2004 suggested that emotion-recognition and emotion-understanding abilities were impaired in both populations, but that deaf and hearing-impaired children raised *without* a natural language (sign language) had the most trouble with both tasks, whereas children raised in a signing-rich environment had an easier time with them. For blind and visually impaired children, the ability to hear vocal tone and rhythm supported both emotional awareness tasks (and both abilities tended to be higher in visually impaired children than in hearing-impaired children); however, being unable to visually receive information about changes in gestures, positioning, and facial expressions impeded both emotion tasks. In general, these emotional impediments lessened over time (and with specific emotion-recognition and emotion-understanding training) in both populations. From Dyck, M. J., C. Farrugia, I. M. Shochet, and M. Holmes-Brown. "Emotion Recognition/Understanding Ability in Hearing or Vision-Impaired Children: Do Sounds, Sights, or Words Make the Difference?" *Journal of Child Psychology and Psychiatry* 45, no. 4 (2044): 789–800.

19. Bischof-Köhler, D. "Empathy and Self-Recognition in Phylogenetic and Ontogenetic Perspective." *Emotion Review* 4, no. 1 (January 2012): 40–48.

20. Being a fiercely stubborn and scathing social critic helps cut through this endless emotional subterfuge, though I have no idea how I would know this, since my own childhood was one of delicate good manners and rainbow fairy tales—*snort.*

21. I have deep concerns about the way this distinction is being used to sort people into greater or lesser levels of humanity. For instance, in his book *Zero Degrees of Empathy* (Allen Lane, 2011), British psychopathologist Simon Baron-Cohen categorizes autistics as being affectively empathic yet cognitively impaired in empathy, and he places psychopaths on the opposite end of this continuum (where psychopaths allegedly have no capacity to empathize affectively but can do so cognitively). This theorizing is very alarming in its willingness both to brand people as psychopaths (which is a rare condition and not completely understood) and to continually exclude autistics from the realm of normal humanity. As a disability rights advocate and friend of many autistic youth and adults, I can't state strongly enough how dangerous this theory is to the lives of autistic people, who are often wildly empathic rather than less so—both cognitively *and* affectively. As an empath, it is very easy to see that autistics are absolutely empaths (and often hyperempaths), though their sensory-processing differences can make their ability to decipher social cues problematic.

    My problem with the categories of affective and cognitive empathy is certainly based on social justice (in that they are used to classify people as less than human), but it is also based on empathic awareness of the actual processes of empathy. In my experience, affective and cognitive empathy are not separate or separable states; rather, I see cognitive empathy as a function of affective empathy, in that you can't effectively perform the process that some people identify as cognitive empathy unless you already have the capacity to *feel* what's going on. In my view, the capacity to separate oneself from the direct feeling and to stand away from the direct experience (and to view it from a kind of emotional eagle's-eye view) is a function of Emotion Regulation and Perspective Taking *added to* a preexisting capacity for Emotion Contagion. Simply put: if you can "cognitively" appreciate the emotional perspective of another, I propose that you already have the "affective" capacity to recognize, share, and understand emotions.

22. I've worked one-on-one with men in maximum-security prisons, including murderers and lifers—I actually looked for psychopathy—yet I didn't find a lack of empathy there. I understand how vital it is to isolate cruel and brutal people from the rest of humanity, and to place them decidedly in a specific category of evil or irretrievable brokenness, but empathically speaking, I am not able to do so in ways that are intellectually and empathically grounded. I'm still studying this, as I have done since toddlerhood, when I endured years of extended physical contact with a person whose clear intention was to dehumanize, control, and harm me. I have strong empathic reservations about identifying seemingly unempathic people as nonhuman—especially since, through the everyday act of "othering" people, you and I can easily make ourselves scathingly unempathic about the plight of people we've identified as our enemies (or, hello, as psychopaths).

23. de Waal, F. *The Age of Empathy: Nature's Lessons for a Kinder Society.* New York: Harmony, 2009.

24. "Studies examining children's concern for others had previously focused on babies' sensitivities to people in distress. At the University of California, Berkeley, researcher Alison Gopnik wanted to find out when children discover that other people feel differently than they do—a prerequisite for empathy. . . . This ability to acknowledge other people's feelings—even when they differ from your own—is essential to understanding when (and how) people want to be comforted. 'To become truly empathic,' Gopnik says, 'you have to say not just "I feel your pain," but "I feel your pain, and I know it's not my own. I should be helping you, not myself."'" From Whyte, J. E. "The Emergence of Empathy in Babies," https://family.go.com/parenting/pkg-toddler/article-825641-the-emergence-of-empathy-in-babies-t/.

25. The episode, which was called "The Empath," focused on a young mute woman who could physically pull the pain and disease out of others and into her own body. Captain Kirk, Mr. Spock, and Dr. McCoy were abducted and put through a series of tortures by alien scientists who wanted to see if the empath, Gem, would sacrifice her own health for the life of another. In the later series *Star Trek: The Next Generation,* a female officer named Deanna Troi was the ship's counselor from an empathic and telepathic race called Betazoids. Like Spock before her, Troi was half-human, and much of her story revolved around trying to fit into both cultures—with the fully empathic and telepathic Betazoids, who didn't require spoken language, and with the unempathic and nontelepathic humans, who regularly used language to avoid, hide, or lie about their emotions.

26. This section about Howard Gardner's work first appeared on pages 39–41 in my book *The Language of Emotions.* There is some controversy about Gardner's work because his categories of intelligence are not quantifiable, and many researchers feel that these categories can therefore only be looked upon as a kind of philosophical musing about how we define intelligence. That's certainly the way I'm using Gardner's work, but I'm also revisiting it here because it's still the only approach to intelligence that includes emotional and social intelligences as valid and equal parts of cognition.

27. This reminds me of something I overheard in 2002 at a table full of yoga instructors at the famous Kripalu yoga retreat. I perked up immediately, because they were talking about how doing a very common pose absolutely correctly (the "downward dog" pose) could cause shoulder injuries in women. I was flabbergasted, because I had always heard yoga touted as a magical curative for every possible physical problem. As it turns out, yoga (and meditation) is just like everything else; you need to make sure that the process fits you and that you're not being forced to fit into the process. If you get injured or you're uncomfortable, but people blame you because you're not doing it right, this is almost always a warning: you may be in the presence of true believers but not in the presence of a truly appropriate (for you) practice or technique.

28. Damasio, A. *Descartes' Error: Emotion, Reason, and the Human Brain.* New York: Picador, 1994 (pp. 192–194).

29. Damasio, A. *Looking for Spinoza: Joy, Sorrow, and the Feeling Brain.* New York: Harcourt, 2003 (pp. 152–155).

30. Damasio, A. *The Feeling of What Happens: Body and Emotion in the Making of Consciousness.* New York: Harvest, 1999 (pp. 61–67).

31. McLaren, Karla. "Emotions: Action-Requiring Neurological Programs." April 16, 2011. http://karlamclaren.com/emotions-action-requiring-neurological-programs/.

32. The full quiz (which focuses on anger, fear, sadness, shame, jealousy, envy, contentment, and anxiety) is in my interactive online course, "Emotional Flow: Becoming Fluent in the Language of Emotions" (Sounds True, 2012).

33. From my book *The Language of Emotions:*

The Difference between Guilt and Shame: In my early teens, I read a popular self-help book that branded guilt and shame as "useless" emotions. The book presented the idea that we're all perfect, and therefore shouldn't ever be guilt-ridden or ashamed of anything we do. That idea seemed very strange to me, so I went to the dictionary and looked up "guiltless" and "shameless" and found that neither state was anything to celebrate. To be *guiltless* means to be free of mark or experience, as if you're a blank slate. It's not a sign of intelligence or growth, because guiltlessness exists only in people who have not yet lived. To be *shameless* means to be senseless, uncouth, and impudent. It's a very marked state of being out of control, out of touch, and exceedingly self-absorbed; therefore, shamelessness lives only in people who don't have any relational skills. Both states—guiltlessness and shamelessness—helped me understand the intrinsic value of guilt and shame.

Fascinatingly, in a dictionary definition, guilt isn't even an emotional state at all—it's simply the knowledge and acknowledgement of wrongdoing. Guilt is a state of circumstance: you're either guilty or not guilty in relation to the legal or moral code you value. You cannot *feel* guilty, because guilt is a concrete state—not an emotional one! Your feelings are almost irrelevant; if you did something wrong, you're guilty, and it doesn't matter if you're happy, angry, fearful, or depressed about it. When you don't do something wrong, you're not guilty. Feelings don't enter into the equation at all. The only way you could possibly ever *feel* guilty is if you don't quite remember committing an offense ("I feel like I might be guilty, but I'm not sure."). No, what you feel is *shame.* Guilt is a factual state, while shame is an emotion.

Shame is the natural emotional consequence of guilt and wrongdoing. When your healthy shame is welcomed into your psyche, its powerful heat and intensity will restore your boundaries when you've broken them yourself. However, most of us don't welcome shame into our lives; we obscure it by saying "I feel guilty" instead of "I feel ashamed," which speaks volumes about our current inability to identify and acknowledge our guilt, channel our appropriate shame, and make amends. This is the real shame, because when we don't welcome and honor our free-flowing and appropriate shame, we cannot moderate our own behavior. We'll continually do things we know are wrong—and we won't have the strength to stop ourselves. In our never-ending shamelessness, we'll offend and offend and offend without pause—we'll *always* be guilty—because nothing will wake us to our effect on the world.

If we continue to use the incorrect statement "I feel guilty," we'll be unable to right our wrongs, amend our behaviors, or discover where our shame originated—which means we'll be unable to experience true happiness or contentment (both of which arise when we skillfully navigate through any difficult emotion). If we don't come out and correctly state "I'm ashamed of myself," we'll never improve. I'll say it again before we go deeper: Guilt is a factual state, not an emotional one. You're either guilty or not guilty. If you're not guilty, there's nothing to be ashamed of. However, if you *are* guilty, and you want to know what to do about the *fact* of your guilt, then you've got to embrace the information shame brings to you. (pp. 198–200)

34. However, there are seventeen emotional categories in *The Language of Emotions.* I'm omitting the suicidal urge from this list due to the amount of time it would take to explain it responsibly. I've included the suicidal urge and depression in the "Emotional Vocabulary List" in the Appendix, so that you'll be able to identify suicidal ideation in others and know how to provide (or steer people to) support.

35. Because our English emotional vocabulary isn't extensive, you'll see that I had to combine many emotions in my vocabulary list. Anger and hatred are in the Anger category; fear, anxiety, and panic are in the Fear category; and so on. It's *hard* to find enough English words to describe distinct gradations of many specific emotions!

36. McLaren, K. "How Much Emotion Is Too Much? (Revisited!)" May 25, 2011. http://karlamclaren.com/how-much-emotion-is-too-much-revisted/.

37. McLaren, K. "Is It a Feeling or Is It an Emotion? Revisited!" March 2, 2012. http://karlamclaren.com/is-it-a-feeling-or-is-it-an-emotion-revisited/.

38. Winerman, L. "Talking the Pain Away: Brain Research Indicates Putting Problems into Words Eases Emotional Distress." *Monitor on Psychology* 37, no. 9 (2006).

39. This is a play off of Antonio Damasio's designation of the "emotionally *competent* stimulus," which he talks about in his book *Self Comes to Mind: Constructing the Conscious Brain* (Pantheon, 2010). I really appreciate Damasio's concept of emotional stimuli, but the word *competent* didn't encompass the lived experience of the emotive process for me.

40. McLaren, Karla. "Building Your Raft: The Five Empathic Skills." *The Language of Emotions.* Boulder: Sounds True, 2010 (125–158).

41. McLaren, Karla. "Befriending Anxiety in 2011. Huzzah!" January 3, 2011. http://karlamclaren.com/befriending-anxiety-in-2011-huzzah/.

42. For instance, Ohio State neuroscientist Randy Nelson and colleagues found that relatively dim light sources during sleep (equivalent to a TV left on in a darkened bedroom)

reduced cognitive speed, reduced activity in the hippocampus, and induced depressive behaviors in hamsters. One suggestion is that the light tricks the body into thinking that it is still daytime and that the sleep-inducing hormone melatonin doesn't activate fully. Therefore, sleep is not as deep or restorative. From Fonken, L. K., E. Kitsmiller, L. Smale, and R. J. Nelson. "Dim Nighttime Light Impairs Cognition and Provokes Depressivelike Responses in a Diurnal Rodent." *Journal of Biological Rhythms* 27 (2012): 319–327.

43. Orthorexia, or extreme healthy eating, was first defined by Steven Bratman, MD, in 1996 at http://www.orthorexia.com/about/.

44. See Dr. Levine's books, audio learning sets, and online courses under the Trauma Healing heading in the Further Resources section.

45. My response about thresholds first appeared in an online newsletter in 2010 and was then included in the text portion of my online course *Emotional Flow* (Sounds True, 2012).

46. Weir, Kirsten. "Fickle Friends: How to Deal with Frenemies." *Scientific American Mind* (June 16, 2011).

47. Wenner Moyer, Melinda. "Eye Contact Quells Online Hostility: Mean Comments Arise from a Lack of Eye Contact More Than from Anonymity." *Scientific American Mind* (September 16, 2012).

48. Conscious Complaining with a Partner was created for a Kripalu workshop and first appeared on my website under the title "New Empathic Skills!" November 1, 2010. http://karlamclaren.com/new-empathic-skills/.

49. McLaren, Karla. "Stress Is a Weasel Word, and Maybe That's Good!" May 15, 2012. http://karlamclaren.com/stress-is-a-weasel-word-and-maybe-thats-good/.

50. See Bal, P. M., and M. Veltkamp. "How Does Fiction Reading Influence Empathy? An Experimental Investigation on the Role of Emotional Transportation." *PLoS ONE* 8, no. 1 (2013); Gabriel. S., and A. F. Young. "Becoming a Vampire without Being Bitten: The Narrative Collective-Assimilation Hypothesis." *Psychological Science* 22, no. 8 (2012).

51. Green, J. A., P. G. Whitney, and M. Potegal. "Screaming, Yelling, Whining, and Crying: Categorical and Intensity Differences in Vocal Expressions of Anger and Sadness in Children's Tantrums." *Emotion* 11, no. 5 (2011): 1124–1133.

52. *Kitten vs. a Scary Thing,* http://www.youtube.com/watch?v=_MqHN-4okZ4.

53. Radvansky, G. A., S. A. Krawietz, and A. K. Tamplin. "Walking through Doorways Causes Forgetting: Further Explorations." *The Quarterly Journal of Experimental Psychology* 64, no. 8 (2011): 1632–1645.

54. An early version of this piece on emotion work first appeared on my site as "An Introduction to Emotion Work." March 6, 2010. http://karlamclaren.com/an-introduction-to-emotion-work/.

55. Some people see the concept of meritocracy as problematic due to our strong privilege structures of race and class, which create and reinforce inequalities, such that a meritocracy might actually just be a collection of elite, white, educated, upper-class males who gained their skills in an unjustly segregated, class-based, and unequal society. See Chris Hayes's *Twilight of the Elites: America after Meritocracy* (Crown, 2012) for an examination of this problem. When I refer to a meritocracy, I'm talking about an idealized version, in which the people who truly perform the job best *get* the job and then have real autonomy.

56. Milliken, F. J., E. W. Morrison, and P. F. Hewlin. "An Exploratory Study of Employee Silence: Issues that Employees Don't Communicate Upward and Why." *Journal Of Management Studies* 40, no. 6 (2003): 1453–1476.

57. My work on gossip began in a post called "A Holiday Gift for Your Emotions." December 17, 2010. http://karlamclaren.com/a-holiday-gift-for-your-emotions/.

58. Waters, Tony. *Bureaucratizing the Good Samaritan: The Limitations of Humanitarian Relief Operations.* Boulder, CO: Westview Press, 2001.

59. Ariely, Dan. *The Upside of Irrationality.* New York: Harper, 2010, 237–241.

60. My three-party empathy model is a nod to Fritz Breithaupt's discussion of three-person empathy; however, my terminology refers to complex group-level behaviors. See Breithaupt, Fritz. "A Three-Person Model of Empathy." *Emotion Review* 4 (2012): 84.

61. McLaren, Karla. "How Do We Detoxify Our Natural Tendency to Create Us-versus-Them Conflicts?" (Facebook post). August 14, 2012. https://www.facebook.com/notes/karla-mclaren/how-do-we-detoxify-our-natural-tendency-to-create-us-versus-them-conflicts/10151111406133390.

62. De Dreu, C. K. W., S. Shalvi, L. L. Greer, G. A. Van Kleef, and M. J. J. Handgraaf. "Oxytocin Motivates Non-Cooperation in Intergroup Conflict to Protect Vulnerable In-Group Members." *PLoS ONE* 7, no. 11 (2012); Rockliff, H., A. Karl, K. McEwan, J. Gilbert, M. Matos, and P. Gilbert. "Effects of Intranasal Oxytocin on 'Compassion Focused Imagery.'" *Emotion* 11, no. 6 (2011).

63. Lalich., J., and K. McLaren. "Inside and Outcast: Multifaceted Stigma and Redemption in the Lives of Gay and Lesbian Jehovah's Witnesses." *Journal of Homosexuality* 57, no. 10 (2010).

Further Resources

EMOTIONS AND EMPATHY

Blakeslee, Sandra, and Matthew Blakeslee. *The Body Has a Mind of Its Own*. New York: Random House, 2007.

Buss, David M. *The Dangerous Passion: Why Jealousy Is as Necessary as Love and Sex*. New York: The Free Press, 2000.

Damasio, Antonio. *Descartes' Error: Emotion, Reason, and the Human Brain*. New York: Picador, 1995.

Damasio, Antonio. *The Feeling of What Happens: Body and Emotion in the Making of Consciousness*. New York: Harvest, 1999.

Damasio, Antonio. *Looking for Spinoza: Joy, Sorrow, and the Feeling Brain*. New York: Harcourt, 2003.

Davidson, Richard J., and Sharon Begley. *The Emotional Life of Your Brain*. New York: Hudson Street Press, 2012.

Decety, Jean, and William Ickes, eds. *The Social Neuroscience of Empathy*. Cambridge, MA: MIT Press, 2009.

de Waal, Frans. *The Age of Empathy: Nature's Lessons for a Kinder Society*. New York: Harmony, 2009.

Eliot, Lise. *Pink Brain, Blue Brain: How Small Differences Grow Into Troublesome Gaps— and What We Can Do About It*. New York: Houghton Mifflin Harcourt, 2009.

Evans, Dylan. *Emotion: The Science of Sentiment*. New York: Oxford University Press, 2002.

Goffman, Erving. *Stigma: Notes on the Management of Spoiled Identity*. New York: Simon & Schuster, 1963.

Goleman, Daniel. *Emotional Intelligence: Why It Can Matter More Than IQ*, 10th anniversary edition. New York: Bantam, 2006.

Grandin, Temple. *Animals in Translation: Using the Mysteries of Autism to Decode Animal Behavior*. New York: Scribner, 2004.

Hochschild, Arlie. *The Managed Heart: Commercialization of Human Feeling*. Berkeley: University of California Press, 2003.

Ickes, Wiliam, ed. *Empathic Accuracy*. New York: Guildford Press, 1997.

Lamia, Mary. *Understanding Myself: A Kid's Guide to Intense Emotions and Strong Feelings.* Washington, DC: Magination Press, 2010.

McLaren, Karla. *Emotional Flow: Becoming Fluent in the Language of Emotions.* Online course. Boulder, CO: Sounds True, 2012.

McLaren, Karla. *The Language of Emotions: What Your Feelings Are Trying to Tell You.* Boulder, CO: Sounds True, 2010.

Milgram, Stanley. *Obedience to Authority: The Unique Experiment that Challenged Human Nature.* New York: Harper & Row, 1974.

Nettle, Daniel. *Happiness: The Science behind Your Smile.* New York: Oxford University Press, 2006.

Rifkin, Jeremy. *The Empathic Civilization.* New York: Tarcher, 2009.

Sher, Barbara, and Annie Gottlieb. *Wishcraft: How to Get What You Really Want.* New York: Ballantine, 1979.

Szalavitz, Maia, and Bruce D. Perry. *Born for Love: Why Empathy Is Essential—and Endangered.* New York: William Morrow, 2010.

Wilson, Edward O. *The Social Conquest of Earth.* New York: Liveright Publishing, 2012.

Zimbardo, Philip. *The Lucifer Effect: Understanding How Good People Turn Evil.* New York: Random House, 2007.

HEALTH AND WELL-BEING

Dement, William. *The Promise of Sleep: A Pioneer in Sleep Medicine Explores the Vital Connection between Health, Happiness, and a Good Night's Sleep.* New York: Dell, 1999.

Engel, Cindy. *Wild Health: How Animals Keep Themselves Well and What We Can Learn from Them.* New York: Houghton Mifflin, 2002.

Mednick, Sara. *Take a Nap! Change Your Life.* New York: Workman, 2006.

Randall, David K. *Dreamland: Adventures in the Strange Science of Sleep.* New York: W.W. Norton, 2012.

COMMUNICATION AND RELATIONSHIP SUPPORT

De Angelis, Barbara. *Are You the One for Me? Knowing Who's Right and Avoiding Who's Wrong.* New York: Delacorte, 1992.

Ellison, Sharon. *Taking Power Struggle Out of Parenting.* Deadwood, OR: Wyatt-MacKenzie, 2007.

Ellison, Sharon. *Taking the War Out of Our Words.* Deadwood, OR: Wyatt-MacKenzie, 2009.

Johnson, Robert. *He: Understanding Masculine Psychology.* New York: Perennial, 1974.

Johnson, Robert. *She: Understanding Feminine Psychology.* New York: Perennial, 1976.

Riera, Michael. *Uncommon Sense for Parents with Teenagers.* Berkeley CA: Celestial Arts, 2004.

TRAUMA HEALING

de Becker, Gavin. *The Gift of Fear: Survival Signals that Protect Us from Violence.* Boston: Little, Brown & Company, 1997.

Lalich, Janja, and Madeleine Tobias. *Take Back Your Life: Recovering from Cults and Abusive Relationships.* Berkeley, CA: Bay Tree Publishing, 2006.

Levine, Peter. *Healing Trauma.* Audiotapes. Boulder, CO: Sounds True, 1999.

Levine, Peter. *The Healing Trauma Online Course.* Online course. Boulder, CO: Sounds
True, 2011.

Levine, Peter. *It Won't Hurt Forever: Guiding Your Child through Trauma.* Audiotapes.
Boulder, CO: Sounds True, 2001.

Levine, Peter. *Waking the Tiger: Healing Trauma.* Berkeley, CA: North Atlantic, 1997.

THE BRAIN AND NEUROSCIENCE

Ariely, Dan. *Predictably Irrational: The Hidden Forces that Shape Our Decisions.* New York:
HarperCollins, 2008.

Ariely, Dan. *The Upside of Irrationality: The Unexpected Benefits of Defying Logic at Work and
at Home.* New York: Harper, 2010.

Blakeslee, Sandra, and Matthew Blakeslee. *The Body Has a Mind of Its Own.* New York:
Random House, 2007.

Burton, Robert. *On Being Certain: Believing You Are Right Even When You're Not.* New York:
St. Martin's Press, 2008.

Damasio, Antonio. *Descartes' Error: Emotion, Reason, and the Human Brain.* New York:
Picador, 1995.

Damasio, Antonio. *Self Comes to Mind: Constructing the Conscious Brain.* New York:
Pantheon, 2010.

Davidson, Richard J., and Sharon Begley. *The Emotional Life of Your Brain.* New York:
Hudson Street Press, 2012.

Gilovich, Thomas. *How We Know What Isn't So: The Fallibility of Human Reason in Everyday
Life.* New York: Free Press, 1993.

Hood, Bruce. *The Science of Superstition: How the Developing Brain Creates Supernatural
Beliefs.* New York: Harper One, 2010.

Marcus, Gary. *Kluge: The Haphazard Construction of the Human Mind.* New York:
Houghton Mifflin, 2008.

Newberg, Andrew. *Why We Believe What We Believe: Uncovering Our Biological Need for
Meaning, Spirituality, and Truth.* New York: Free Press, 2006.

Ramachandran, V. I., and Sandra Blakeslee. *Phantoms in the Brain: Probing the Mysteries of
the Human Mind.* New York: Quill William Morrow, 1998.

Sacks, Oliver. *Hallucinations.* New York: Knopf, 2012.

Sacks, Oliver. *The Man Who Mistook His Wife for a Hat: And Other Clinical Tales.* London:
Duckworth, 1985.

Tavris, Carol, and Elliot Aronson. *Mistakes Were Made (But Not by Me): Why We Justify
Foolish Beliefs, Bad Decisions, and Hurtful Acts.* New York: Harcourt, 2008.

SHADOW WORK AND MYTHOLOGY

Barks, Coleman. *The Essential Rumi.* San Francisco: HarperSanFrancisco, 1995.

Bly, Robert. *A Little Book on the Human Shadow.* San Francisco: HarperSanFrancisco, 1988.

Johnson, Robert. *Owning Your Own Shadow.* San Francisco: HarperSanFrancisco, 1993.

Meade, Michael. *The Water of Life: Initiation and Tempering of the Soul.* Seattle: GreenFire
Press, 2006.

Somé, Malidoma. *The Healing Wisdom of Africa.* New York: Viking, 1999.

Somé, Malidoma. *Ritual: Power, Healing, and Community.* Portland, OR: Swan Raven, 1993.

Somé, Sobonfu. *Welcoming Spirit Home.* Novato, CA: New World Library, 1999.

Storr, Anthony, ed. *The Essential Jung.* New York: MJF Books, 1983.

Zweig, Connie, and Jeremiah Abrams, eds. *Meeting Your Shadow: The Hidden Power of the Dark Side of Human Nature.* New York: Tarcher/Putnam, 1991.

Index

About the Author

KARLA McLAREN IS an award-winning author and pioneering educator whose empathic approach to emotions has taken her through the healing of her own childhood trauma into an empathic healing career and now into the study of sociology, neurology, cognitive and social psychology, anthropology, and education. She is the author of books, audio learning programs, and online courses that focus on emotions and empathy.

Karla has taught at such venues as the University of San Francisco, Omega Institute, Naropa University, Kripalu, and the Association for Humanistic Psychology. In addition, as a prison arts educator with the William James Foundation, she has used singing, poetry, drumming, and drama to help men in maximum-security prisons explore and heal long-held emotional traumas.

In her academic career, Karla served as a researcher and editor on the books *When Killing Is a Crime* (2007), by Tony Waters, and *Take Back Your Life: Recovering from Cults and Abusive Relationships* (2006), by Janja Lalich. With Dr. Lalich, Karla has coauthored a sociological research study on the multiple stigmatizations that gay, lesbian, bisexual, transgender, and questioning people experience in fundamentalist religions,[63] and she is coauthoring a study about children who grew up in cults and escaped. She is currently developing new forms of empathy and social-interaction curricula for neurologically diverse people.

Karla lives in Sonoma County, California, with her husband, Tino Plank, who is a master's-level nurse educator working in hospice and end-of-life care.

About Sounds True

SOUNDS TRUE IS a multimedia publisher whose mission is to inspire and support personal transformation and spiritual awakening. Founded in 1985 and located in Boulder, Colorado, we work with many of the leading spiritual teachers, thinkers, healers, and visionary artists of our time. We strive with every title to preserve the essential "living wisdom" of the author or artist. It is our goal to create products that not only provide information to a reader or listener, but that also embody the quality of a wisdom transmission.

For those seeking genuine transformation, Sounds True is your trusted partner. At SoundsTrue.com you will find a wealth of free resources to support your journey, including exclusive weekly audio interviews, free downloads, interactive learning tools, and other special savings on all our titles.

To learn more, please visit SoundsTrue.com/bonus/free_gifts or call us toll free at 800-333-9185.

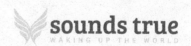

sounds true
WAKING UP THE WORLD